Franchthi Paralia
The Sediments, Stratigraphy, and Offshore Investigations

Excavations at Franchthi Cave, Greece

T.W. Jacobsen, General Editor

FASCICLE 6

Franchthi Paralia

The Sediments, Stratigraphy, and Offshore Investigations

T.J. WILKINSON and
SUSAN T. DUHON

with contributions by
John A. Gifford
Sytze Bottema

INDIANA UNIVERSITY PRESS
Bloomington & Indianapolis

Library of Congress Cataloging-in-Publication Data

Wilkinson, T. J. (Tony J.)
Franchthi Paralia—the sediments, stratigraphy, and offshore investigations / T.J. Wilkinson and Susan T. Duhon, with contributions by John A. Gifford, Sytze Bottema.

(Excavations at Franchthi Cave, Greece; fasc. 6)
Bibliography: p.
1. Franchthi Cave Site (Greece) 2. Paralia Site (Greece) 3. Stone age—Greece 4. Excavations (Archaeology)—Greece. 5. Greece—Antiquities
I. Duhon, Susan T. II. Title. III. Series.
GN816.F73W55 1990 551.4'1'094952—dc20 89-26712
ISBN 0-253-31978-1

1 2 3 4 5 94 93 92 91 90

CONTENTS

FOREWORD (T.W. Jacobsen) xi

PREFACE xiii

A NOTE ON TERMINOLOGY xv

PART I The Onshore Investigations

Chapter One *Geomorphology of Franchthi Paralia* 3

The Limestone Outcrop

The Debris Slopes

Deposits of the Modern Debris Slopes

The Formation of the Paralia Embayment

Chapter Two *Soil Profiles through Selected Sedimentary Sequences* 15

Soil Profiles

Chapter Three *Classification of the Excavated Sediments* 37

Class A: Stony Red Colluvium

Class B: Lower Gravelly Loam

Class C: Stone-free Silt Loam

Class D: Red-hued Sediments with Serpentinites (Upper Reds)

Class E: Dark Gray Stony Clay Loams

Class F: Upper Stony Loam and Class G: Talus Accumulation

Class H: Light Gray Silt Loam

Class J: Fills of Cut Features and Disturbances

Class K: Topsoil

Chapter Four *Processes of Deposition of Selected Sediment Classes* 47

Free Talus Movement

Impeded Talus Movement

Addition of Cultural Debris

Post-depositional Alteration of Archaeological Sediments

Chapter Five *The Stratigraphic Succession* 55

Summary of Stratigraphic Sequence

Chapter Six *Discussion and Conclusions* 71

General Discussion of the Paralia Sediments

The Chronological Development of Sedimentary Deposits

Maximum Extent of the Paralia Settlement

PART II The Offshore Investigations

Chapter Seven *Analysis of Submarine Sediments Off Franchthi Cave* (John A. Gifford) 85
Introduction
Methodology
Laboratory Analyses (with reports by J.M. Hansen and D.S. Reese)
General Discussion and Conclusions
Chapter Eight *Holocene Environment of the Southern Argolid: A Pollen Core from Kiladha Bay* (Sytze Bottema) 117
Introduction
Core Location, Geography, Climate, and Vegetation
Malacology
Dating
Methods
Discussion of the Kiladha Pollen Diagram
Comparison of the Kiladha Diagram with Other Palaeobotanical Information from Greece
Environmental Changes and Human Habitation in the Southern Argolid at the End of the Fourth Millennium B.P.

APPENDIXES The Onshore Investigations: Supporting Data

Appendix A *The Stratigraphic Contexts of the Paralia Walls* 141
Appendix B *Catalogue of Strata* 145
Appendix C *Field and Laboratory Methods* 175
Field Methods
Laboratory Methods
Appendix D *Clay Mineralogy* 179
Appendix E *Miscellaneous Samples* 181
Appendix F *Tables of Laboratory Data* 183

NOTES 199
REFERENCES 201
PLATES 209

FIGURES

1. Geomorphology of Franchthi Paralia 4-5
2. Slope Profiles Showing Archaeological Accumulation within Colluvial Footslopes 8-9
3. Section of Eroded Debris Slopes in Northern Paralia 10
4. Histograms Showing Distribution of Stones of >10 cm from Selected Paralia Deposits 12
5. Relationship Between Slope Inclination and Rock Creep on Mancos Shale Hillslopes (after Schumm 1967) 13
6. Plan of Paralia Indicating Sampling Locations of Soil Profiles in Relation to Prehistoric Features 16
7. Soil Profile Q: Percent Clay 19
8. Soil Profile Q: Chemistry 20
9. Soil Profile Q: Glycolated X-Ray Diffraction Patterns 21
10. Soil Profile R: Percent Clay 23
11. Soil Profile R: Chemistry 24
12. Soil Profile S: Percent Clay 26
13. Soil Profile S: Chemistry 27
14. Soil Profile T: Percent Clay 28
15. Soil Profile T: Chemistry 29
16. Soil Profile L: Percent Clay 31
17. Soil Profile L: Chemistry 32
18. Soil Profile L: Glycolated X-Ray Diffraction Patterns 33
19. Soil Profile L: Calcium Carbonate Equivalent 34
20. Plan of Paralia Excavated Area Showing Contoured Surface of Paleosol 39
21. Relationship of Sedimentary Classes and Soil Chemistry 42
22. Orientation of Potsherds and Tabular Stones in North Section of Q6N 43
23. X-Ray Diffraction Pattern for Final Neolithic Sherd 45
24. Vectors of Rock Creep on a Progressively Diminishing Angle of Slope 48
25. Schematic Plan of Paralia Walls 52
26. Stratigraphic Flow Diagram: L5 56
27. Stratigraphic Flow Diagram: O5 58
28. Stratigraphic Flow Diagram: P5 60
29. Stratigraphic Flow Diagram: P5-Q6-Q5 62
30. Stratigraphic Flow Diagram: Q6N 67
31. Stratigraphic Flow Diagram: QR5 68
32. Hypothetical Sediment Sequence on Slope and Hypothetical Transverse Section 72-73
33. Main Wall Phases in Grid Squares Q5, P5, Q6, and QR5 75
34. Slope Profile Through Grid Squares Q4-Q6, Extended into Kiladha Bay 79
35. Master Section Drawing, L5 East 80
36. Present General Setting of the Paralia Site and Environs 86
37. Perspective View of Outer Kiladha Bay between the Franchthi Headland and Koronis Island 90
38. Index Map Showing Locations of Cores Taken in 1985 91

39. Variation of Grain-Size Fractions with Depth 97
40. Triangle Plot Showing Distribution of Grain-Size Fractions 98
41. Cumulative Grain-Size Plots of Four Core Samples 99
42. Cumulative Grain-Size Plots of Basal Sediment Samples 100
43. Variation of Four Components of Core Samples with Depth 101
44. Areal Distribution of Particles in Core Samples 113
45. Areal Distribution of Particles in Core Samples 114
46. Map of Greece Showing Locations of Pollen Sites 118
47. Pollen Diagram for OK 85/11 (Kiladha) *Facing page 122*
48. Pollen Zones, Time, and Cultural Periods in the Argolid 128
49. Main Part of Trikhonis Pollen Diagram 130
50. Main Part of Halos Pollen Diagram 131
51. Main Part of Aghia Galini Pollen Diagram 132
52. Abnormally Dry and Wet Areas in Greece, January 1955 136

TABLES

1. Paralia: Sedimentary Classes 50
2. Summary of 1985 Ormos Kiladha (OK) Cores 89
3. Radiocarbon Age Determinations (Uncorrected) on OK Core Samples 93
4. Particles/Gram in the Coarse and Fine Granule Fractions of OK85 Basal Sediments 95
5. Marine Invertebrates Identified from the 1985 Bulk Basal Core Samples 104-105
6. Identification of Botanical Remains from OK85 Cores 107

PLATES

1. Balloon Photograph of Franchthi Paralia
2. Views of Paralia, Cave, and Backwall
3. General View of Outer Kiladha Bay
4. Components of the Corer
5. Coring Operations, 1981
6. Coring Operations, 1981
7. Mud Plaster Fragments from Coring
8. Neolithic Sherds from Coring

FOREWORD

In late July 1969, after the completion of the third season of excavation at Franchthi Cave, one of our Greek workmen sharply spotted the remains of what appeared to be a human skull protruding slightly from the eroded scarp along the shore in front of and below the mouth of the cave. That discovery, coupled with the abundance of Neolithic potsherds and other artifacts that we had observed in the scarp and on the surface along the shore since first visiting the site in 1966, made clear to us the need to test this part of the site before bringing our excavations to a conclusion. Circumstances did not permit us to initiate a formal investigation of the area until July 1971. A grid of five-meter squares was laid out on the slope above the shoreline and beach (cf. Jacobsen and Farrand 1987:10-14), and a small cut was then opened in grid square Q5 to examine the environs of the eroding skull (which actually lay in square Q6). The concentration of surface finds in this area had suggested to us that this was a promising place to begin our investigation, and subsequent work has shown that most of the exposed prehistoric structures were located here. Thus commenced our excavation of Franchthi "Paralia" (Greek "seashore").

The 1971 operation on Paralia was of rather modest scale, but considerably more earth was moved in subsequent field seasons: 1973, 1974, and 1976. Indeed, as excavation in the cave itself wound down, we were able to devote increasingly more time and resources to the exposure of this complex but very interesting part of the site. Eventually, we were able to open up an area of more than 100 m^2 and bring to light a substantial archaeological deposit belonging exclusively to the Aegean Neolithic period. While the area of our excavations was relatively small (probably no more than 5% of the potentially excavatable area), it was sufficient to reveal evidence of considerable human occupation and to suggest to us, at least as early as 1974, that these remains belonged to a more extensive site, much of which may now lie beneath the waters of Kiladha Bay. This in turn led to the geophysical and coring operations conducted in the bay in 1979, 1981, and 1985, the results of which are discussed in this volume as well as elsewhere in this publication series (van Andel and Sutton 1987).

The objective of this fascicle is to present the results of what might be considered the geoarchaeological investigations that complemented the strictly archaeological excavations on Paralia. The volume thus lays the foundation for our interpretation of the Paralia remains. The authors articulate the complex processes involved in the formation and evolution of the site and provide us with the basis for the stratigraphic succession. The bulk of the volume (Part I and Appendixes) is devoted to a description and discussion of the Paralia sediments and stratigraphy by T.J. Wilkinson and Susan Duhon. As their manuscript approached final form, the preliminary results of the coring in the bay under the direction of Dr. John Gifford became available. It seemed reasonable, therefore, to incorporate those findings in this publication as well. Accordingly, Part II is devoted to a final report of the 1981 and 1985 coring operations and includes an analysis by Dr. Sytze Bottema of the valuable pollen remains from one of the cores. The manuscript of Part I was essentially complete by the summer of 1988, while Part II attained its present form by summer 1989.

The reader should understand from the outset that these remains belong entirely to the Neolithic period. Unlike the situation in the nearby cave, there is no evidence of pre-Neolithic human activity on Paralia. This means that, in terms of the coarsest absolute chronology (*uncalibrated* C-14 determinations), the limits of prehistoric occupation range from ca. 6000 b.c. (8000 B.P.) to ca. 3000 b.c. (5000 B.P.). This is based on synchronisms with the dated sequence in the cave and, unfortunately, cannot be confirmed by radiocarbon measurements from Paralia itself. Charred material suitable for radiocarbon dating was strikingly rare in the excavations, especially in contexts that were archaeologically well defined. The overall cultural phasing must await the final presentation of the cultural remains themselves in other fascicles of this series (e.g., Vitelli, forthcoming a-b).

While the coring in the bay tends to support our hypothesis of a more extensive open site outside the cave and one that is now largely submerged, Gifford's work has shown that the precise nature of this site cannot be determined without proper underwater excavation. I hasten to add, however, that our project has no intention of undertaking such a costly operation. That, along with further excavation in the cave itself, will remain for a future generation of archaeologists.

The general editor would like to thank Ms. Mary Downs, Ms. Kimberly Gardner, and, especially, Dr. Jeffrey Harlig of Indiana University for their extremely valuable help in preparing this volume for publication. I also wish to acknowledge with considerable gratitude the cooperation of our colleagues at the Indiana University Press and the continued financial support of the Interpretive Research Program of the National Endowment for the Humanities and the Indiana University Foundation (Edward A. Schrader Endowment).

T. W. JACOBSEN

PREFACE

Archaeological deposits on a site accumulate as part of a process of interaction between human activity and the land surface upon which the activity takes place. The cultural deposits must be interpreted in the context of this interaction.

Since the Paralia part of the Franchthi Cave site is located at the foot of a steep hillslope, the archaeological deposits can be understood only if natural hillslope processes are understood and their contributions to the deposits and their influence on human activity are taken into account. Since the Paralia deposits are also truncated by the sea, the site that we see may be only the margin of a much larger site, now eroded away, or submerged and buried by water-laid sediments. Our interpretation of the features and artifacts from the Paralia must in some way take into account the portion of the site that we cannot see.

An additional factor, essential to the interpretation of the deposits, is time. In the case of Paralia, laws of superposition are complicated by a downslope component of movement. This in turn can result in inverted stratigraphy, with apparently earlier deposits overlying deposits containing later artifacts. In such cases, an understanding of slope processes is crucial to an interpretation of the chronological sequence.

In Part I of this fascicle, the natural processes that regulated the laying down of the deposits while the Paralia was occupied and those that modified the deposits subsequently are explained and interpreted on the basis of field descriptions and chemical and physical analyses of sediment samples. Part II is a presentation of the results of underwater investigations conducted by Gifford and his colleagues in Kiladha Bay.

Our aim in this fascicle is to provide a guide to the Paralia that will clarify its complex stratigraphy and provide additional context for its artifacts and features. The fascicle can be read for an overview of the physical site, but, since it is also intended to be read in conjunction with other fascicles dealing with the artifactual and other finds from the site, the relevant stratigraphic and analytic data are included.

The archaeological layers were described in the field by T. J. Wilkinson in 1974, 1976, and 1979, and finally in Bloomington, using samples gathered for analysis during the foregoing seasons. Many of the data presented in the catalogue of strata are based on 1974 descriptions, although where possible they were checked against the soil profile descriptions. The soil profiles were described and sampled in 1976 by Carolyn Olson. Soil profile descriptions were checked and soil horizon designations assigned in 1979 by Susan Duhon. The quantitative data are from the work of Duhon (1982) and are fully tabulated in Appendix F.

A NOTE ON TERMINOLOGY

In this report archaeological *layers* are *sediments* or *deposits* laid down by human or natural agencies often influenced by human activities within recognized archaeological sites. In Part I, a lithostratigraphic sequence based on excavation stratigraphy and pedological studies has been formulated. In Part II, because of the nature of the core samples and the inherent difficulties of underwater work, more strictly sedimentological techniques were used to establish a lithostratigraphic sequence. In particular, the Phi grain-size scale was used as described in the text. However, for both the onshore and offshore work the conceptual framework for excavation stratigraphies explained in Jacobsen and Farrand (1987:7) was used.

In Part I, *soils* are considered to be pedogenically altered *sediments*. This distinction permits us not only to define episodes of deposition on the land surface, but also to recognize episodes of non-deposition during which subaerial weathering (soil formation) took place. In order to take advantage of this distinction, conventions of soil descriptive terminology are followed in Part I as detailed below and in the text.

Soil descriptive terminology is based upon that used by the U.S. Department of Agriculture Soil Survey Manual (USDA 1951, 1962), the main attributes described being as follows:

a. *Depth below ground surface*. See position of soil profiles on section drawings.

b. *Nature of horizon boundaries or stratigraphic interfaces*. These are given both in the text descriptions of Chapter 2 and in the stratigraphic catalogue (Appendix B). In the latter, they are classified according to the following types:

1. Boundaries of cuts and disturbances: pits, burials, wall-construction trenches, wall-robbing trenches.
2. Clear stratigraphic breaks, usually representing stratigraphic unconformities: clear boundary, gross difference in sediment type on either side of interface.
3. Break in sequence as a result of additions of archaeological materials: floors, dumps on surfaces, etc.
4. Moderately distinct boundary indicated by color or texture change, or both; not as clear as in 2 or 3 above.
5. Gradual boundary to difference in soil color, texture, or stone content.

N.B. Although stratigraphic breaks of type 2 may indicate that an unconformity occurs in the sequence, the absence of distinct boundaries does not necessarily imply continuity of deposition. For example, talus deposits often exhibit merging boundaries throughout, but the deposits actually include many depositional hiatuses.

c. *Soil colors* are described according to Munsell soil color charts.

d. *Soil texture* refers to the relative proportion of sand, silt, and clay in the soil. Textures of the fine earth fraction have been described according to the U.S. Department of Agriculture's terminology (USDA 1951:210). The following terms refer to the fine fraction (<2 mm): clay, silty clay, sandy clay, *silty clay loam*, sandy clay loam, *clay loam*, silt, *silt loam*, *loam*, sandy loam, loamy sand, and sand. (The textures in italics were found on the site.)

The coarse fraction is subdivided into gravel (or pebbles) (2-60 mm), cobbles (60-300 mm), and boulders (>300 mm). These are angular or subangular unless stated otherwise. "Stony" refers to a poorly sorted mixture of gravel and cobbles contained within the fine matrix. Where necessary, the gravel fraction is subdivided into fine (2-5 mm), medium (5-25 mm), and coarse (25-60 mm) categories. The relative abundance of stones, or other inclusions, is described as absent (<1%), rare (1-5%), occasional (6-25%), common (16-35%), or abundant (36-70%). The matrix, i.e., the fine material surrounding the stones, is described as sparse, moderate, or extensive.

e. *Soil structure* refers to the aggregation of primary soil particles into compound particles or clusters of primary particles separated from adjoining aggregates by surfaces of weakness (USDA 1951, 1962).

f. *Soil consistence* refers to the degree and kind of cohesion and adhesion in soil material or to its resistance to deformation or rupture. Although consistence and structure are interrelated, structure pertains to the shape, size, and definition of natural aggregates that result from variations in the forces of attraction within a soil mass, whereas consistence pertains to the strength and nature of such forces themselves (USDA 1951, 1962).

In addition, faunal disturbances, root abundance, and worm holes or casts are described and presented where appropriate. Other properties such as the presence of calcium carbonate ($CaCO_3$), serpentinite pebbles, and land snail concentrations are also noted.

The following points refer especially to the catalogue of strata (Appendix B). In "Description," "S.D." refers to the horizon reference used by Susan Duhon (see Chapter 2). This reference is followed by the appropriate soil horizon letter. Where possible, a single letter (A to K) is assigned in accordance with the classification presented in Chapter 3.

Other terms used in the text and Appendix B include the following:

a. *Continuous re-sorting*. Particle movement has continuously taken artifacts from their original context and redeposited them downslope. This often occurs in a series of cycles.

b. *Cross-cut layers*. Cross-cut layers are layers which have been inadvertently excavated across their mutual boundary to incorporate artifacts from both layers into a new but arbitrary layer.

c. *Fall sorting*. Large, heavy stones fall further downslope, by virtue of their greater momentum, than light stones. This results in a coarse, stony deposit downslope and finer, stony deposits upslope.

d. *Openwork*. This refers to gravel, usually angular or subangular, which exhibits large voids among the individual stones.

Archaeological periods. In the text we have used the preliminary terminology employed during excavation (Jacobsen 1976), which is as follows: Early Neolithic (ca. 6000-5000 b.c.), Middle Neolithic (ca. 5000-4500 b.c.), Late Neolithic (ca. 4500-4000 b.c.), and Final Neolithic (ca. 4000-3000 b.c.). The absolute dates are based on uncalibrated radiocarbon measurements (Libby half-life).

PART I

The Onshore Investigations

CHAPTER ONE

*Geomorphology of Franchthi Paralia**

Franchthi Cave is located in a prominent limestone headland on the coast of the southern Argolid, Greece. The archaeological site consists of two parts, the cave itself and the Paralia (Jacobsen and Farrand 1987:Plate 2). The latter is a low bench of deposits located along the beach outside and below the cave entrance.

The headland is one of several blocks of massive limestone of middle Jurassic age which have been thrust over somewhat younger units of thinly bedded limestone and calcareous sandstone, collectively known as flysch, and serpentinite (Jacobsen and Farrand 1987:Plate 1). As a result of this structural history, the immediate region surrounding the cave is one of limestone peaks and ridges separated by valleys floored by serpentinite and flysch. Within the valleys, minor prominences correspond to outcrops of harder units of the flysch.

THE LIMESTONE OUTCROP

The Paralia embayment is bounded to the east by a steep bedrock slope or "backwall," which extends roughly north-south from the northern wall of the cave (Figure 1 and Plate 2). The surface of the vertically bedded and highly jointed limestone slopes between 50° and 75° to the horizontal except at two locations where shallow re-entrants have developed along beds of less resistant limestone. This backwall or "free face" is the original source of much of the rock debris on the slopes below.

Two limestone spurs limit the Paralia at the north and the south. The southern spur continues the approximate line of the southern cave wall whereas the northern spur forms an east-west extension of the backwall, itself an extension of the northern wall of the cave. Submarine springs issue from below both spurs (Figure 1). Much of the northern spur actually consists of boulders cemented into a solid mass by a calcareous, reddish-yellow, silty deposit (travertine-cemented boulders). Flow banding in one or two places in the northern spur suggests localized precipitation by pre-existing springs. Toward the debris slopes to the south, calcium carbonate occurs as

* We wish to thank the following for their advice and help during the fieldwork and post-excavation analysis: T.W. Jacobsen, W.R. Farrand, C. Olson, R.V. Ruhe, K.D. Vitelli, S. Kopper, C. Runnels, P. Murray, Tj.H. van Andel, S. and R. Payne, C. Perlès, and J. Shackleton. We are especially grateful to Dan Pullen for his painstaking work on the section drawings. The balloon photograph (Plate 1) was taken by J. W. Myers and processed by R. Heron. This report also incorporates much advice from, and, we hope, answers at least some of the questions that were raised by, a stimulating Franchthi field team, which included D. Keller, L. Talalay, J. Hansen, M. Fotiades, T. Cullen, and D. Williams.

KEY TO FIGURE 1

LIMESTONE BACKWALL

LIMESTONE SHOWING DIRECTION OF BEDDING PLANES

OTHER LIMESTONE OUTCROPS

TRAVERTINE-CEMENTED ROCKS

CEMENTED TALUS

MAIN TALUS

MIDSLOPE/FOOTSLOPE BOUNDARY

ARCHAEOLOGICAL TRENCH

GRAVEL BEACH

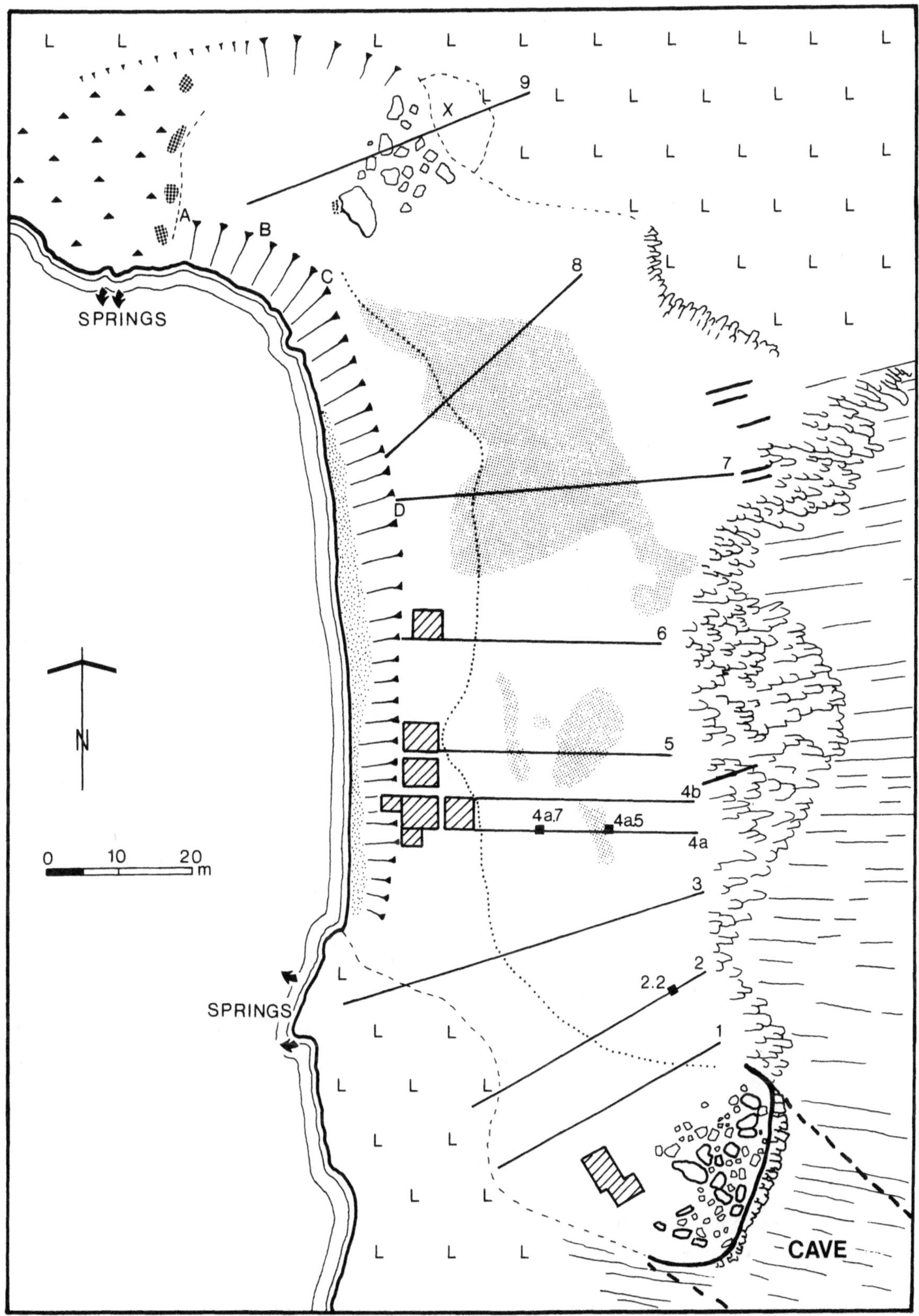

Figure 1. Geomorphology of Franchthi Paralia showing surveyed slope profiles (1-9), soil pits (2.2, 4a.5, and 4a.7), and archaeological trenches (grid squares, hatched). (For section drawing of A-D, see Figure 3.)

nodules characteristic of those found in soil carbonate horizons, which suggests that precipitation of carbonate took place in a subaerial environment.

THE DEBRIS SLOPES

The debris slopes have three components: the midslope, the footslope, and terrain of low gradient with rock debris of all sizes. The term midslope, previously used by M. J. Selby (1982), is applied on the Paralia to steep slopes covered by limestone debris of all sizes derived from the adjacent backwall, which replaces the upper slope of Selby's terminology. Slope gradients vary between 22° and 31°, but a gradient of 25° is characteristic for the main stretch of Paralia (Figure 1 and Figure 2, profiles 3-7). In Figure 1 the midslope is distinguished from the footslope by a dotted line. The midslope can be seen to form an apron beneath the backwall, and at least one third of its area is littered with loose talus or scree (see below: *Talus Deposits*).

Talus slopes usually have characteristic gradients between 28° and 46°, more commonly 30° to 38° (Selby 1982). Those at Franchthi fall within or below the lower end of this range, and, although it appears that rockfall has contributed the main mass of debris to the slopes, the thickness of the talus is probably not sufficient for it to be the primary determinant of the angle of repose of the slope. Instead, the underlying stony red colluvium (Chapter 3) appears to have controlled the slope angle.

The footslope fringes the talus-covered midslope and has a gradient of less than 20° (usually less than 15° [Plate 2]). On the Paralia today, the footslope consists of a low bench of mostly cultural material which aggraded during the period of occupation. Although dominantly fine-grained (grain size less than 2 mm in diameter), the deposits also include intrusive material deriving from the talus. The natural and cultural processes which interacted to produce this bench constitute the principal subject of this report. The bench is truncated on the seaward side by a low wave-cut escarpment (Figure 3).

Terrain of low gradient with rock debris of all sizes is located in the vicinity of the cave mouth and in the northern Paralia between the bedrock spur and the talus-covered midslope. Common boulders and the presence of a large mass of limestone (at point *x* in Figure 1), with bedding planes 10° to 15° out of alignment with the surrounding bedrock, suggest that rock collapse is responsible for slope morphology in these locations.

The sedimentary stratigraphy of the footslope is well exposed in the archaeological excavation trenches and, to a lesser extent, in the wave-cut escarpment truncating the slope. The stratigraphy of the midslope and of the rest of the debris slopes must be extrapolated primarily from these exposures, but three soil pits (at profile locations 2.2, 4a.5, and 4a.7 in Figure 1) provide additional data.

DEPOSITS OF THE MODERN DEBRIS SLOPES

Apart from an unknown (but probably minor) input of aeolian sediment, the deposits on the debris slopes derive from the following sources:

1. boulder collapse, backwall weathering, and the resultant release of stones;
2. wash of fine sediment from the hillslopes above;
3. recycling of the stony red colluvium;
4. archaeological debris, notably wall constructions (see Appendix B) and addition of domestic rubbish.

These deposits accumulated upon a basal layer of stony red colluvium, a dominantly Pleistocene substratum (see Chapter 3).

Boulder Collapse

On Paralia, boulders have been accumulating on the slopes throughout the period of deposition, but the only major collapse episodes have been recorded near the cave mouth (Farrand, forthcoming). Boulders usually appear to have rolled well downslope to come to rest in sometimes precarious positions, leaving large voids between the boulders and the underlying surface. These voids then become filled with talus or sometimes with large numbers of dead land snails, *Helix* sp. being especially common.

Large groups of boulders are not necessarily the product of wholesale collapse of the backwall, but more often they appear to have resulted from the progressive trapping of newly arrived boulders by those already present. The great momentum gained by some falling boulders is illustrated by the case of a large boulder (ca. 120 cm in length) which arrived in grid square Q4 sometime after the Early Neolithic occupation. Its shattered apex exhibited cracks up to 3 mm wide, which were later filled with loam. The soil immediately adjacent on one side and below, unlike nearby soils, exhibited a massive structure, possibly the result of compression on impact. A few stones were also oriented parallel to the boulder face. Field observations suggest that the boulder might have penetrated as much as 30 cm into the pre-existing archaeological sediment, and its shattered end indicates that the final impact, or one made in transit, was substantial. No other example of boulder penetration was observed, however. In other talus environments, ''bump holes'' have been recorded as elliptical depressions roughly 1 m long by 50 cm deep (Rapp 1960). Rapp's work demonstrates that boulder trajectories can be oblique to the slope gradient. On Paralia, a single calcite-veined boulder could be traced to its source on the backwall; in this case, a lateral movement of three to five meters occurred before the boulder came to rest a few meters upslope from grid square Q4.

Talus Deposits

Loose deposits of angular to subangular talus litter the midslope and occasionally penetrate to the footslope. The more extensive northern sheet focuses on the broad reentrant developed in the backwall from which most of the talus presumably was derived. Along the backwall, joints and other planes of weakness have been enlarged by solution, root growth, or the release of stress as a result of boulder collapse. In addition, the progressive disintegration of rockfall is probably a significant source of smaller stones (Selby 1982). Many talus stones appear to have been reworked from the red colluvium. Freeze-thaw processes, which contribute much talus debris in high latitudes or altitudes, appear to have been of limited significance at Franchthi during the past 25,000 years (Farrand, forthcoming). The rather sporadic production of debris is reflected in the talus deposits, which are discontinuous in space and colonized in places by grass and lentisk shrubs.

Three shallow soil pits were excavated into the talus slopes at profile locations 2.2, 4a.5, and 4a.7 (Figures 1 and 2). These are described as follows:

Pit 2.2	0-40 cm	Dark brown (10YR 4/3 dry, 10YR 3/3 moist) loam; granular; soft, sparse-to-moderate matrix containing abundant medium-to-coarse angular gravel.
	40-55 cm	Dark brown (7.5YR 4/4 dry), sparse matrix; tightly packed medium-to-coarse angular gravel with thin, reddish brown (5YR 3/3) coatings.

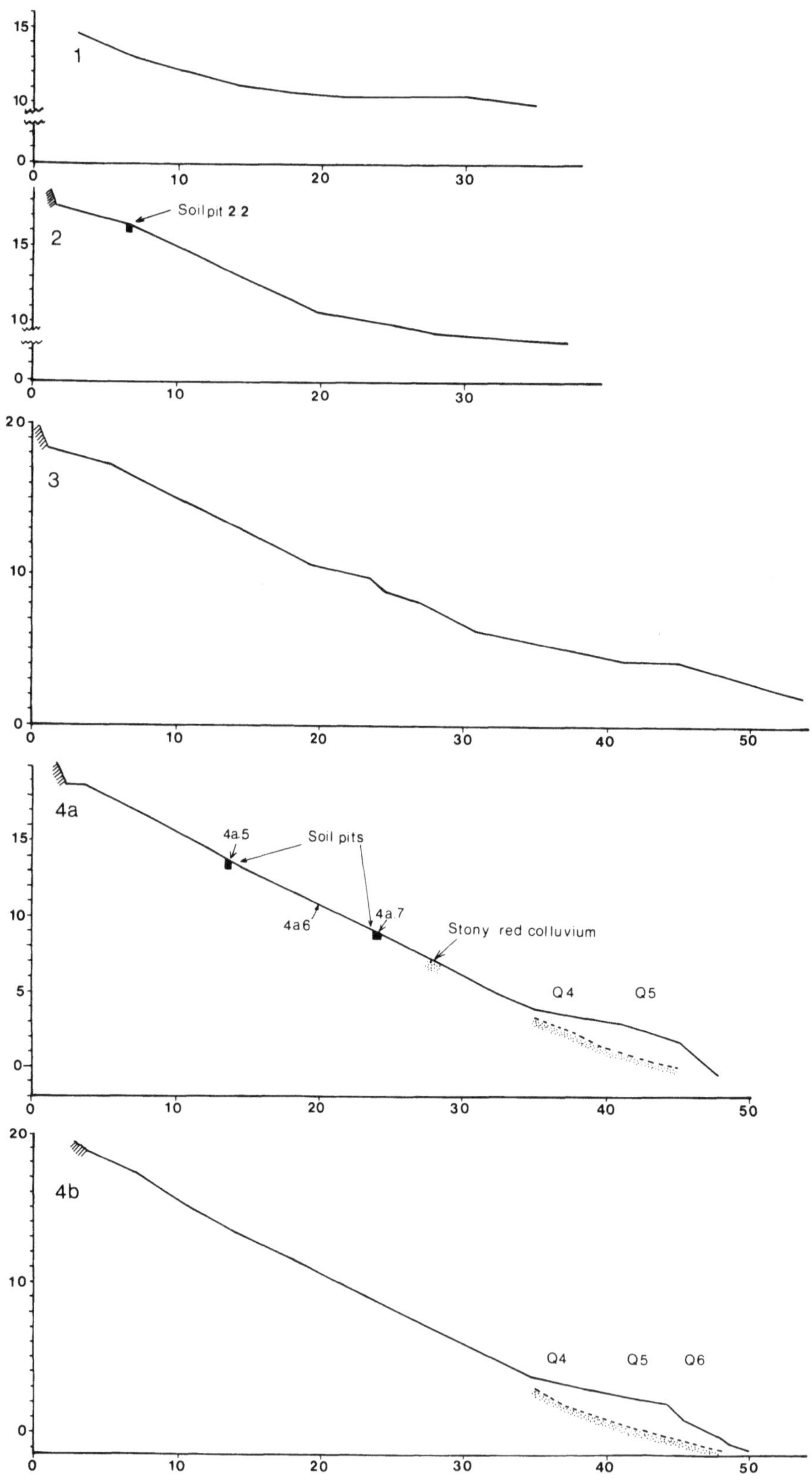

Figure 2. Surveyed slope profiles showing archaeological accumulation within colluvial footslopes. Stony red colluvium stippled; talus particle size determined at 4a.6 and 7.7.

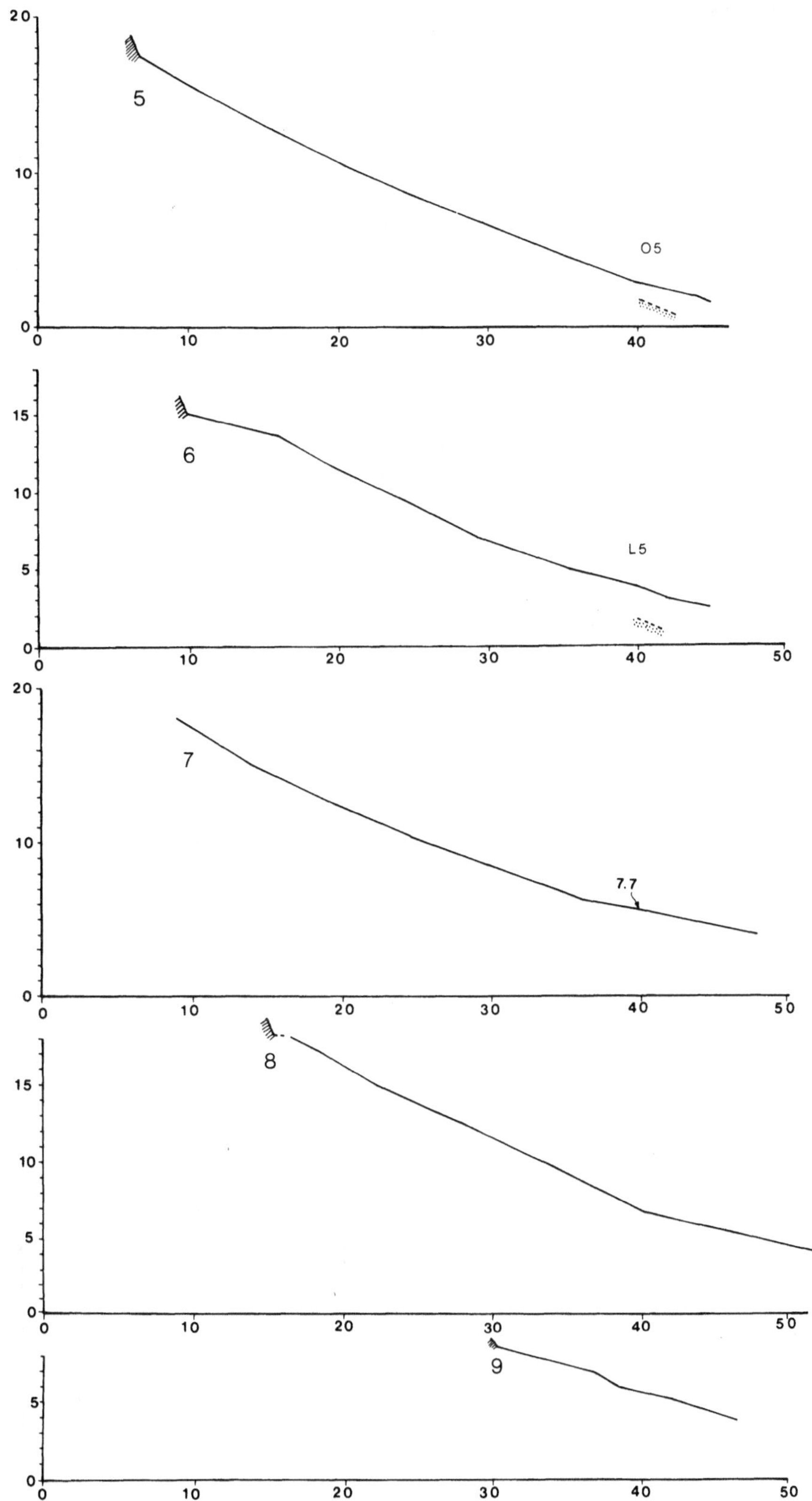

Figure 2 (continued).

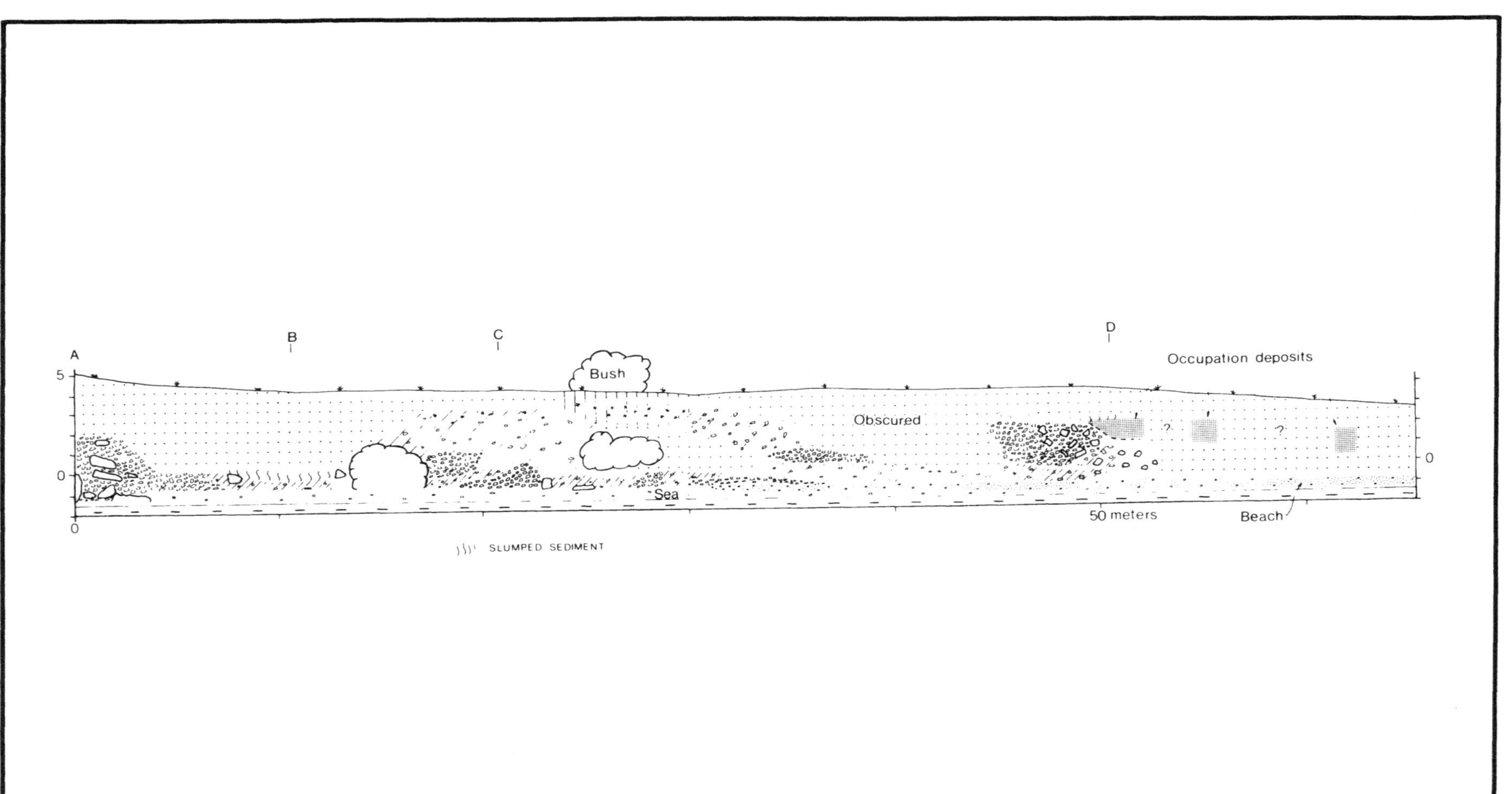

Figure 3. Long section of eroded debris slopes in northern Paralia. Conventions are as for the main section drawings except where otherwise indicated. (Cf. Jacobsen and Farrand 1987:Plate 42.) For clarity, the sparse yellowish red matrix has been omitted from the talus deposits. (See also Figure 1.)

Pit 4a.5	Surface cover	Light grass cover, nearest bush ca. 1 m distant; angular gravel-cobbles form thin talus; occasional boulders in vicinity on surface and within soil; to northeast, minor exposure of cemented talus; surface moderately stable; nearest active talus located 2 m downslope.
	Stones	Poorly sorted, angular to subangular gravel-cobbles, maximum dimension 10 cm; all limestone, some have vein calcite, others thin, pink coatings of calcium carbonate.
	Matrix 0-25 cm	Dark brown (10YR 4/3 dry, 10YR 3/3 moist), gravelly loam; medium granular structure; soft; fine root hairs; moderately extensive matrix separates stones by up to 1 cm.
	Below 25 cm	Dark brown (7.5YR 4/4 dry, 7.5YR 3/2 moist) gravelly loam; soft; otherwise as from 0-25 cm; pit terminated at 40 cm due to presence of boulder.
Pit 4a.7	Surface cover	Lightly grassed with poorly sorted angular to subangular gravel-cobble surface; lightly cemented red colluvium exposed a short distance downslope.
	0-20 cm	Brownish yellow (10YR 6/6 dry) or dark yellowish brown (10YR 4/4 moist), fine gravelly loam with fine subangular blocky structure; abundant root hairs.
	20-30 cm	Medium-coarse subangular to angular gravel with sparse, yellowish red cemented matrix.

Artifacts were rare in all three deposits:

Pit 2.2	Two sherds, one of which probably dates to the Final Neolithic.
Pit 4a.5	Several sherds, worn, but probably Final Neolithic.
Pit 4a.7	One sherd, probably Final Neolithic; another, possibly Byzantine or Classical; several marine shells.

The talus also includes a significant component of non-limestone rocks assumed to have been introduced by the prehistoric inhabitants of the site or by others. In an area of 75 m^2 of talus to the north of grid square L5 (locus 7.7; see Figures 1, 2, and 4), 27 cobble-sized ''imports'' were counted, a density of one per 2.8 m^2. The introduced rocks are mainly sandstones, perhaps originally from the Kiladha valley, but they also include several chunks of limestone bored by the mollusc *Lithophagus* (a marine organism) and two lumps of unworked chert of uncertain origin.

In a few locations on the midslope, three or four stones (200-400 mm, long axis) were found aligned, as if they had been deliberately placed there. It is possible that such stones were placed on the midslope to control or reduce the movement of talus down the slope. The occurrence of these possible ''retaining walls'' and the sparse scatter of pottery sherds on the midslope suggest that the prehistoric people used the midslope as well as the footslope for their activities, especially in the later period of occupation.

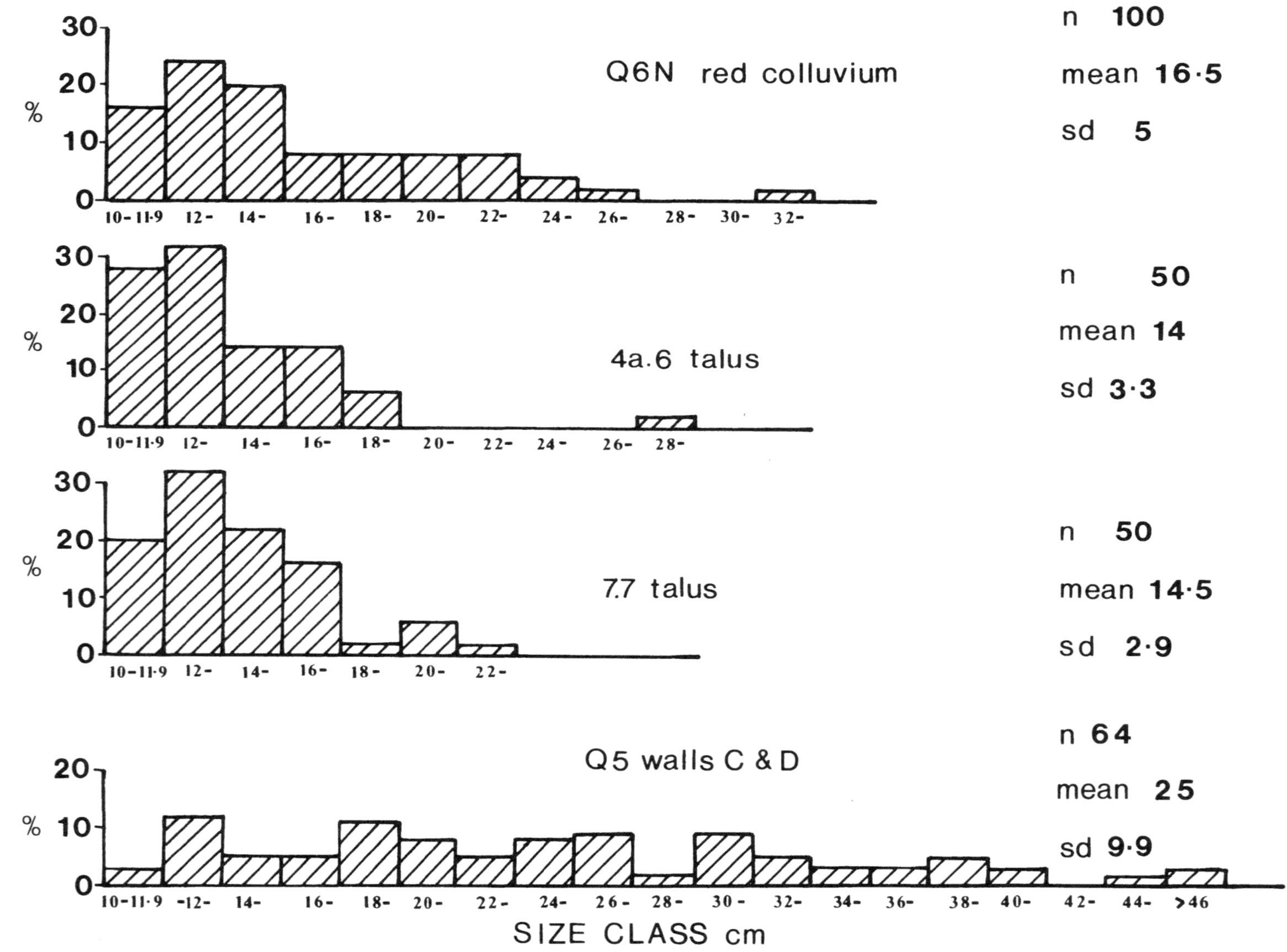

Figure 4. Histograms showing distribution of stones of >10 cm (max. dimension) from selected Paralia deposits. Note the coarse "tail" of Q6N red colluvium and general unavailability in colluvium and talus of large stones suitable for wall building.

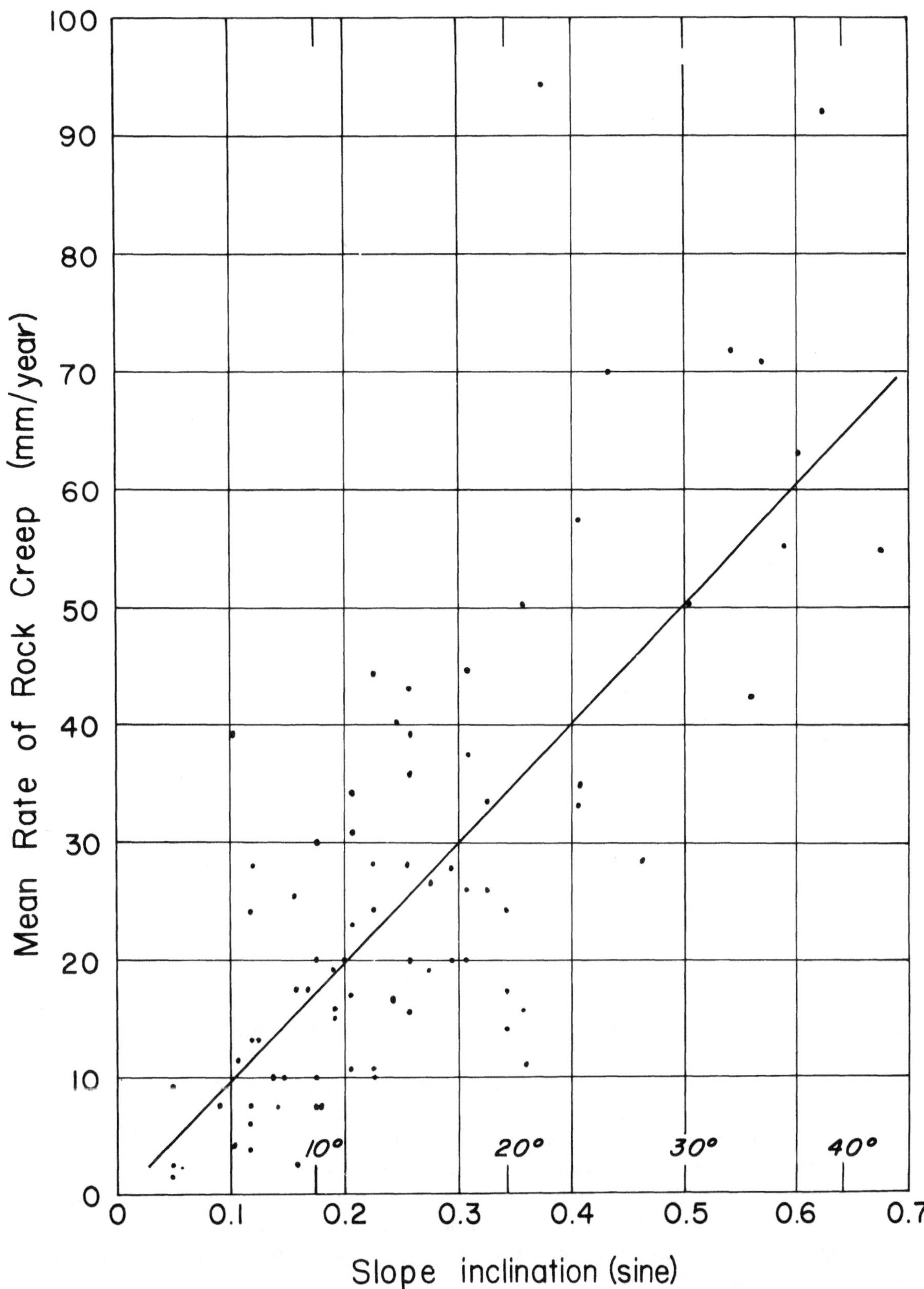

Figure 5. Relationship between sine of slope inclination and rate of movement of rock fragments (in mm/year) on Mancos Shale hillslopes. Standard error is 11.8 mm; correlation coefficient is 0.77. (Redrawn from Schumm 1967:Figure 1.)

The presence of exotic stones not derived from the nearby limestone outcrop, artifacts, and reworked colluvium emphasizes the heterogeneity of the talus and the instability of the slope. These characteristics must be kept in mind when the deposits on the footslope are considered.

Talus Movement

The progressive creep of rock particles downslope, although slow, is inevitable, and temperature changes in hot or cold seasons, as well as the passage of animals, humans, falling rocks, or storm runoff will contribute to stone movement (Davison 1888). The rate of "rock creep" is directly proportional to the sine of the slope angle (Schumm 1967). This relationship, shown in Figure 5, was derived by Schumm on shale slopes in western Colorado, and it is likely that a similar, although not identical, relationship prevails at Franchthi. Unlike the long trajectories of falling boulders, such movements are small. As a result, any impediment to creep (e.g., a wall across the slope) will cause stones to accumulate at the break of slope. Such accumulation will produce localized aggradation as discussed in Chapter 4.

Transport of sand, silt, and clay by water percolating through or flowing across the talus will also lead to localized accumulations behind slope barriers. The disruptive effect of man and animals on the sediment fabric tends to increase sediment yield and transport. Consequently, the balance between talus creep and slope wash may have been altered during the Neolithic.

On very active talus slopes, basal erosion of the footslope can result in the rapid readjustment of the slope profile with stones from upslope rolling down to fill the resultant scar (Howarth and Bones 1972). Such readjustment has clearly not taken place on the Franchthi Paralia, where marine truncation of the footslope has had little apparent effect on the slope above. Instead, the slope profile appears to be largely controlled by the slope of the underlying stony red colluvium, on which the talus merely forms a shallow veneer.

THE FORMATION OF THE PARALIA EMBAYMENT

Together, the cave, its southern continuation below the two collapsed openings, and the Paralia backwall are aligned approximately northwest-southeast. The alignment implies that the embayment could have resulted simply from the collapse of a pre-existing northwestern extension of the cave. The resultant hollow would then have become filled with collapsed debris and later with the products of subaerial weathering (J. S. Kopper, personal communication 1974). Alternatively, the Paralia embayment might have evolved by subaerial erosion of the backwall (free-face retreat). Such erosion would have been aided by localized solution or collapse, possibly as a result of "sapping" by large or long-lasting springs (Sweeting 1973:215).

An origin of the embayment by collapse is attractive in view of the presence of the cave, and it is also supported by the presence of a large collapsed doline at nearby Dhidhima. Cave roof collapse, however, has frequently been overemphasized in the interpretation of many karst features, and the more mundane process of subaerial erosion or solution must not be dismissed in this case. Furthermore, the absence of data on the thickness of the stony colluvium and on any former northward extension of the cave means that the collapse hypothesis, although preferred by the authors, cannot be proven.

CHAPTER TWO

Soil Profiles through Selected Sedimentary Sequences

The bulk of the archaeological deposits along the coastal strip of Paralia accumulated as part of the colluvial footslope defined above. The deposits, which are up to 2 m thick, must have originally formed a wedge-shaped deposit extending well beyond the present shoreline, but coastal erosion has trimmed this wedge into the truncated bench now visible.

The stratigraphy and sedimentary history of the footslope were studied primarily in exposures created by the archaeological excavations. Extensive field descriptions by the authors and subsequent laboratory analyses of selected sequences by Carolyn Olson and Susan Duhon form the basis of this account.

From this work, a generalized description of 10 sedimentary classes or facies emerges. In Chapter 3 these classes are designated by the capital letters A through K and are roughly sequential from the base of the exposed sections to the modern surface. They are based on physical properties, including the presence or absence of cultural debris, but *not* on date. Hence, particular deposits, e.g., those of class C (see Chapter 3), are not necessarily restricted to one archaeological period. Suggestions as to the likely processes producing each class or facies are made in Chapter 4. A more detailed examination of certain processes fundamental to the understanding of the stratigraphic sequence is also included in Chapter 4.

A more detailed stratigraphic history is given for each excavation trench in Chapter 5. The strata are designated by Roman numerals, and correlation with archaeological excavation units is attempted wherever possible (Appendix B). Although a relative chronology is produced in this manner, it cannot be viewed as a site phasing in the archaeological sense. Instead, the chronological scheme merely represents a sequence as interpreted from the trench sections in the field, from section drawings, and from site notebooks, supplemented by available laboratory data. It must be emphasized that the definition of any given stratum is subjective. ''Splitters'' would have defined many more strata, ''lumpers'' rather less.

SOIL PROFILES

A detailed interpretation of a sedimentary sequence must take into account episodes of deposition and erosion and periods during which sediments were neither laid down nor removed, but weathered in place. Formal soil profile descriptions are an important basis for such interpretations.

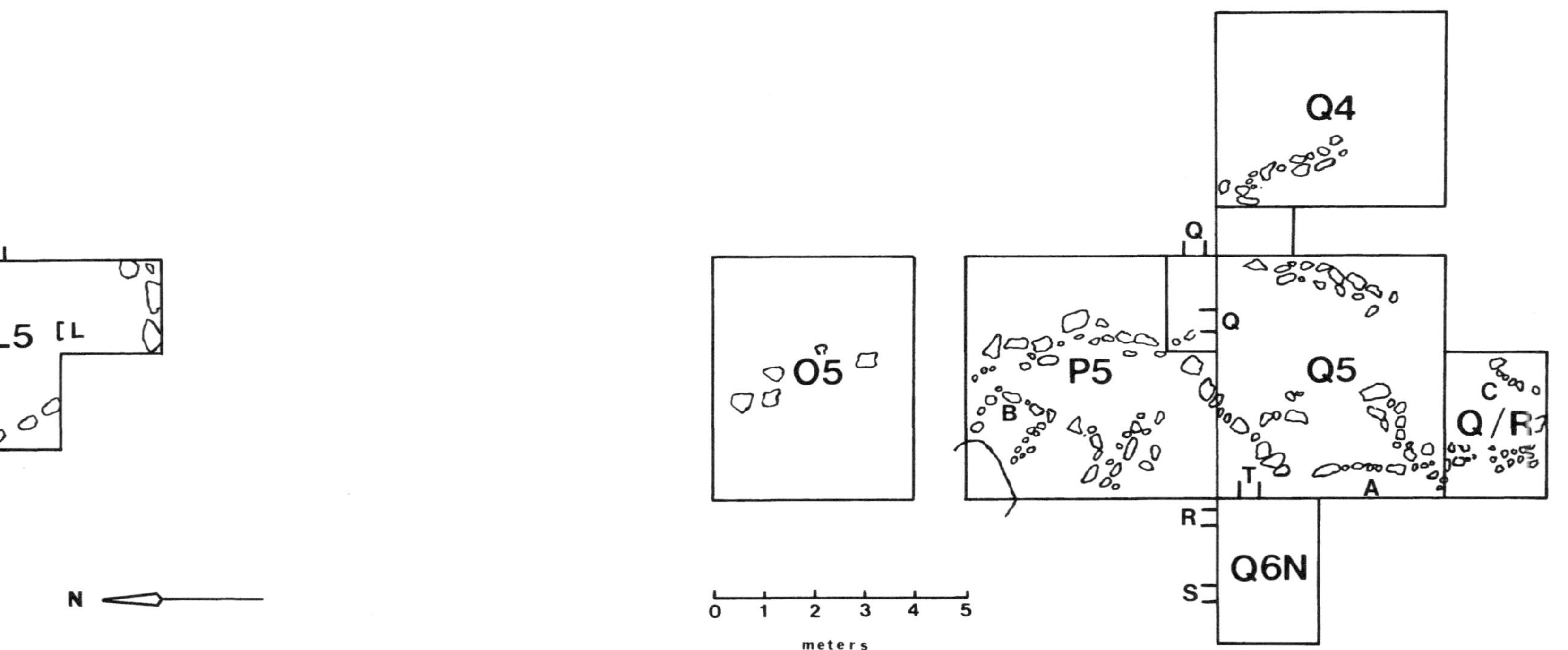

Figure 6. Plan of Paralia indicating sampling locations in relation to Neolithic walls. Labels L, Q, R, S, and T show locations of soil profiles. Labels A, B, and C show location of independent soil samples.

Five profiles were described and sampled as an aid to establishing stratigraphic relationships among the archaeological deposits on the Paralia. The data from these profiles furnish part of the framework on which the general classification of the sediments discussed in the next chapter rests. The locations of the five profiles are shown in Figure 6 (see also Jacobsen and Farrand 1987:Plates 40 and 41). They are labeled Q, R, S, T, and L. Profiles Q, R, S, and T are in approximate alignment and constitute a short traverse perpendicular to the slope contours. Profile L is located more than 20 m north of Profile Q, but at approximately the same elevation on the slope. Profiles L and Q are complete from the present ground surface, but profiles R, S, and T are truncated at the top, where overlying sediments were removed in the course of archaeological excavation. Formal descriptions of the profiles are also presented in the text below. In addition to these five profiles, four isolated samples, not part of any profile, were also collected. These, labeled A, B, C, and D, are discussed in Appendix E.

Profile Q (Figures 7-9) is the longest and most complete profile sampled. In order to sample a complete profile from the surface topsoil into the red substratum, it was necessary to take the samples from two locations (indicated on Figure 6). The samples above the broken line were taken from a spot to the east and slightly to the north of the lower part of the profile. The profile has been subdivided into soil horizons, layers approximately parallel to the surface, based upon characteristics observed in the field. These layers can be either sedimentary in origin or superimposed by pedogenic processes on pre-existing sedimentary strata. Such processes can include the activities of organisms and plant growth, water movement, diffusion, dispersion, flocculation of clay-sized material, expansion and contraction, weathering and clay enrichment (Bear 1964). The layers or horizons described approximate strata summarized in Chapter 5 and catalogued in more detail in Appendix B.

The morphology of profile Q is as follows. The colors in all profile descriptions are on dry soils unless specified as moist.

Sample	*Depth (cm)*	*Horizon*	
1	0-20	A1	Brown/dark brown (10YR 4/3) clay loam, dark brown (10YR 3/3) moist; weak fine-to-medium granular structure; hard; many roots and angular limestone cobbles.
2	20-38	A3	Brown/dark brown (7.5YR 4/4) clay loam, dark brown (7.5YR 3/4) moist; weak medium granular structure; hard; rootlets and angular and rounded gravels.
3	38-53	B21	Light yellowish brown to light brown (10YR-7.5YR 6/4) clay loam, dark brown (7.5YR 3.5/4) moist; weak medium granular structure; hard; rare rootlets and angular cobbles.
4	68-83	B22	Light yellowish brown (10YR 6/4) clay loam, dark brown (7.5YR 3/4) moist; weak medium granular structure; slightly hard; common angular cobbles.
5	83-108	IIB23	Light brown (7.5YR 6/4) loam, dark brown to dark reddish brown (7.5YR-5YR 3/4) moist; very weak medium subangular blocky structure; hard; rounded serpentinite gravels; abrupt boundary to:

6	108-123	IIIC1	Light brownish gray (10YR 6/2) loam, very dark grayish brown (10YR 3/2) moist; massive; soft; rare angular gravels.
7	123-158	IIIC2	Light brownish gray (10YR 6/2) silt loam, very dark grayish brown (10YR 3/2) moist; single grain; soft; common angular cobbles.
8	158-181	IIIC3	Brown (7.5YR 5/4) loam, brown/dark brown (7.5YR 4/4) moist; massive; soft; many angular cobbles.
9	181-228	IVB21b	Reddish yellow (5YR 6/6) silty clay loam, yellowish red (5YR 4/6) moist; moderate medium subangular blocky structure; hard; many boulders and cobbles.
10	228-253	IVB22b	Reddish yellow (5YR 6/6) clay loam, yellowish red (5YR 4/6) moist; moderate coarse subangular blocky structure; very hard; common boulders; charcoal.

In profile Q, a weakly developed solum has formed in the upper 108 cm. The solum comprises the A and B horizons and is the zone of soil formation. The A1 horizon, distinguished by its dark color and by the presence of organic matter, is the layer of maximum biological activity. The A3 horizon is transitional to B. The A1 and A3 horizons usually correspond to sediment class K or topsoil in the general classification scheme (Chapter 3). The B horizon is recognized here by its strong color and structure. The latter refers to aggregates of soil particles, specified according to their size, shape and arrangement, distinctness and durability. The C horizon is a layer of weathered, unconsolidated material, where the expression of pedogenic processes is minimal.

The Roman numeral prefixes (not related to the Roman numeral stratum designations discussed in Chapter 5) indicate lithologic discontinuities. The distinction is thus made between different parent materials in the same soil horizon or between pedogenic horizons and those of geologic or archaeological origin (USDA 1951, 1962). The first change to a redder, more coarsely textured horizon (IIB23) in which serpentinite pebbles (foreign inclusions) are present occurs in this profile at a depth of 83 cm. This horizon falls in sediment class D. At a depth of 108 cm there is an abrupt change to a silty horizon (IIIC1) which is brownish gray in color and contains quantities of pulverized charcoal in the silt-sized fraction. This horizon and the two immediately below, IIIC2 and IIIC3, are soft, loose, massive, and without soil structure. They are included in sediment class C.

At the base of the section, the reddish yellow horizons with structure are identified as parts of a buried B horizon. This paleosol formed on the pre-Neolithic landscape in the past and was subsequently buried by the deposits which overlie it. Its stronger color and more distinct structure (compared to the ground soil referred to above) imply a greater degree of soil development. These horizons are in sediment class A.

Samples taken from the profile were analyzed with respect to particle size, chemistry, and mineralogy. (Methods of analysis are discussed in Appendix C.) The solum of the ground soil and the paleosol have relatively high clay contents compared to the low clay and high silt content of horizons IIIC1, IIIC2, and IIIC3 (Figure 7).

The chemical parameters analyzed include organic carbon, iron and manganese oxides, calcium carbonate equivalent, cation-exchange capacity (hereafter CEC), extractable cations, and

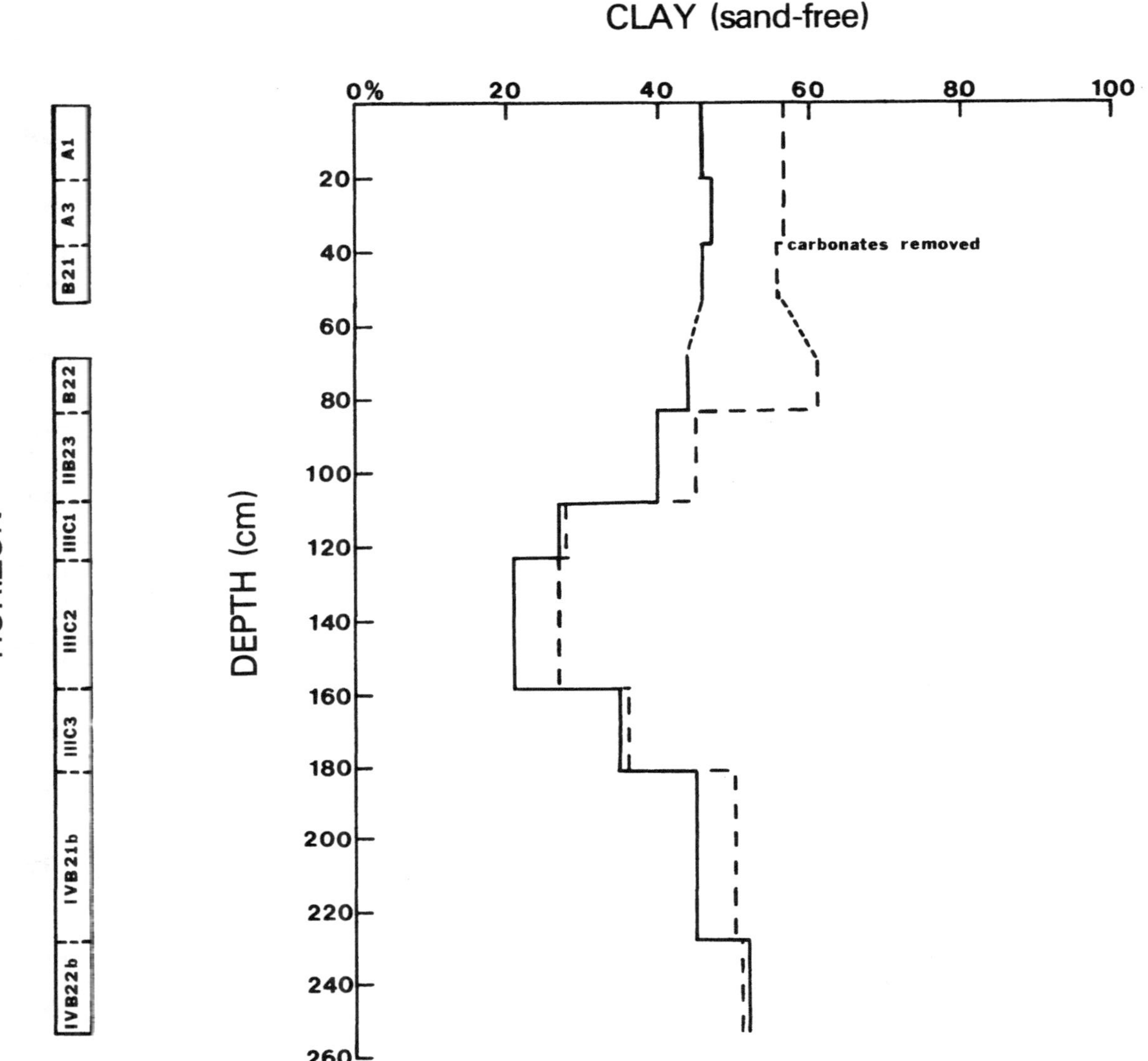

Figure 7. Soil profile Q: Percent clay expressed on a sand-free basis. Broken lines show the same information for samples from which carbonates were removed prior to particle-size analysis (see Appendix C).

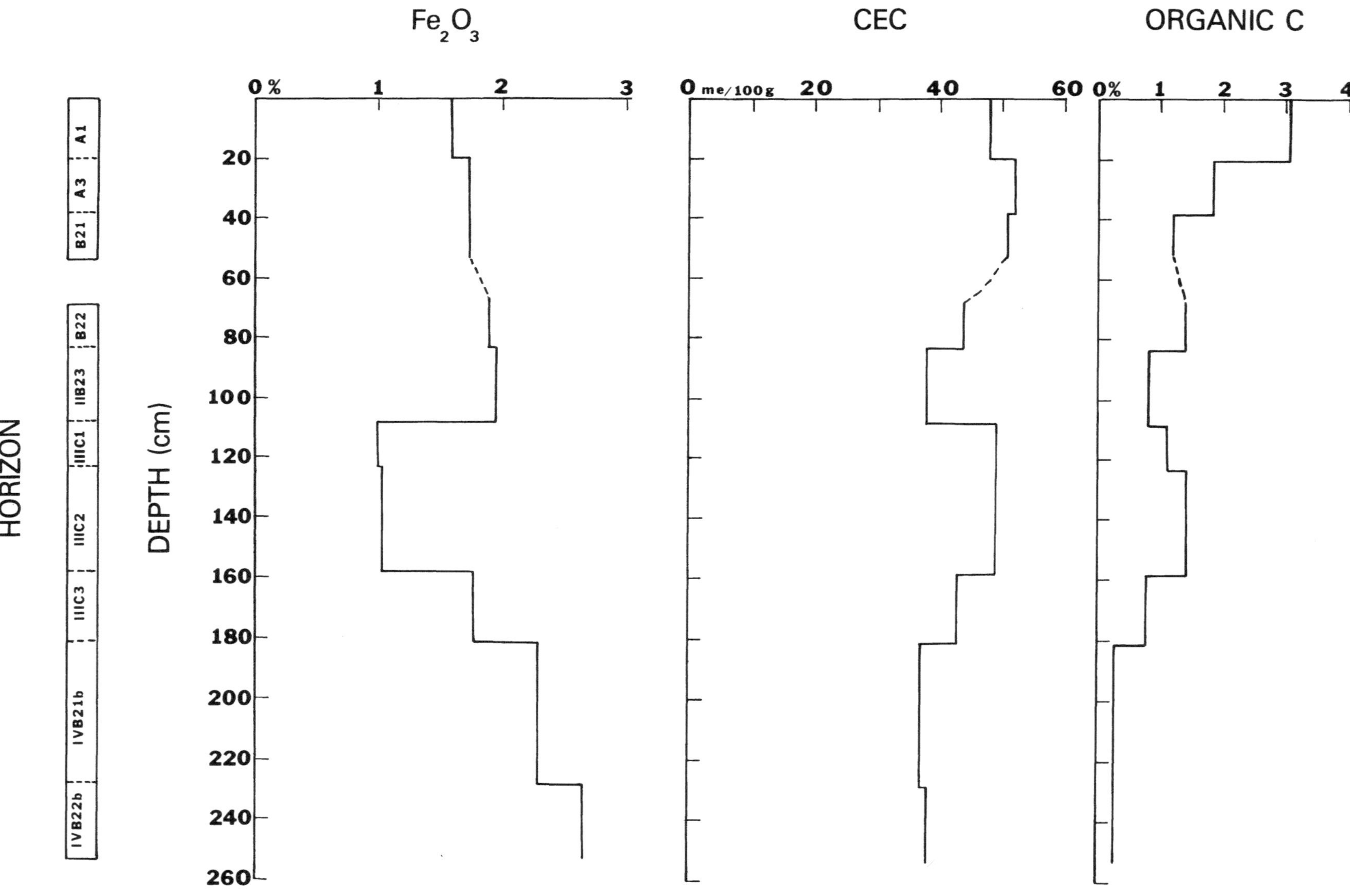

Figure 8. Soil profile Q: Chemistry.

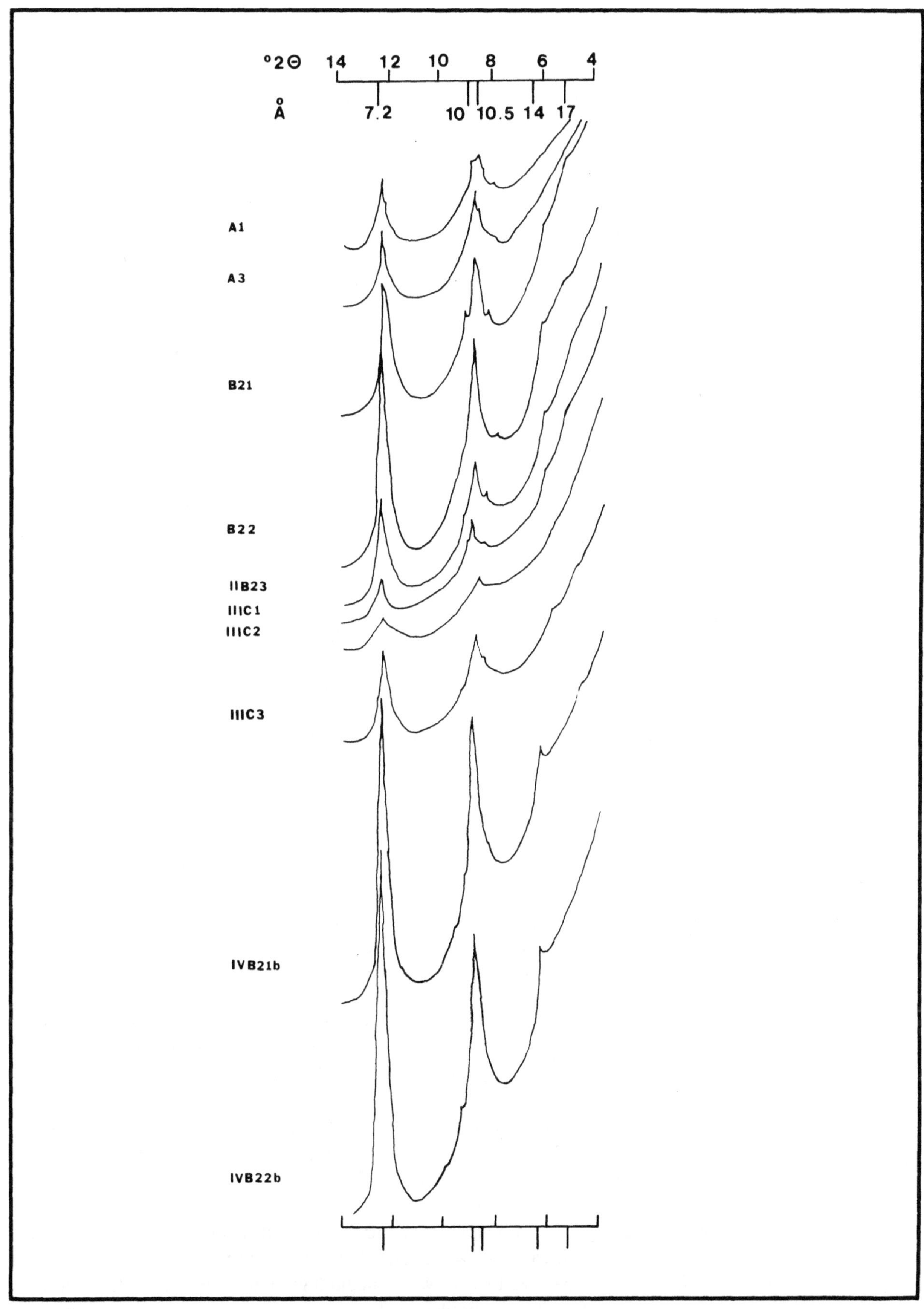

Figure 9. Soil profile Q: Smoothed and aligned glycolated x-ray diffraction patterns of the <2μm fraction.

pH (Figure 8). The consistently high values for calcium carbonate observed in the profile and elsewhere on Paralia are not surprising: limestone is a common rock locally and the rainfall is low, precluding effective leaching of the soil. The neutral or somewhat alkaline pH values are also expected in calcareous soils. Iron and manganese oxides form in the soil as part of the weathering process. Iron oxides are in large part responsible for the reddish and yellowish hues observed. This correspondence can be seen in profile Q by comparing the iron oxide curve with the Munsell colors reported in the profile description. Samples relatively high in iron oxide, as in samples Q5 and Q10, tend to have a redder hue—7.5YR or 5YR in the Munsell system. Note also the rough parallelism of the iron oxide curve with the curve for percentage of clay. Organic carbon is predictably high in the A horizon of the ground soil. It decreases with depth except for moderately high values in the IIIC horizons. In profile Q, CEC is relatively high in the upper 83 cm and in horizons IIIC1, IIIC2, and IIIC3. It is comparatively low in the IIB23 horizon and in the paleosol.

Mineralogically, as determined by x-ray diffraction and by examination of the sand fractions under the microscope, profile Q has abundant calcite and quartz in the coarse fractions. The calcite occurs in the form of limestone and shell fragments, as well as cement for aggregates of particles. The <2 micrometer (μm) fraction includes calcite, quartz, and clay minerals. The clay mineralogy of the profile is characterized by a suite dominated by kaolinite and illite, with varying amounts of chlorite, expandable minerals and minor palygorskite. (The identification of the clay minerals is discussed in Appendix D.) Figure 9 shows aligned, glycolated x-ray diffraction patterns for profile Q. The peaks of kaolinite (7.2 Å) and illite (10 Å) are sharpest and most intense in the B horizon of the ground soil and also of the paleosol. In the paleosol, distinct chlorite peaks (14 Å) are also present. In contrast, the peaks for horizons IIIC1, IIIC2, and IIIC3 are much more subdued.

Profiles R, S, and T are located a few meters downslope from profile Q. Profiles R and S are similar and are discussed together. Profile T, in spite of its proximity to the others, is very different. Since much of it is missing, profile T is only briefly discussed.

Profile R (Figures 10 and 11)

Sample	*Depth (cm)*	*Hori-zon*	
1	0-30	B21	Grayish brown (10YR 5/2) loam, very dark grayish brown (10YR 3/2) moist; weak-medium-granular-to-subangular-blocky structure; slightly hard, roots and gravel.
2	30-52	B22	Light brownish gray (10YR 6/2) loam, very dark grayish brown (10YR 3/2) moist; weak-medium-granular-to-fine-subangular-blocky structure; slightly hard; cobbly.
3	52-80	C1	Light brownish gray (10YR 6/2) loam, dark brown (10YR 3/3) moist; massive-to-very-weak medium granular structure; soft to slightly hard; cobbly.
4	80-103	C2	Light brownish gray (10YR 6/2) silt loam, very dark grayish brown (10YR 3/2) and dark reddish brown (5YR 3/2) moist; massive-to-very-weak medium granular; slightly hard; cobbly; carbonate nodules.

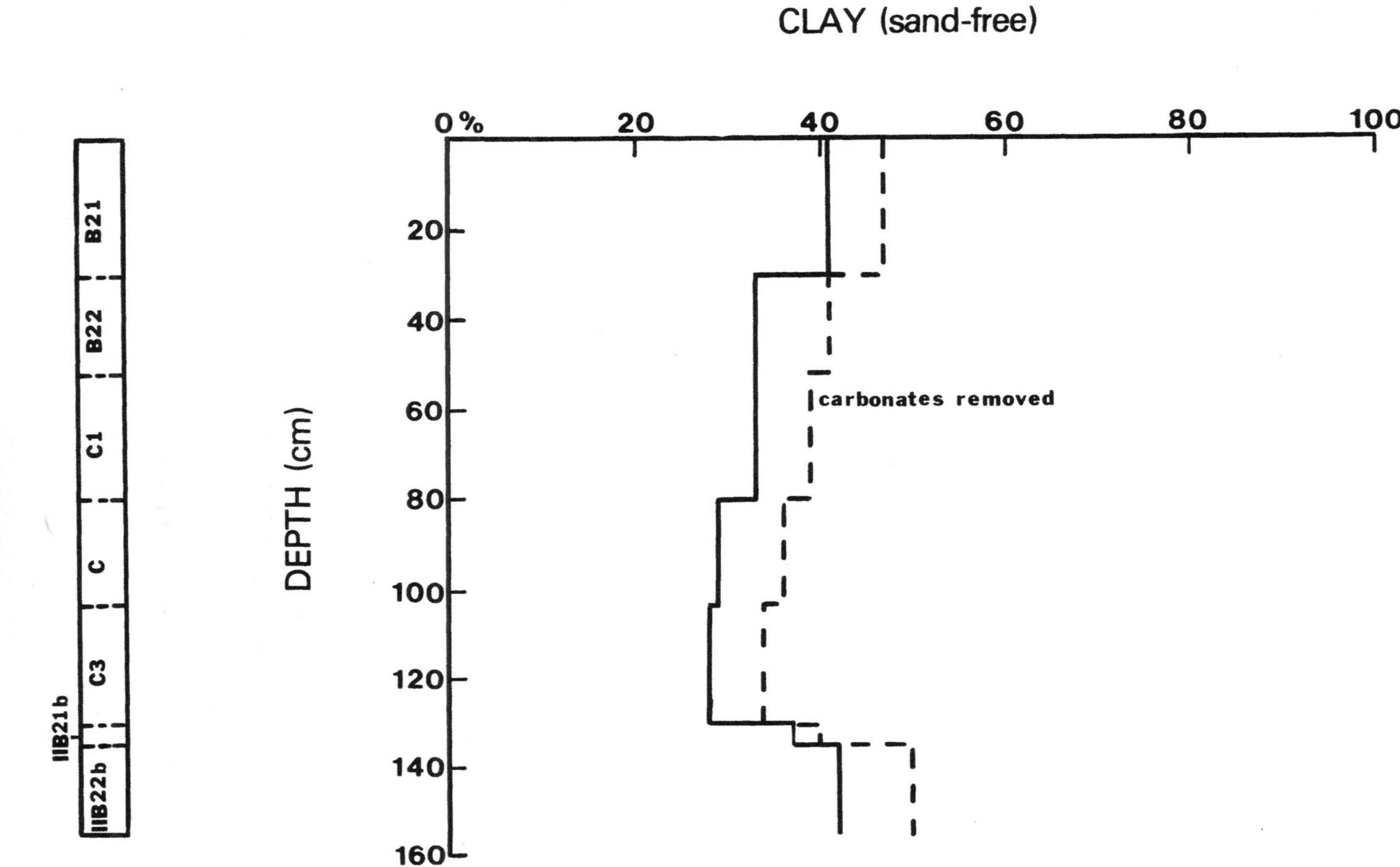

Figure 10. Soil profile R: Percent clay expressed on a sand-free basis, with and without removal of carbonates.

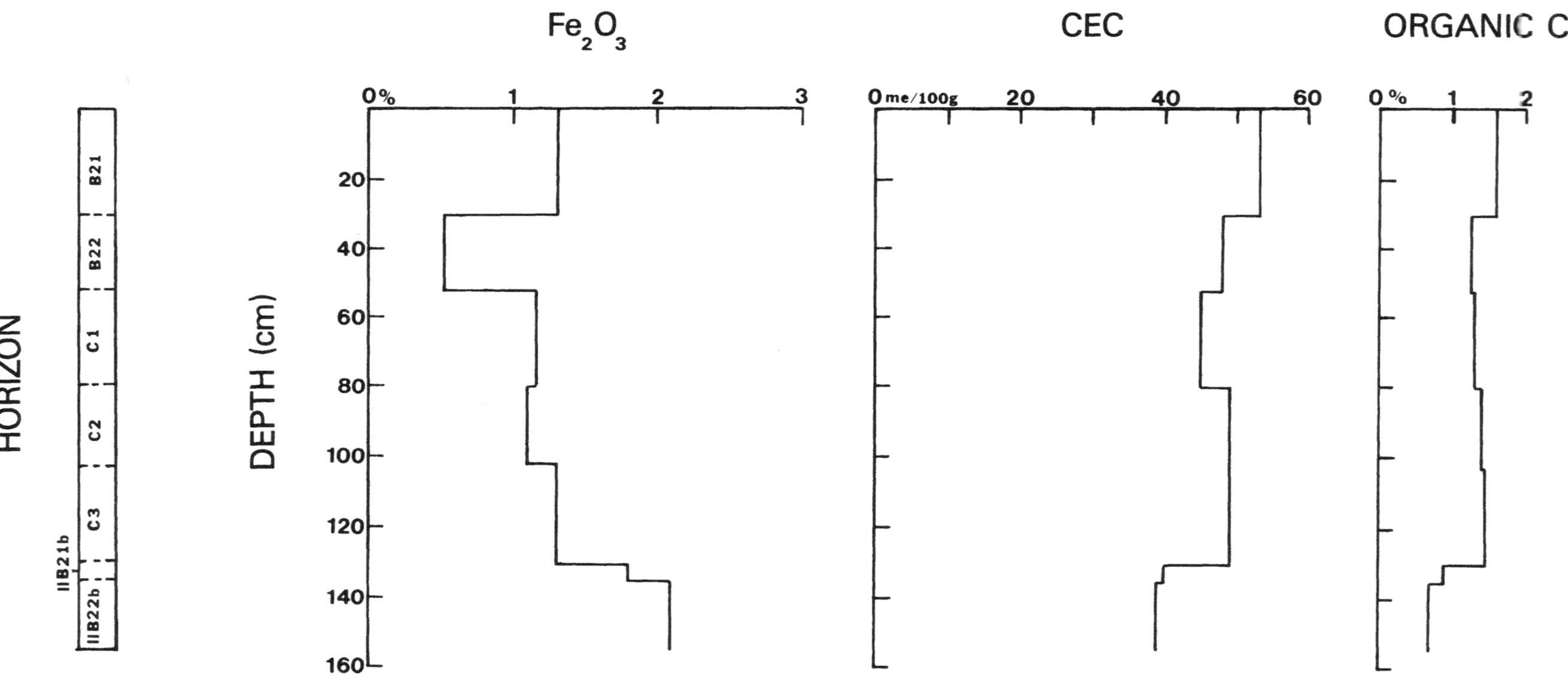

Figure 11. Soil profile R: Chemistry.

5	103-130	C3	Brown (10YR 5/3) silt loam, dark brown (7.5 YR 3/2-10YR 3/3) moist; massive-to-very-weak medium granular; slightly hard; cobbly; carbonate nodules.
6	130-135	IIB21b	Light brown (7.5YR 6/4) clay loam, brown/dark brown (7.5YR 4/4) moist; weak medium subangular blocky structure; slightly hard; cobbly; much charcoal.
7	135-155	IIB22b	Brown (7.5YR 5/4) clay loam, dark brown (7.5YR 3/4) moist; moderate medium subangular blocky structure; hard; cobbly; many small gastropods.

Profile S (Figures 12 and 13)

1	0-20	B21	Light brownish gray (10YR 6/2) silt loam, very dark grayish brown (10YR 3/2) moist; weak medium granular structure; slightly hard; cobbly.
2	20-40	B22	Brown (10YR 5/3) loam, dark brown (10YR 3/3) moist; weak medium granular structure; slightly hard; cobbly.
3	40-55	B23	Light brownish gray (10YR 6/2) loam, very dark grayish brown (10YR 6/2) moist; weak medium granular structure; slightly hard; cobbly.
4	55-70	C1	Light brown (7.5YR 6/4) loam, dark brown (7.5YR 3/4) moist; massive-to-very-weak medium granular structure; slightly hard; cobbly.
5	70-85	C2	Light brownish gray (10YR 6/2) loam, very dark grayish brown (10YR 3/2) moist; massive; slightly hard; cobbly; bee holes.
6	85-90	IIA1b	Brown (7.5YR 5/4) clay loam, dark brown (7.5YR 3/4) moist; weak medium subangular blocky; slightly hard; cobbly; includes a discontinuous layer of carbonate accumulation.
7	90-100	IIB2b	Yellowish-red-to-strong-brown (5-7.5YR 5/6) clay loam, yellowish red to strong brown (5-7.5YR 4/6) moist; moderate medium subangular blocky; hard; cobbly.

Profile T (Figures 14 and 15)

	0-70		Missing.
1	70-92	B21	Pink (7.5YR 7/4) silt loam, dark brown (7.5YR 3/4) moist; very weak fine granular to subangular blocky; slightly hard; cobbly.

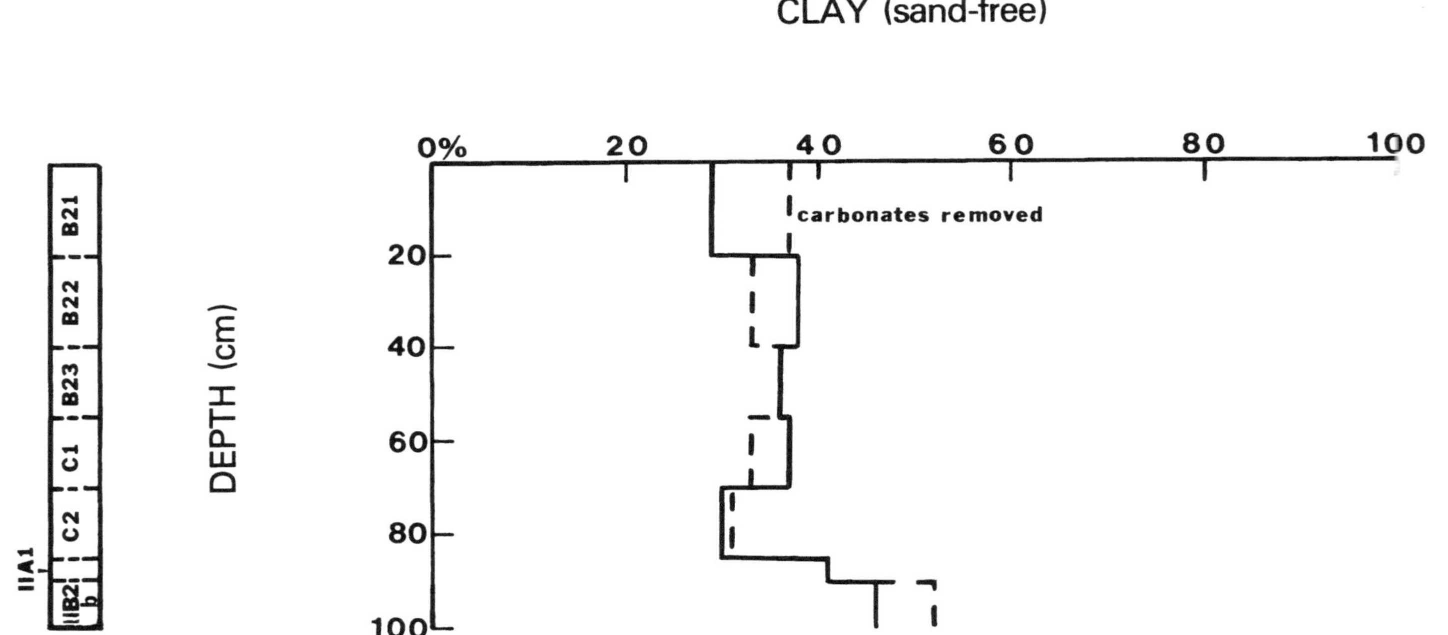

Figure 12. Soil profile S: Percent clay expressed on a sand-free basis, with and without removal of carbonates.

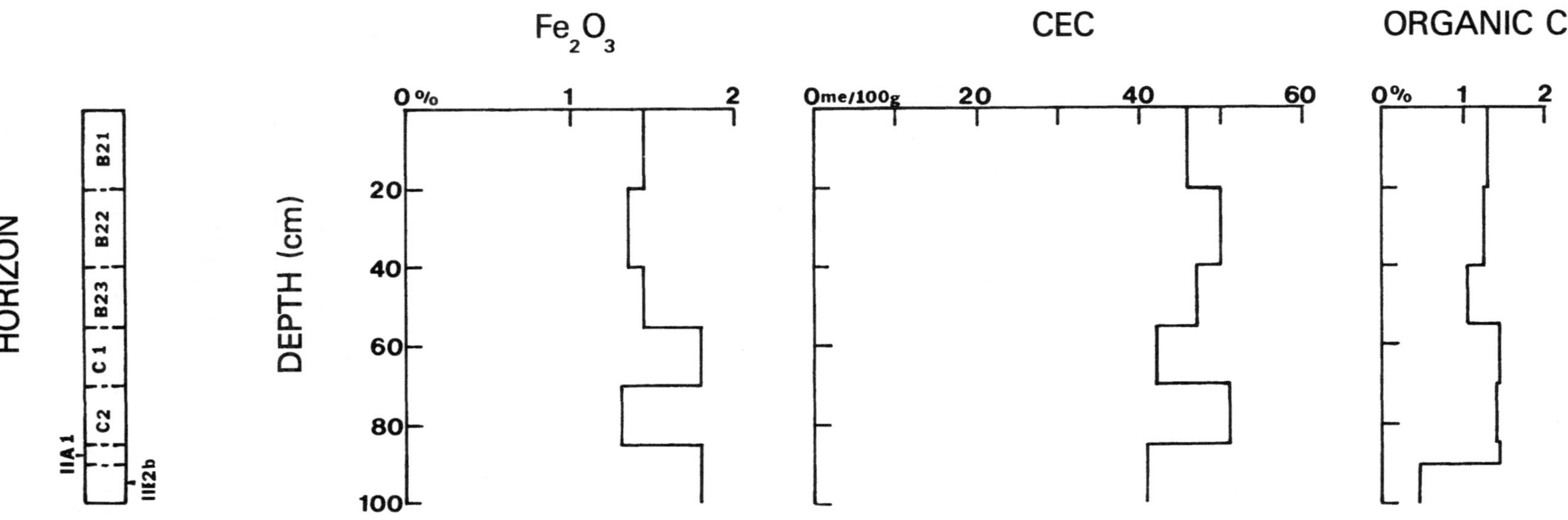

Figure 13. Soil profile S: Chemistry.

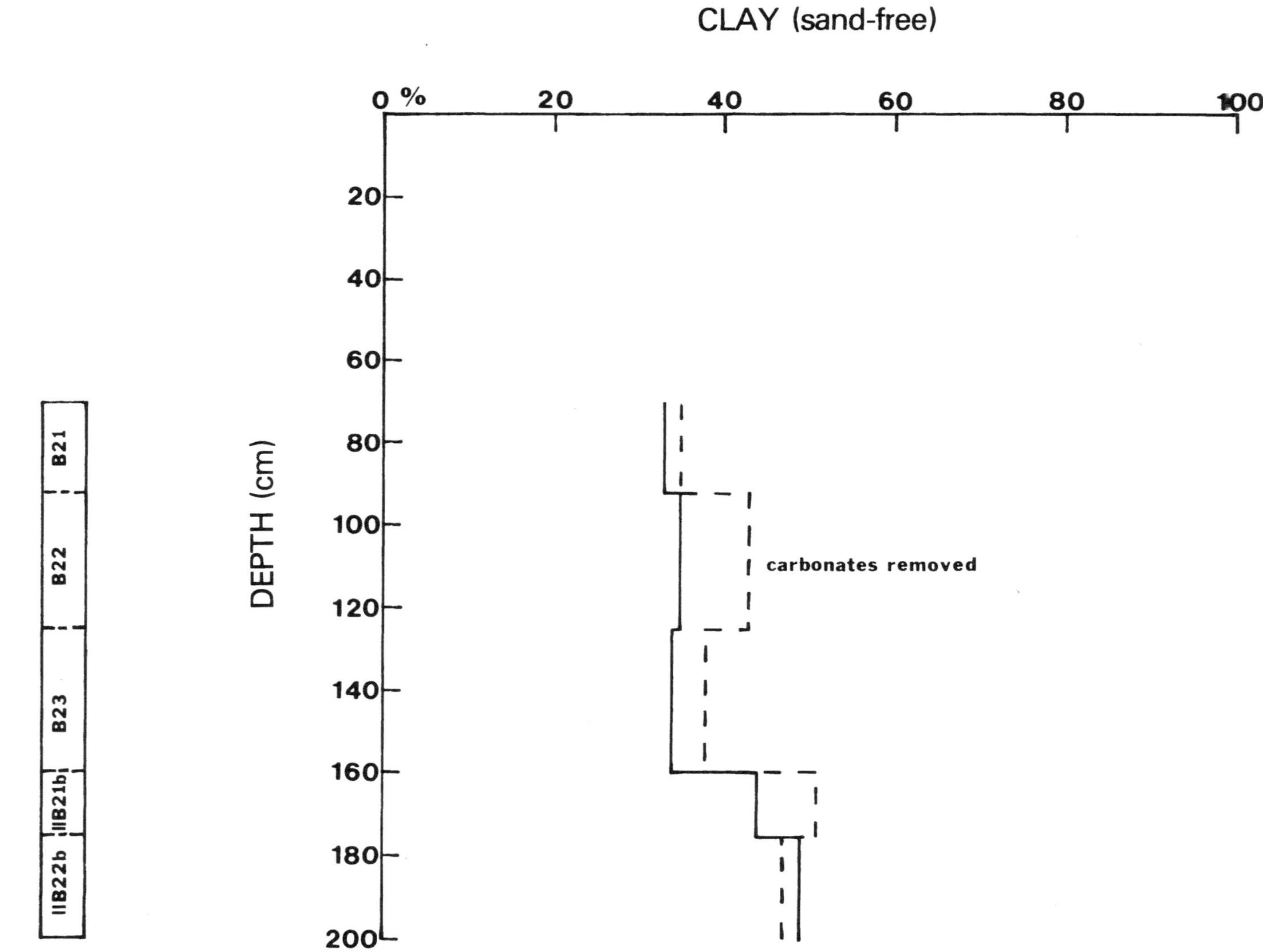

Figure 14. Soil profile T: Percent clay expressed on a sand-free basis, with and without removal of carbonates.

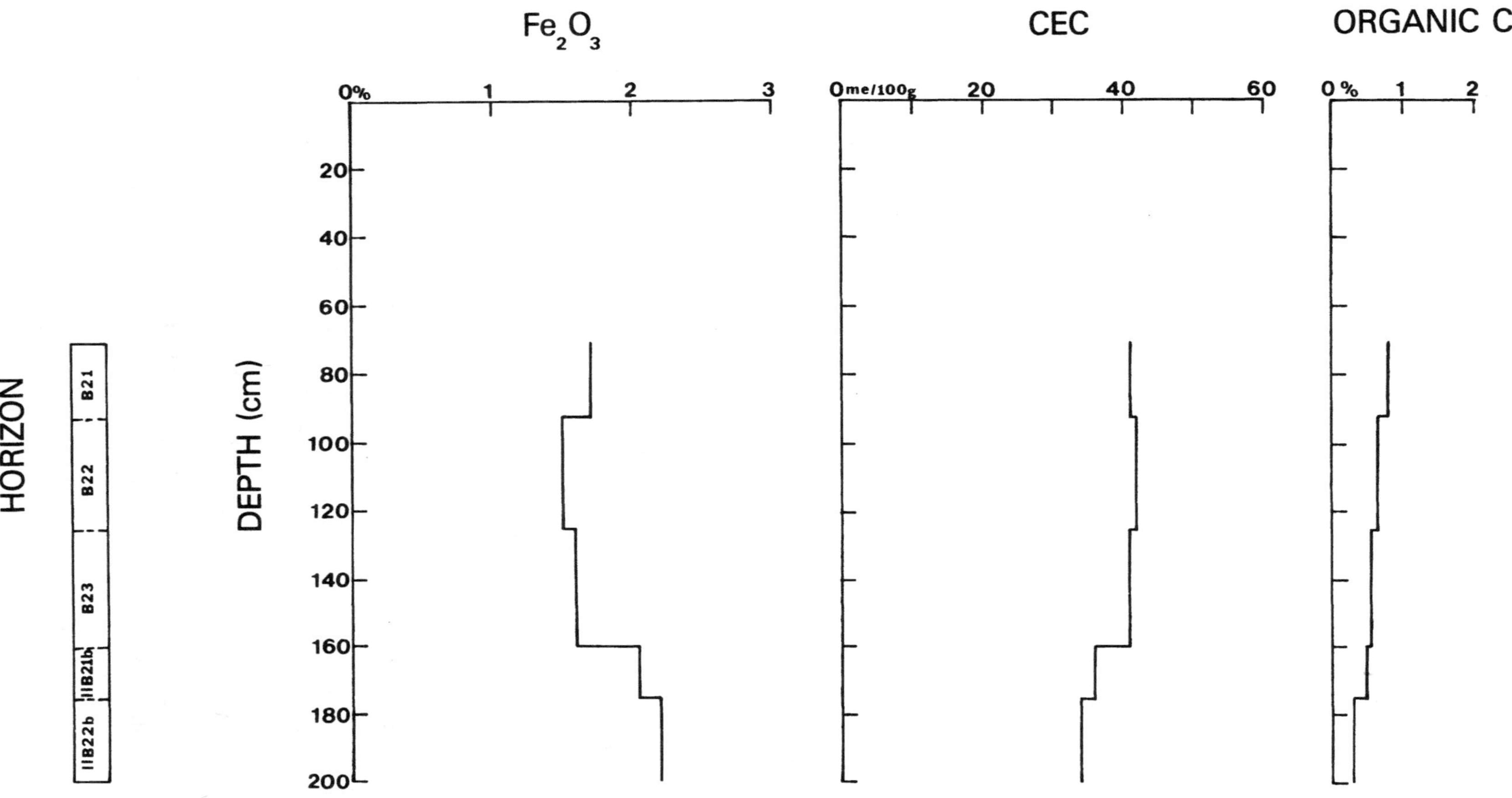

Figure 15. Soil profile T: Chemistry.

2	92-125	B22	Light brown (7.5YR 6/4) loam, yellowish-red-to-dark-brown (5YR 4/6-7.5YR 3/4) moist; very weak medium subangular blocky; slightly hard; cobbly; band of marine shells.
3	125-160	B23	Light brown (7.5YR 6/4) silty clay loam, dark brown (7.5YR 3/4) moist; very weak medium subangular blocky; slightly hard; cobbles and boulders.
4	160-175	IIB21b	Brown (7.5YR 5/4) clay loam, dark brown (7.5YR 3/4) moist; weak medium subangular blocky; slightly hard to hard; cobbly.
5	175-200	IIB22b	Yellowish red (5YR 5/6) clay loam, yellowish red (5YR 4/6) moist; moderate medium subangular blocky; hard; cobbly; charcoal.

In profiles R and S, a weakly developed ground soil is again observed overlying a moderately developed paleosol. The A1 horizon of the ground soil is missing, having been removed during excavation. The B horizon, recognized by the presence of soil structure, grades gradually into the C horizon. A buried A1 horizon associated with the paleosol is recognized in profile S on the basis of its dark color, the presence of structure, and content of organic matter. This horizon is absent or indistinguishable in profile R. The buried B horizon is recognized by its strong color and moderate structural development.

In contrast to profile Q, the entire ground soil of profiles R and S is formed in silty materials of brownish gray to brown (10YR) hues. These sediments belong in class E. Lenses of more reddish (5-7.5YR) materials are present, however. Finely divided charcoal is abundant. Organic carbon is consistently high in the B and C horizons of the ground soil, but iron oxide content and CEC are variable. In particular, iron oxide values are high and CEC is low in horizon C1 of profile S (Figures 11 and 13). The paleosol in both profiles (formed in sediment class A material) is characterized by increases in clay (Figures 10 and 12), in iron and manganese oxides, and by a relatively low CEC, but these properties are expressed less strongly than in profile Q.

The mineralogy of profiles R-T does not differ from that of profile Q. Calcite and quartz are abundant in the coarser fractions, and kaolinite and illite dominate the clay minerals. The buried soil formed in sediment class A materials is identifiable at the base of profile T by the increase in clay (Figure 14), but the boundary between it and the ground soil developed in overlying material is diffuse. Although the upper 70 cm of the profile is removed, a B horizon associated with the missing surface appears to be present, judging by the observed soil structure. Organic carbon and CEC are low throughout the profile (Figure 15). Mineralogically, profile T is similar to profiles Q, R, and S.

Profile L (Figures 16-19) is located approximately 25 meters north of profiles Q, R, S, and T. The last sample of the profile was taken from a location slightly to the south and west of the rest of the profile in order to be sure of including the red substratum. Its morphology follows. The broken line indicates a point of offset within the section, the lower section being near I in Figure 35.

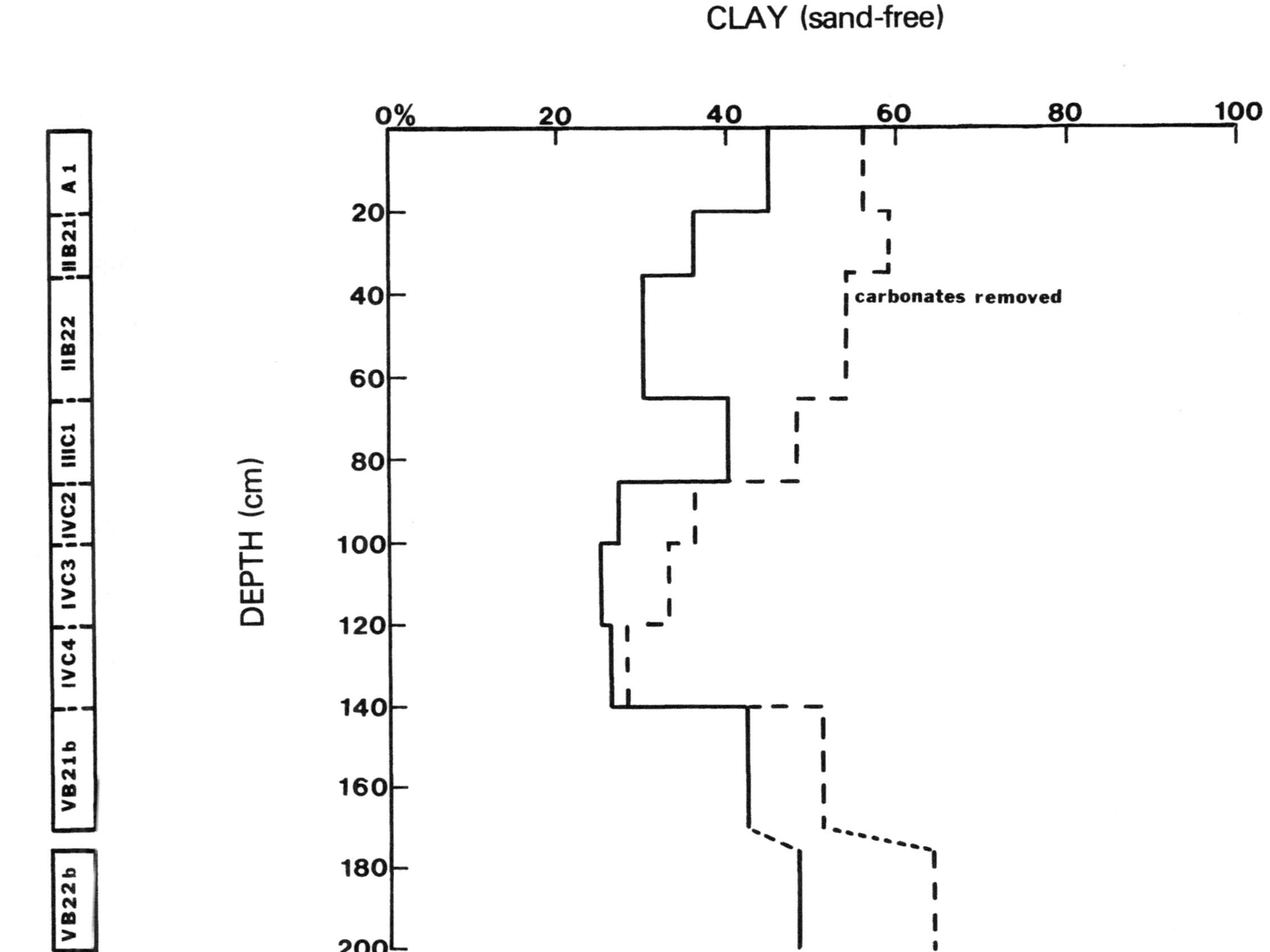

Figure 16. Soil profile L: Percent clay expressed on a sand-free basis, with and without removal of carbonates.

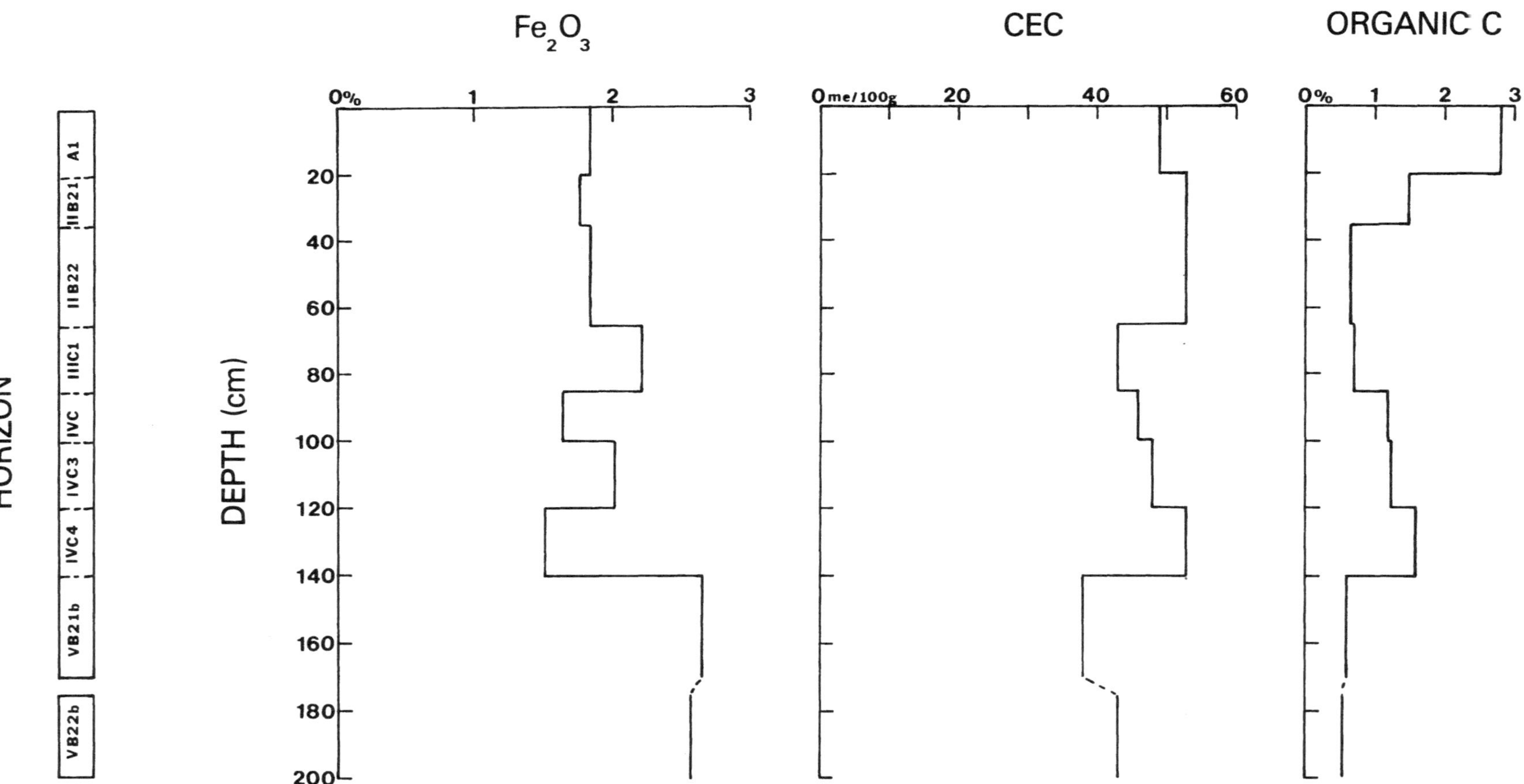

Figure 17. Soil profile L: Chemistry.

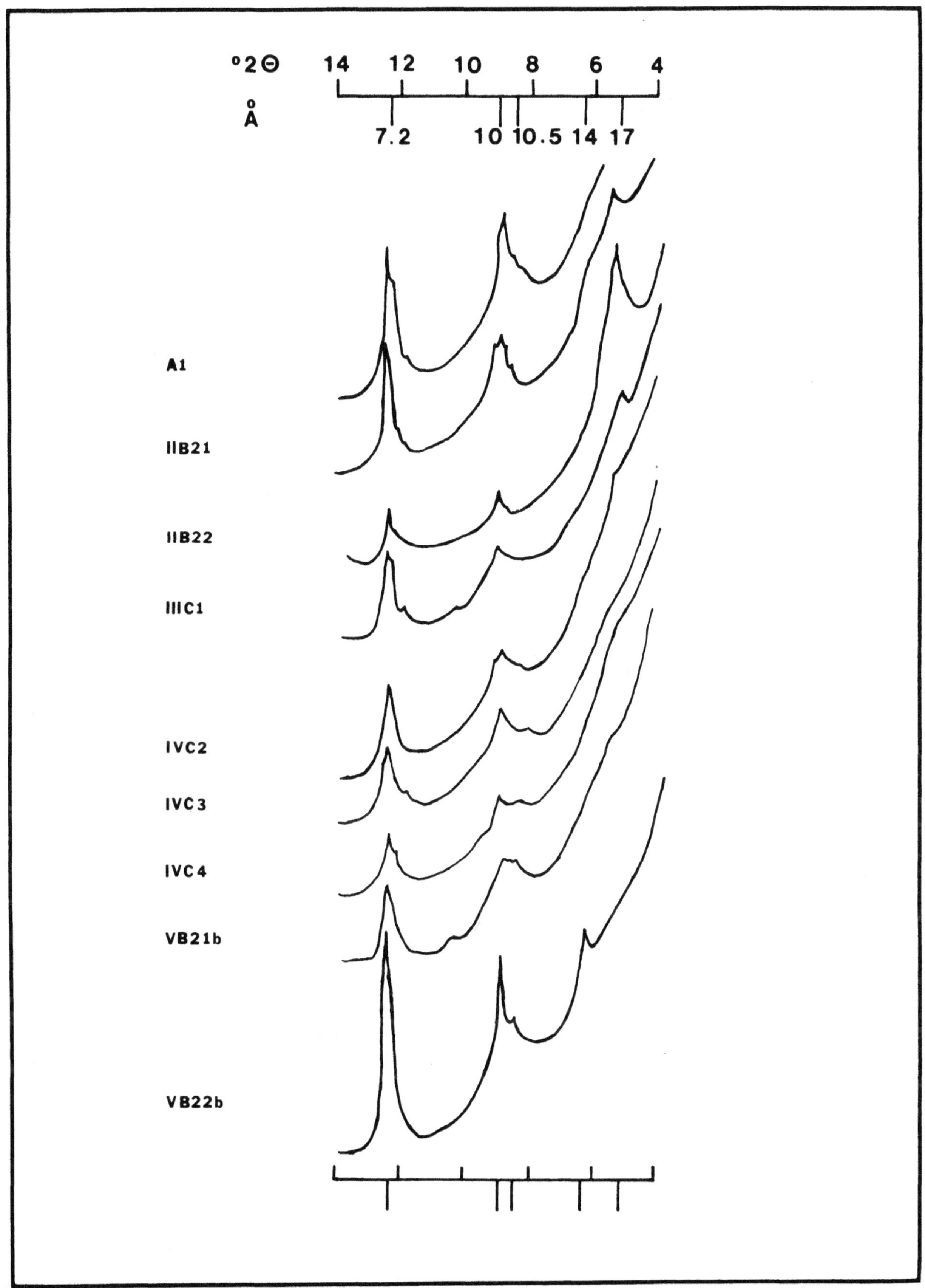

Figure 18. Soil profile L: Smoothed and aligned glycolated x-ray diffraction patterns of the <2μm fraction.

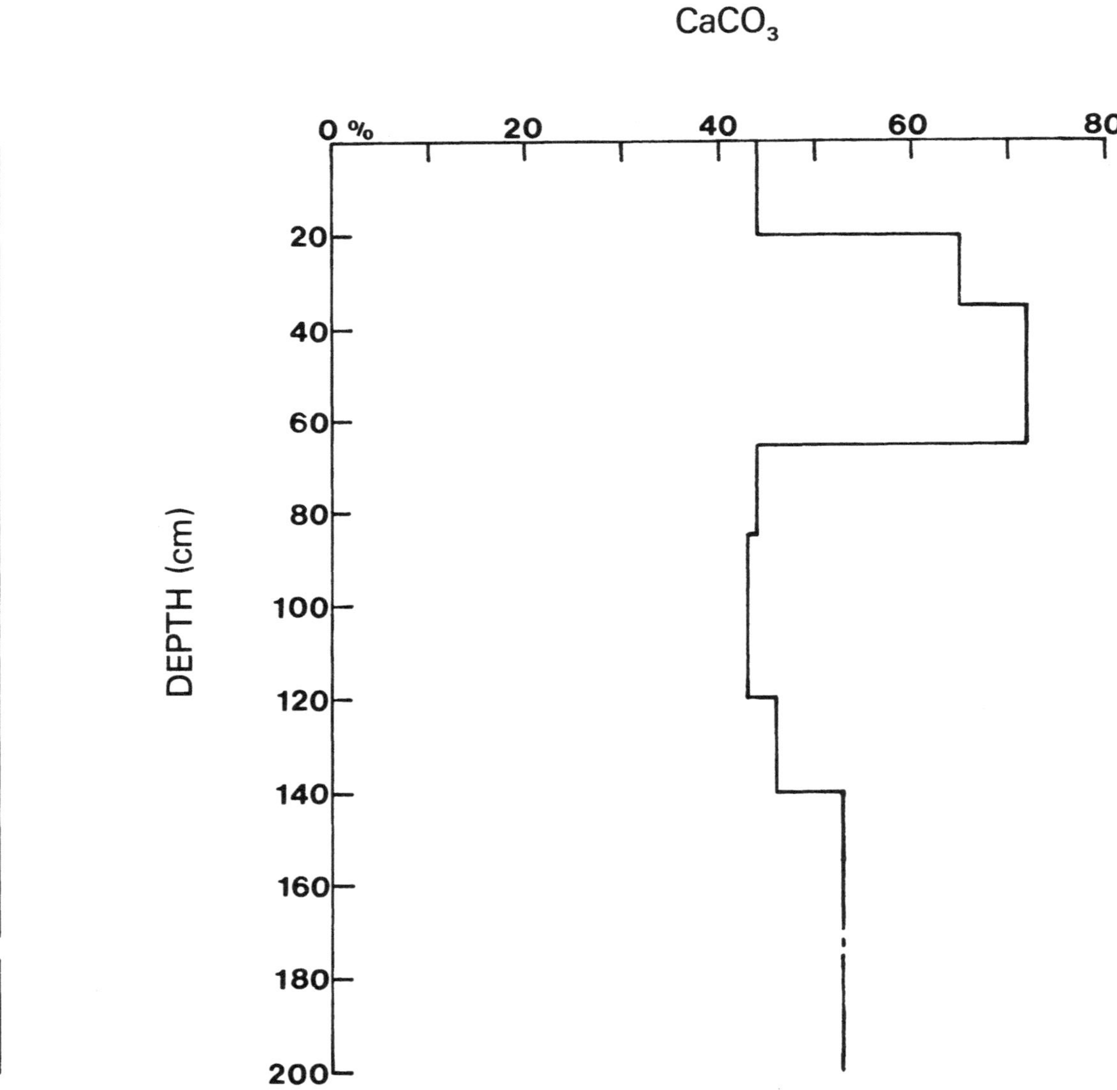

Figure 19. Soil profile L: Calcium carbonate equivalent.

Sample	*Depth (cm)*	*Horizon*	
1	0-20	A1	Brown (10YR 5/3) clay loam, dark brown (10YR 3/2) moist; weak medium subangular blocky; slightly hard; large carbonate nodules; roots; rare cobbles and boulders.
2	20-35	IIB21	Light yellowish brown (10YR 6/4) silty clay loam, dark brown to brown (7.5YR 3/2-10YR 4/3) moist; weak medium subangular blocky; slightly hard; large carbonate nodules and finely divided dispersed carbonates; cobbly.
3	35-65	IIB22	Pink (7.5YR 7/4) silt loam, reddish-brown-to-brown/dark-brown (5YR 5/3-7.5YR 4/4) moist; weak medium subangular blocky; very hard; much finely divided dispersed carbonate; rare gravels.
4	65-85	IIIC1	Light brown (7.5YR 6/4) clay loam, dark-reddish-brown-to-dark-brown (5-7.5YR 3/4) moist; massive; hard; cobbly.
5	85-100	IVC2	Pale brown (10YR 6/3) silt loam, dark brown (10YR 3/3) moist; massive; slightly hard; cobbly.
6	100-120	IVC3	Pale brown (10YR 6/3) silt loam, dark brown (7.5YR 3/2) moist; massive; slightly hard; cobbly; roots.
7	120-140	IVC4	Brown (10YR 5/3) silt loam, dark brown (10YR 3/3) moist; single grain; soft; cobbly; charcoal under rocks.
8	140-170	VB21b	Reddish yellow (5YR 7/6) loam, yellowish red (5YR 4/6) moist; weak medium granular; slightly hard; very cobbly, sparse matrix.
9	170-200	VB22b	Reddish yellow (5YR 6/6) clay loam, yellowish red (5YR 5/6) moist; moderate medium subangular blocky to medium granular; hard; cobbles and boulders.

Profile L resembles profile Q in its broad features, but it differs in detail. A weak soil profile is formed in the upper part, and the paleosol is recognized at the base of the section by its reddish yellow hue and moderate structure.

The lithologic changes are of some importance. The first of these occurs at a depth of 20 cm and is marked by high carbonate content. Carbonate equivalent averages 68% from 20 to 65 cm (horizons IIB21-22) in profile L, compared to about 41% for the rest of Paralia (Figure 19). This lithologic stratum is in sediment class H. The calcium carbonate is in large part secondary, occurring as soft lumps and finely dispersed in the soil matrix. The latter causes colors of high value (6-7) and moderate chroma (4) in the dry soil, giving it a whitish appearance. The occurrence of this whitened soil is observed elsewhere in grid square L5 to be discontinuous and frequently localized in pits. Smectite is a dominant component of the clay mineral suite in horizons IIB21 and IIB22, and it is also present in the IIIC1 and IVC2 horizons.

The next lithologic change, which occurs at a depth of 65 cm, is to a massive, reddish (5-7.5YR) clay loam (horizon IIIC1) included in sediment class D. Horizon IIIC1 overlies a sequence of massive pale brown to brown silt loam (IVC2, 3, 4) belonging to sediment class C, which begins at a depth of 85 cm.

The final lithologic change occurs at a depth of 140 cm at the top of the paleosol. In its upper part, the paleosol is a very stony loam with sparse matrix.

Particle size and soil chemistry are shown in Figures 16 and 17. Organic carbon is high in the A1 horizon and decreases with depth, but it increases again in the IVC horizons. The curve is subparallel to the organic-carbon curve in profile Q. CEC also is similar in profiles L and Q, being higher in the solum of the ground soil and in the organic-rich, grayish brown, silty C horizons. Iron oxide is somewhat variable in profile L, but it is highest in the paleosol.

The mineralogy of this profile is comparable with that observed in other profiles, except for the presence of smectite as mentioned above. Figure 18 shows the aligned, glycolated patterns for the <2 μm fraction of profile L. Subdued peaks, especially for the 10 Å mineral, are observed in the central part of the profile, particularly in the IVC horizons.

CHAPTER THREE

Classification of the Excavated Sediments

The Paralia sediments were described in the field by T. J. Wilkinson during the 1974, 1976, and 1979 seasons. In 1979, the preliminary field sections were redrawn and fully checked, with particular attention given to soil properties, layer boundaries (interfaces), stone content, and stone/potsherd orientation. Descriptions of all significant archaeological layers are given in the stratigraphic catalogue (Appendix B). In the following discussion, a *stratum* is a body of sediment that differs from adjacent sedimentary bodies by its color and/or texture. A single stratum can include minor changes in stone content or texture, and these are designated by lowercase letters where appropriate. If the stratum was laid down primarily as the result of human activity in the past, it is an archaeological stratum, but it may not necessarily have accumulated during a single chronological phase. Its role in building up a stratigraphic sequence is discussed in Chapter 5.

Ten sedimentary classes are described below. They are based primarily on the field observations referred to above, supplemented by data from laboratory analyses. These sedimentary classes and their associated strata are summarized in Table 1 (Chapter 4). Following the description of these classes, the process of deposition of certain deposits is examined in more detail.

CLASS A: STONY RED COLLUVIUM

The lowermost unit that has been exposed is a stony, red colluvium. It is the foundation upon which the cultural deposits of the footslope rest, and it also apparently underlies the midslope. In fact, the large number of exposures suggests that this deposit underlies the entire area of the debris slopes.

A long section, demonstrating the variability of the deposit, has been eroded by the sea along the shoreline (Figure 3), and smaller exposures occur on the mid- or footslope. Stony red colluvium was also encountered during archaeological excavation, where it was loosely termed "Pleistocene Red" or "Basal Red." In the soil profiles, it is recognized as the parent material of the B horizon of a buried soil. Since the correspondence is nearly exact, its properties are in part sedimentary and in part pedogenic.

Stone size in the deposit varies from large boulders in excess of one meter in diameter down to angular or subangular gravel (2-60 mm, long axis). Along the marine cut, boulders are more frequent near the bedrock spurs (talus accumulations dominate elsewhere), but boulders can and do occur throughout the deposit.

The fine matrix (mean diameter less than 2 mm), although variable, is normally yellowish red (5YR 5/6 or 5YR 4/6, dry) clay loam. It ranges from extensive, where stones are matrix supported, to very sparse, where "openwork" talus has developed. The chaotic variation of stone size, content, and matrix illustrated in Figure 4 would appear to result from varying amounts of boulder collapse, talus accumulation, and intervening zones of fine sediment deposition.

Rocks within the colluvium are invariably limestone. This fact is important for the interpretation of the archaeological deposits because non-limestone rocks must therefore have been introduced by man. Occasional charcoal flecks or artifacts noted within the red colluvium near its interface with the overlying cultural sediments probably result from contamination or mixing. The deposit is relatively hard since it has been partly cemented by the precipitation of calcium carbonate.

The stony red colluvium of the Paralia closely resembles sediments found at the base of the cave sequence. Radiocarbon determinations on charcoal from the red-hued cave sediments yielded dates ranging from 22,000 B.P. to 10,000 B.P., that is, within the late Pleistocene. Similar deposits, but with variable stone contents, occur to the east of the cave in the Kiladha valley, where they were called "old red" sediments by van Andel et al. (1980). These deposits, termed the "Loutro alluvium" at their type exposure, have yielded radiometric dates of 280,000 +50,000/-33,000; 52,000 ± 4000; and 35,000 ± 3000 years B.P., again placing them within the later Pleistocene (Pope et al. 1984:Table 3; see also van Andel and Sutton 1987). A geophysical reflective layer, below present sea level within Kiladha Bay, probably corresponds with the downslope members of the stony red colluvium (van Andel et al. 1980), and this again supports a pre-Holocene date for the red colluvial deposit.

Although the Paralia stony red colluvium was mainly archaeologically sterile, a thin, red-hued talus (L5 II, Figure 35, subclass A2 in Table 1) containing Early Neolithic sherds accumulated within the upper part of the stony red colluvium in grid square L5. This suggests that the upper skin of the red colluvium might have remained active during the early Holocene.

The stony red colluvium accumulated during the late Pleistocene as a result of a complex of processes. Relatively fine-grained sediments, which may have been red-hued and clay-rich due to weathering prior to transport, were washed from the surrounding limestone hillslopes to accumulate as a matrix around the locally derived rock debris. Debris flows moving downslope may also have contributed poorly sorted masses of clayey, stony material to the footslope deposits.

Prior to the accumulation of Neolithic cultural deposits on the footslope, a soil profile developed in the colluvium thus accumulated, resulting in further reddening and clay enrichment. The development of the soil profile at this time implies a relatively stable land surface and marks a hiatus in rapid erosional or depositional processes. The beginning of the period of soil formation cannot be determined exactly, but a late Pleistocene date is reasonable on the basis of the dates cited above. Soil formation slowed and then ceased in the early Holocene, when Neolithic occupation of the Paralia began and sediments again accumulated rapidly. The colluvial deposit upon which the archaeological deposits lie therefore accumulated during the later Pleistocene, but the soil which developed in this deposit formed during late Pleistocene and early Holocene times. Figure 20 illustrates the contoured surface of the strong red colluvium based upon the excavated sections.

CLASS B: LOWER GRAVELLY LOAM

This class usually occurs in a stratigraphically low position. It generally overlies A and grades into C. Sediments in this class are mainly pale brown or light brownish gray silt loams or loams. Where they overlie the stony red colluvium, they are frequently brown (7.5YR hues) or reddish (5YR hues) in their lower parts. They are relatively soft and contain numerous stones

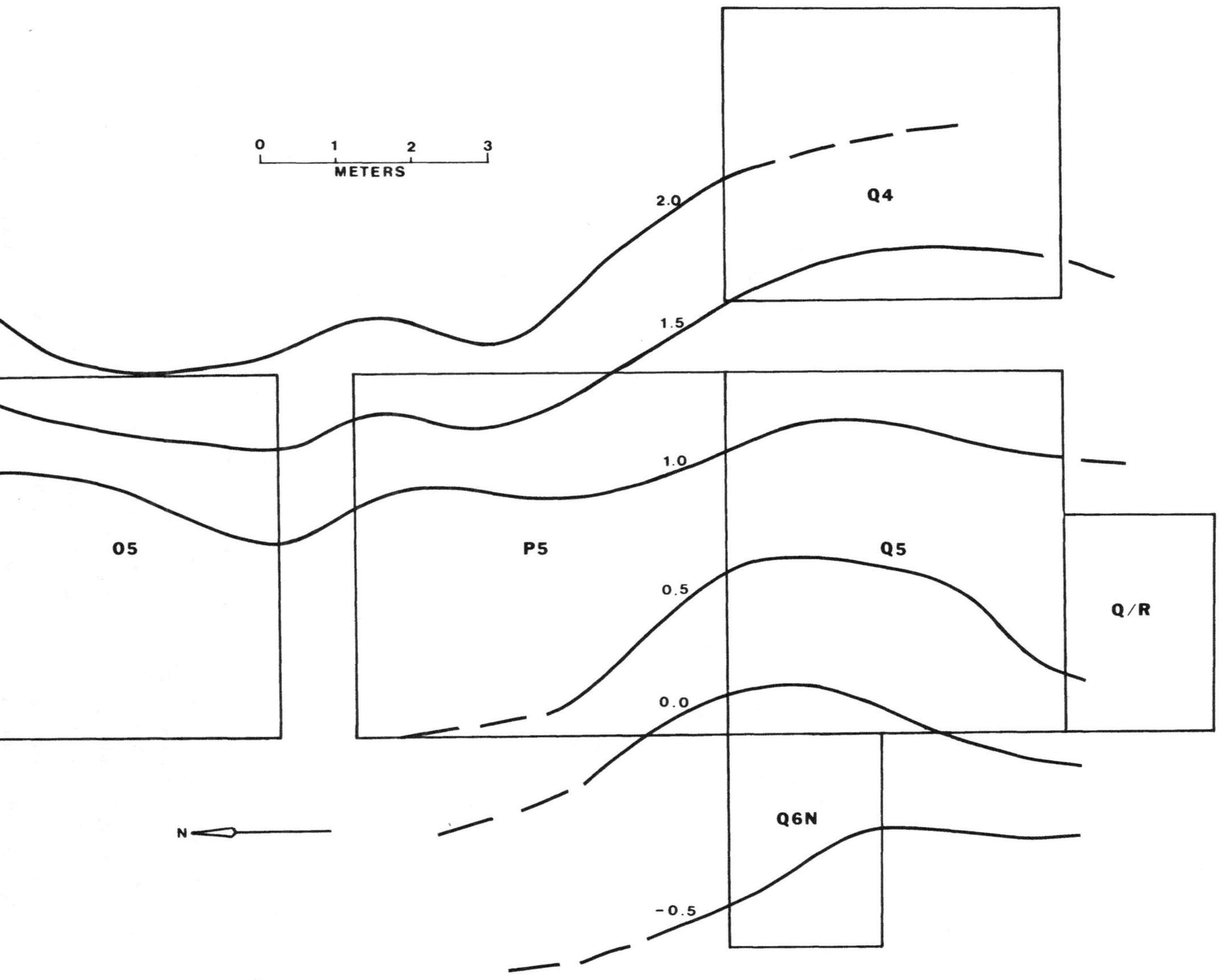

Figure 20. Contoured surface of the Paralia paleosol in meters above/below sea level, based upon measurements recorded in 1979. Tied into the Greek datum (Γ.Υ.Σ.) (Cf. Jacobsen and Farrand 1987:13-14).

up to 15 cm (long axis), but bedding, if apparent, is weak. They have less Fe_2O_3 and more organic carbon than the colluvium beneath, and, as with the stone-free silt loam (C), the grayish hues probably result from a high content of pulverized charcoal as well as organic carbon.

A reddish-hued, gravelly deposit occurs in places between A and B (A2): for example, L5 II and Q5 II (Appendix B). In these cases Q5 II was archaeologically sterile, whereas L5 II contained artifacts throughout. The origin of this accumulation is not certain, but it is evident that, in some cases at least, it accumulated after early Neolithic occupation had commenced.

The sedimentary environment varies slightly from case to case. In general, class B deposits result from the aggradation of talus and other sediments initially on steep slopes (20-25°), but later, more gentle slopes developed behind barriers on the slope (see Chapter 4). The best examples of this are L5 III (soil sample L7) and Q5 III/IV (Appendix B) (soil sample Q8).

CLASS C: STONE-FREE SILT LOAM

The matrix is similar to that of class B, but fewer stones are present. These sediments are significantly siltier than the red colluvium and slightly siltier than the later dark gray stony clay loams (class E). Stones and potsherds are frequently horizontal, and, in L5, two thin red-hued layers (L5:37 and L5:50; Figure 35 and Jacobsen and Farrand 1987:Plate 44) may have been floors. Again, gray hues may result from a high content of pulverized charcoal and/or organic carbon. Iron oxide and organic carbon are the same as class B. The sediment accumulated by the steady accretion of fine sediments on sub-horizontal surfaces, and the possible floors in L5 imply that there was habitation in that area at least. Class C deposits in grid square O5 (strata V, VI, and VII, Jacobsen and Farrand 1987:Plate 47) appear to have accumulated much more rapidly than in squares L and Q, but the process of deposition still was by accretion on sub-horizontal surfaces. A scheme suggesting the mode of formation of specific class B and class C sediments is given in Chapter 4.

CLASS D: RED-HUED SEDIMENTS WITH SERPENTINITES (UPPER REDS)

These sediments have colors in the 5YR/7.5YR range. They frequently occur on top of or adjacent to walls. Although they may be well defined in sections and section drawings, subtle or diffuse boundaries were often observed in the course of excavation. It was rarely possible during excavation to demonstrate them to be the remains of walls or floors, but in the clearest examples, such explanations seemed most plausible.

The upper reds are of loam, clay loam, or silty clay loam textures, that is, very similar to the red colluvium. Iron oxide and organic carbon contents were identical to the those of the red colluvium, but limestone fragments were less frequent.

Significantly, small, usually well-rounded, serpentinite or greenstone pebbles up to 1 cm in diameter were relatively common. They occasionally formed the nuclei of well-developed carbonate concretions of a type normally associated with soil horizons B and C.

In section, these sediments normally contrast markedly with those above and below, and this fact, together with their relationship to walls, strongly suggests an anthropogenic origin. The presence of calcium carbonate nodules (many of which were hard-cored) in greater amounts than in other sedimentary strata on the site suggests that the nodules were already present in the class D sediments before occupational deposits accumulated. They may have originally formed in B or C soil horizons which already contained serpentinite pebbles. The nodules, within their red soil matrix, were then transported to the archaeological site, possibly for use in the construction of floors and buildings. From the associated sherds and the stratigraphic positions of the sediments, a Middle Neolithic date for much of this transport seems most likely. Some of the calcium carbonate nodules, however, may have formed after the sediments accumulated on site. (The various types of $CaCO_3$ accumulation found on the site are treated in Chapter 4.)

Today, serpentinite crops out across Kiladha Bay from Franchthi, and serpentinite gravels are incorporated in exposures of reddish paleosol near the village of Kiladha. Serpentinites are also common in sediments to the north of Franchthi headland in the bay near Ayios Ioannis. The source of this reddish sediment is therefore postulated to be exposures of paleosol beyond the Paralia, probably within the area now submerged.

One pocket of "upper red" (Q6N:20-22 and 27) contained abundant marine shells of *Cerastoderma glaucum* (cockle), and others in Q5 west section (stratum XXVII) contained unarticulated human bone and a significant amount of rolled pottery probably reworked from earlier deposits. Although this artifactual evidence is inconclusive, the presence of serpentinites, with or without carbonate concretions, and the general similarity of these sediments to the various red colluvia of the region argue in favor of their introduction from outside the site.

CLASS E: DARK GRAY STONY CLAY LOAMS

Although variable, these sediments are usually gray brown loams, silt loams or clay loams. In the type section in Q6N, these deposits became browner (7.5YR hues) as well as siltier to the south. They have been designated gray-hued clay loams on the section drawings, but these sections encompass a rather broad textural range. Occasional lenses of upper reds are also present within class E, but they do not always appear on the section. The texture is intermediate between that of the red colluvium and that of the stone-free silt loams (see Figure 21). Iron oxide and organic carbon contents are similar to sedimentary types B and C, and again the gray hues appear to result from a high proportion of pulverized charcoal. Large angular to subangular stones were found to be common in most locations, and in Q6N large potsherds were common, frequently exhibiting fresh breaks. In Q6N, most of these stones and large unabraded sherds are above Unit 23 (Jacobsen and Farrand 1987:Plate 56).

In the top 20 cm of Q6N, stratum VII (i.e., above Unit 13, Figure 22) and in stratum VIII above, sherds and tabular stones lie parallel to the slope with a slight northerly orientation. The mean angle of dip is about 24°, but the scatter ranges from 9° to 45°. The mean angle is approximately parallel to that of the talus midslope above. In the 40 cm beneath, i.e., down to approximately Unit 23, dips are still to the west, but they are gentler, the mean of the westerly dipping sherds being 13°. Below this point, down to approximately the base of stratum VII, sherd orientation appeared chaotic with dips to both east and west. The sediments contain foreign stones, both serpentinites and marine-mollusc-bored limestones, as well as introduced sediments, "upper reds."

The texture of class E deposits is intermediate between that of the red colluvium and the textures of sediments such as the stone-free silt loams (class C). The latter include much material probably washed from upslope.

The absence of an openwork structure, the deposits' general dissimilarity to modern or ancient talus deposits on the Paralia, the unabraded state of most of the sherds, and the presence of significant quantities of introduced materials argue against this type of deposit being a true talus. Tentatively, class E sediments can be interpreted as follows: a relatively rapid accretion

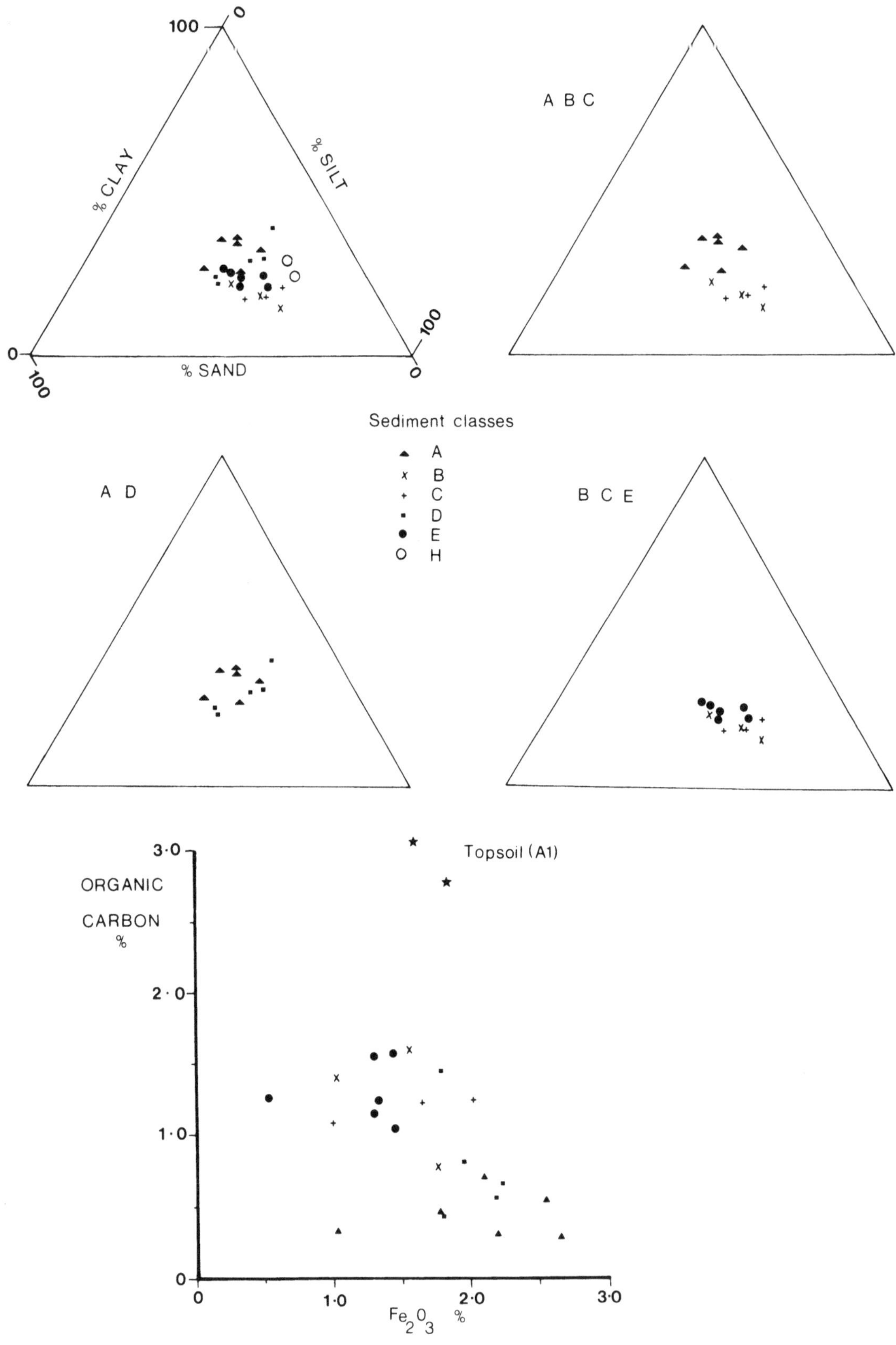

Figure 21. Above: Selected sediment classes plotted on textural triangles. Top left: All analyses of sediment classes A-E and H. Top right: Sediment classes A, B, and C. Middle left: Sediment classes A and D. Middle right: Sediment classes B, C, and E. Plotted from particle-size classes (including carbonates) determined by S. Duhon (Appendix F). Bottom: Relationship between soil organic carbon and Fe_2O_3 for sediment types A-E (Appendix F).

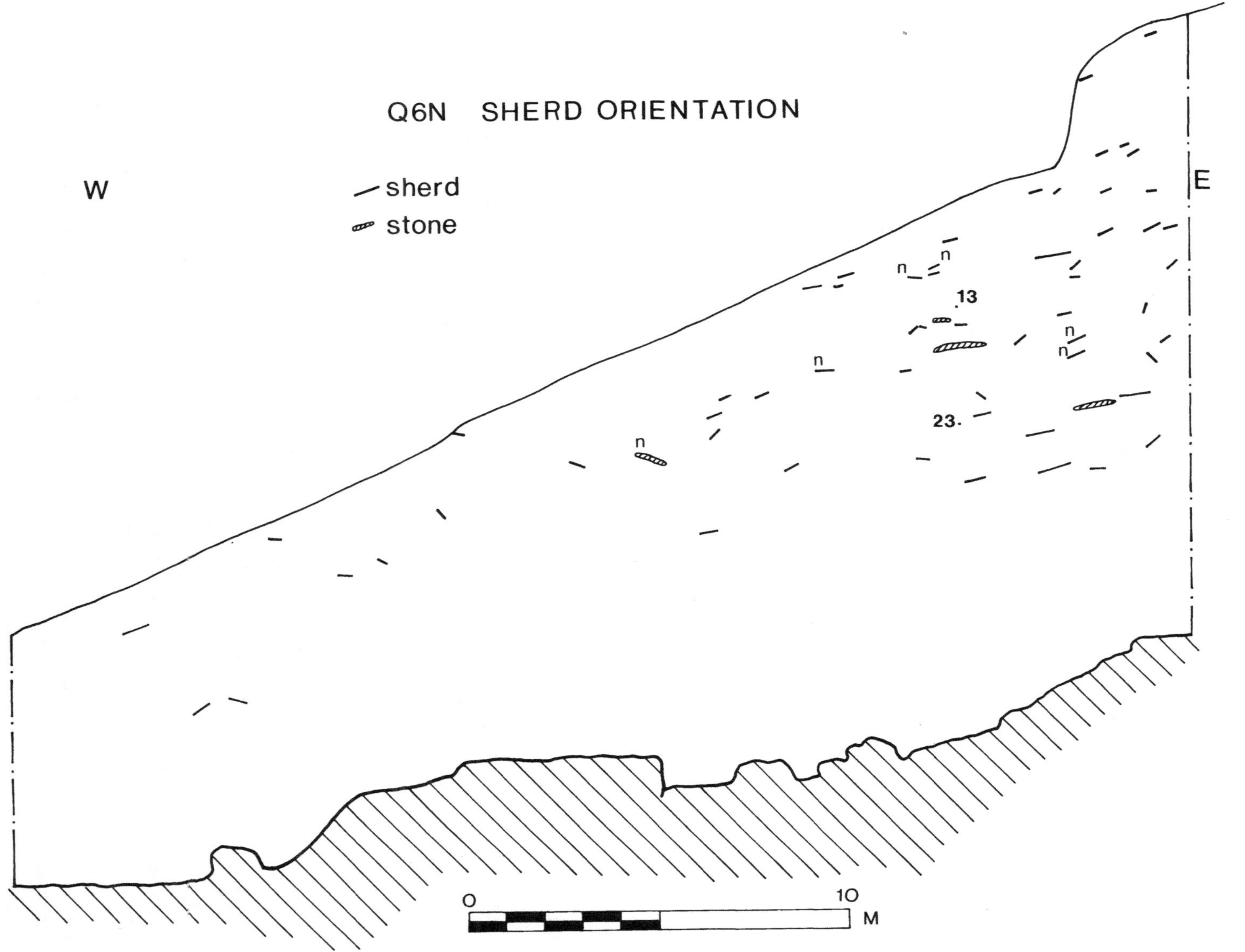

Figure 22. Orientation of potsherds and tabular stones in north section of Q6N. Those marked n also exhibited a significant northerly dip.

of cultural deposit, which included introduced sediments, occurred upon an initially sub-horizontal surface, and which gradually steepened until it approached the angle of the present talus midslope (the latter corresponding to layers with more steeply dipping sherds). The time scale of accumulation is uncertain, but preliminary information from the ceramics suggests that it occurred fairly rapidly during the Middle Neolithic. The process of accumulation cannot have resembled talus creep, which usually resulted in the random orientation of sherds. A relatively rapid, non-talus environment of deposition therefore probably prevailed; possibilities include either periodic accumulation of domestic refuse or the deliberate dumping of backfill on a progressively steepening slope.

Similar sediments occurred in the west of Q5N and also in the southwestern quadrant of P5. A possible occupation surface existed in the P5 sediments in the vicinity of Units 46, 57, and 68 (Jacobsen and Farrand 1987:Plate 55), and the >2.8-mm fraction of these deposits contained frequent serpentinite pebbles. This surface appears to overlie stratum VII of Q6N, but the sediments of the two are otherwise similar.

CLASS F: UPPER STONY LOAM AND CLASS G: TALUS ACCUMULATION

Classes F and G are variable in both matrix and stone content. They are in stratigraphically high position, usually Middle Neolithic and later, and F, especially, overlies many of the later walls on the site.

Class F deposits contain occasional or common stones among which the matrix dominates, except in parts of grid square QR, where small talus lenses were noted. In places, these deposits appear to be differentiated from those above and below by the presence of a weakly developed soil B horizon, for example in soil profile Q: samples Q3 and Q4 (Chapter 2). This horizon is visible on the section drawing as P5 X and XVI (Jacobsen and Farrand 1987:Plates 48 and 54). In such cases, the slight increase in clay content, as well as a discernable difference in color, appears to result from weathering and the secondary enrichment of the pre-existing deposit with clay washed from the overlying A horizon. Class F deposits should not therefore be viewed as depositional layers because in many cases their final form may result from the action of pedogenic processes within a variety of different parent materials.

Class G sediments are similar, but they contain more stones, some of which exhibit the virtual openwork structure of active talus. These deposits can form extensive sheets, as in O5 X, or smaller lenses, such as P5 VII. In one case at least, P5 IV, they accumulated behind a wall (Wall K, north section, see Appendix A; Jacobsen and Farrand 1987:Plate 48) of apparently Middle Neolithic date. The largest body of talus material, O5 X, with outliers P5 IV, VI, and VII, appears in transverse section to be occupying a trough in the east section of squares O5 and P5. In its stratigraphic context, it relates to a major phase of talus accumulation which postdates the construction of Wall K and precedes the Final Neolithic deposit of O5 XI.

Sediment classes F and G represent a continuum of slope activity from virtually stable slopes with little talus movement but some soil horizon development, on the one hand (F), to more active talus accumulation but less soil development on the other (G). Both sediment classes appear to include reworked and rolled potsherds from upslope as well as, in certain cases (e.g., O5 XIX), the stones of a collapsed wall.

CLASS H: LIGHT GRAY SILT LOAM

This distinctive sediment is limited to two locations, L5 VI and O5 XI (Figure 34; Jacobsen and Farrand 1987:Plates 44 and 54). It is light gray or very pale brown with a silt loam or silty

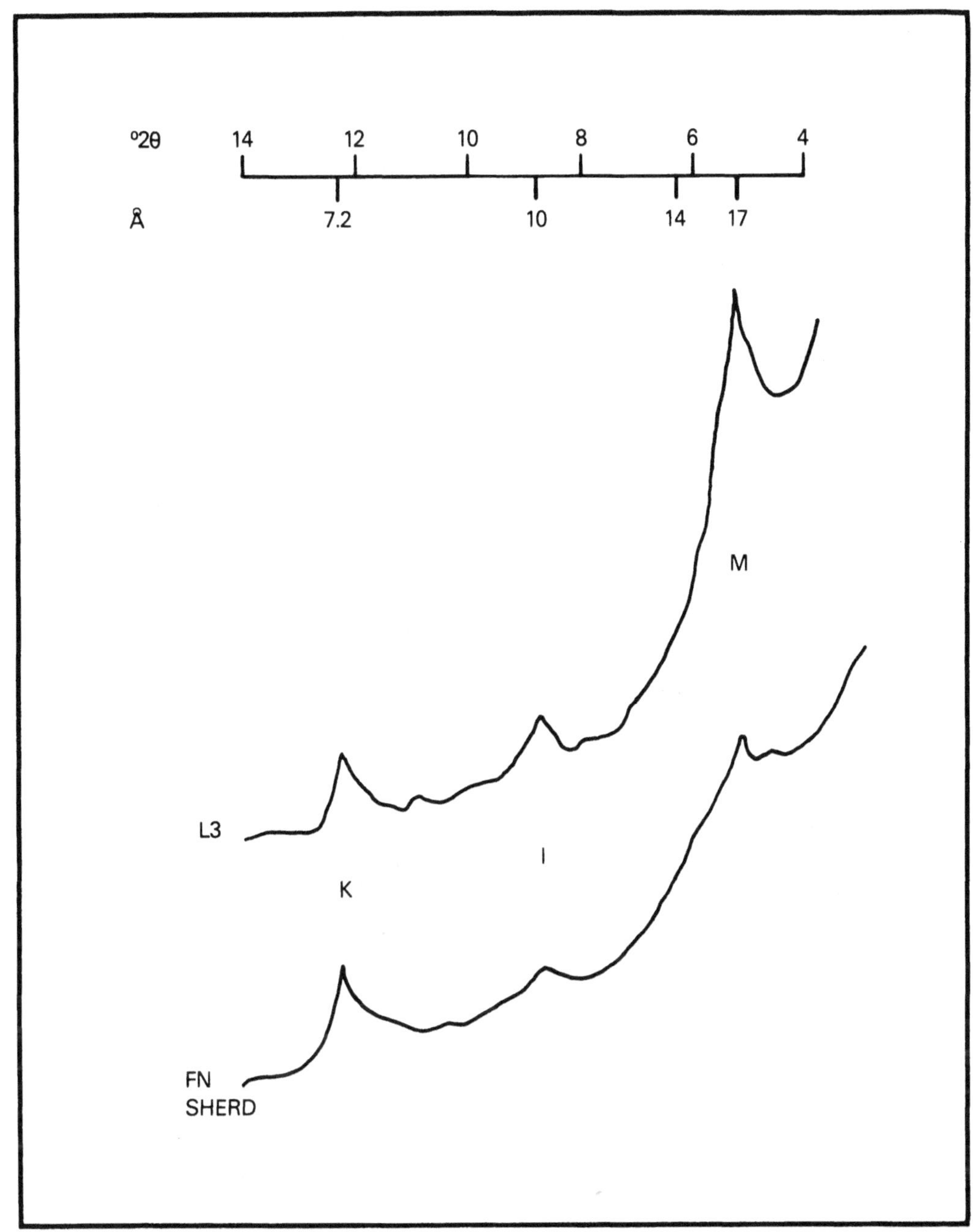

Figure 23. X-ray diffraction pattern for Final Neolithic potsherd aligned with similar trace for sample L3, grid square L5NE. (See note 1.)

clay loam texture. More details are given in samples L2 and L3 of soil profile L; both occurrences are stratigraphically high.

The presence of the clay mineral smectite (montmorillonite) and the very high proportion of $CaCO_3$ distinguish class H from other Paralia sediments. The deposit appears to have been introduced from elsewhere, maybe for an industrial use such as the manufacture of clay vessels, or it may contain the residue from disintegrated, poorly fired vessels (Vitelli, forthcoming b).[1]

CLASS J: FILLS OF CUT FEATURES AND DISTURBANCES

These are not restricted to any particular sediment class. Sediments of class J are frequently softer than the adjacent strata into which a cut presumably has been made, although the cut itself is not always visible. These deposits also comprise lumps or patches of sediment apparently derived from the nearby cut strata. For example, Q5 VII probably resulted from the cutting of pre-existing layers to accomodate Wall A. In contrast, that in L5 (VII) may have resulted from cuts made during the robbing of an earlier wall or for other reasons. Other forms of cuts, such as pits and graves, will be considered in another fascicle in this series (Cullen and Cook, forthcoming).

CLASS K: TOPSOIL

The modern A horizon has a relatively high organic carbon content of 2.5-3.0%, moderately high Fe_2O_3 content and was developed in a variety of sediment classes (Figures 8 and 17). This development, together with an underlying weakly developed B horizon argues in favor of moderate slope stability since major human occupation ceased in the Final Neolithic (ca. 5000 B.P.).

CHAPTER FOUR

Processes of Deposition of Selected Sediment Classes

Although it is very difficult to identify a "norm" for archaeological sediments, those of the Franchthi Paralia deviate markedly from most cultural deposits on open archaeological sites by virtue of the processes active on the slope. Before discussing sources of the sediments and how cultural deposits may be altered through time, it is therefore necessary to describe the dynamics of sediment movement downslope.

FREE TALUS MOVEMENT

Talus movement, whether by rock creep or rolling, will lead to the continuous transport of sediment through a given slope sector without any buildup of sediment. Consequently, aggradation will occur only behind boulders. At the same time, complementary accumulations of stone-free sediments will form on the lee side of boulders. This type of accumulation can be seen in P5 V and VIII (Jacobsen and Farrand 1987:Plates 48 and 54), where lenses of stone-free sediments occur within talus bodies which otherwise must have entailed considerable downslope movement.

IMPEDED TALUS MOVEMENT

If a barrier is constructed across a slope, sediment will start to accumulate on its upslope side. This rather obvious statement requires some elaboration, and the example of Q5 north section (Jacobsen and Farrand 1987:Plate 56) is used to demonstrate how aggradation upslope of a barrier may lead to the differentiation of the sediment into coarse and fine accumulations. The following discussion relates to the accumulation behind Wall C, which was most clearly visible in the south section of Q5N (see wall below Wall A [Jacobsen and Farrand 1987:Plate 56] and associated strata; illustrated diagrammatically in Figure 24). This sequence was, moreover, virtually identical to that shown in the north section. The full sequence is summarized in Chapter 5, and more details are given in Appendix B.

During the accumulation of stratum II, there was virtually free talus movement downslope and no evidence of human occupation in the vicinity. During the accumulation of III, occupational input commenced, and a talus deposit with a sparse loam matrix aggraded on a slope which decreased in gradient from ca. 17° to ca. 5°. During the accumulation of stratum IV, there was then an increase in the fine sediment matrix and a decrease in stone content, although the stones

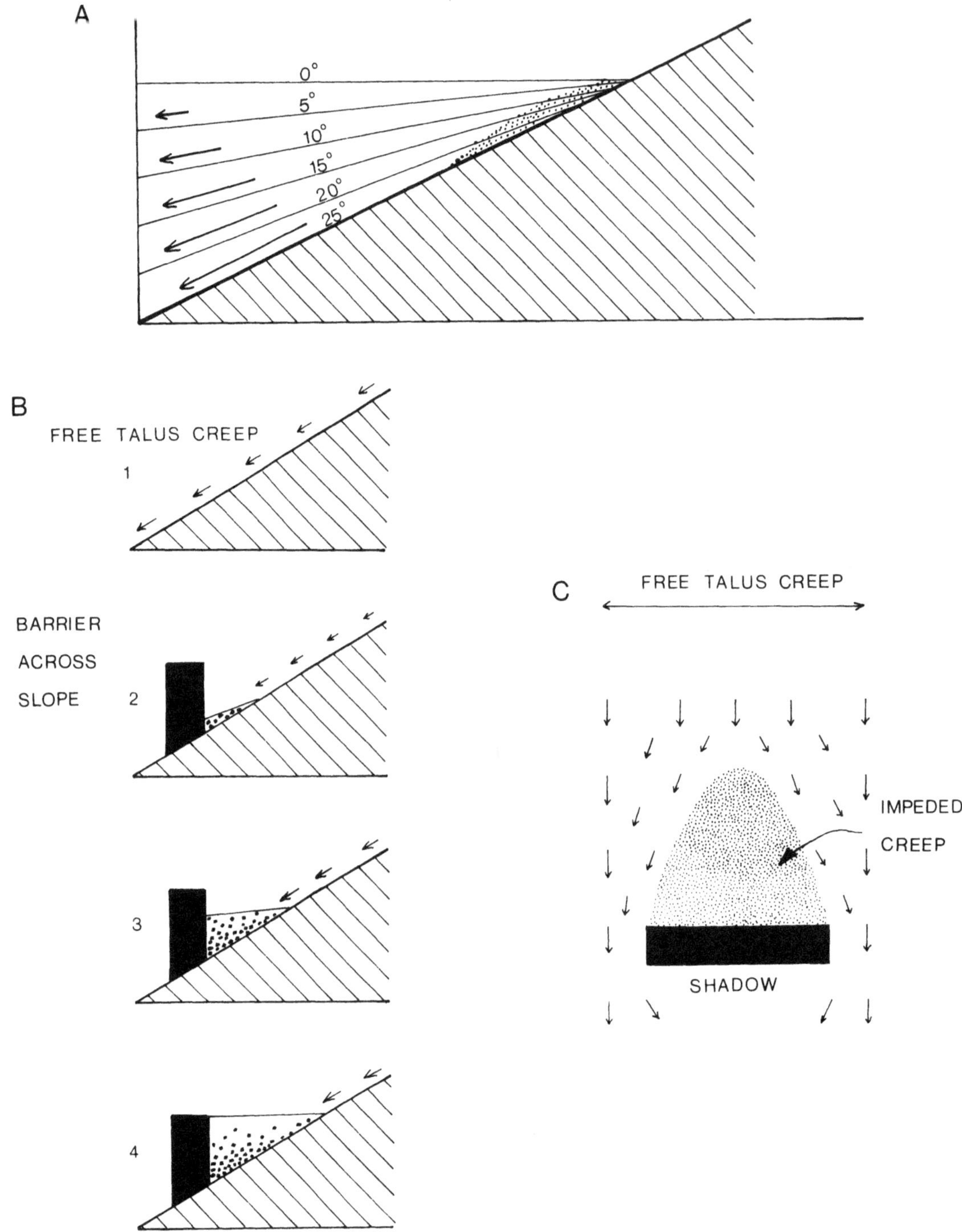

Figure 24. A. Vectors of rock creep on a progressively diminishing angle of slope in accordance with the relationship obtained by Schumm (1967: Figure 5). The arrows are proportional to the distances moved in cm/100 years. The stipple shows how, for a given period, the stone accumulation zone will remain close to the original slope or be confined to the earlier deposits. B. Hypothetical accumulation of stones behind barrier built across slope. C. Plan of same barrier showing free talus movement upslope and "stone shadow" downslope.

were slightly larger in size than in stratum III. By the end of this stage a virtually horizontal bench had been formed, and stone movement had decreased until very few stones occurred in proportion to the quantity of fine sediments. Finally, during the accumulation of stratum V, stone arrivals were rare, and fine sediments continued to aggrade the surface in small increments.

During this cycle the slope gradient first flattened out, and then the fine matrix increased in proportion to the talus. This change in sediment type can be explained in terms of the changing relative transport rates of the coarse and fine sediments. During the accumulation of stratum II, the free talus movement stage, the coarse fraction moved by rock creep, whereas fine sediments were transported by flowing water both across the surface and through the talus interstices to the toe slopes beyond. Following wall construction, both fine and coarse sediments started to accumulate, and the slope gradient lessened. The stones then apparently accumulated in accordance with the relationship derived for rock creep by Schumm (1967). In this model, the rate of rock movement on a slope is directly proportional to the sine of the slope angle (Figure 5). Relative vectors of particle movement are indicated on Figure 24 in accordance with this relationship. It is evident that, as the slope gradient lessens behind the barrier, the distance moved by stones in a given time interval will also decrease. Consequently, the total transport rate will decrease, and stones will start to accumulate on the slope. By the time the bench had a gradient of <5°, very few stones would be able to traverse the widening bench in the time available before a given increment of fine sediment had accumulated. This fine sediment aggradation may also be supplemented by additions of fine material introduced for domestic or building purposes.

The erection of a barrier across the slope would therefore produce the following results (Figure 24):

a. upslope: aggradation of coarse sediments beneath and adjacent to the original slope, a predominance of fine sediment above.
b. the exclusion of most sediment from the "wall shadow" downslope.
c. the continuation of free talus movement on either side, that is to the right and left, of the barrier to give a truncated or attenuated sequence. Here only isolated aggradation or shadows will occur as a result of the presence of small obstacles or boulders. On Franchthi Paralia this contrast between aggradation and free talus movement is clearest in the northern section of Q5 (aggradation) and in P5, the northern part of the east section (free talus movement). In square P5 there was apparently a sedimentary hiatus between strata IIIa and IV (Jacobsen and Farrand 1987:Plate 54), possibly during the Early Neolithic, while there was aggradation in Q5. Aggradation did not commence in P5 until stratum IV accumulated, probably during the Middle Neolithic.

ADDITION OF CULTURAL DEBRIS

In square Q5, by the time the lower gravelly loam and stone-free silt loams had started to accumulate, a significant cultural input had commenced. In addition to obvious artifacts, this input included finely divided charcoal and occasional rounded serpentinite pebbles. Although most angular serpentinites were a residue from soft-stone working, the round pebbles may have arrived with introduced sediments, although these pebbles were never as common as in the "upper reds."

Figure 21 indicates the variation in soil texture, Fe_2O_3 content, and organic carbon for selected Paralia sediments, both cultural and archaeologically sterile. It is evident that class E deposits, although of similar organic carbon and iron oxide content to those of classes B and C, were slightly clay enriched. This enrichment probably resulted from the addition of more clay-rich sediments for building purposes. The conspicuous additions are the "upper reds" (class D). These are more clayey than sediment classes B and C and are close in texture to those of class E (Figure 21). The occurrence of the upper reds as lenses within the class E sediment and the presence of serpentinite pebbles throughout class E imply that the upper reds have contributed to its fine matrix. At some time in the history of class E deposits, the charcoal content became finely divided and some of the added upper reds may have become mixed in until the sediment acquired a generally dark gray hue.

In Table 1, the upper reds designated by a superscript lay immediately above or adjacent to walls. Stratigraphically, this phase of addition of upper reds postdated the Early Neolithic occupation. The most probable sources of the upper reds and other introduced materials are within the area of Kiladha Bay, now flooded by the Holocene marine transgression.

TABLE 1

PARALIA: SEDIMENTARY CLASSES

Class	*Brief Description*	*Stratigraphic Reference Numbers*
A	Stony red colluvium	L5 I; Q5 I, Ia, Ib; Q6 I; P5 I, II; O5 I
A2	Red hued talus	L5 II; Q5 II
B	Lower gravelly loam	L5 III; Q5 III, IV, VIII, XVI; P5 IIIa?; O5 II
C	Stone free silt loam	L5 IV; Q5 V; P5 IIIb, V; O5 V, VI, VII; O5 XIV?
D	Upper reds	Q5 VI[a], XIII[a], XVII[a], XXI[a], XXVII[a]; QR II; Q6 VI, VIIb; P5 XII[a], XIV[a]; O5 IX[a]
E	Dark gray stony clay loams	Q5 XXII, XXIII, XXIV; Q6 VII; P5 VII, VIII
F	Upper stony loam	L5 VIII; Q5 XIX, XX, XXIX, XXX; QR V, VI; P5 IX, X, XVI; O5 XIX
G	Talus accumulations	Q5 XXXI; P5 IV, VII; O5 X, XIII
H	Light gray silt loam	L5 VI, O5 XI
J	Cuts/disturbances	L5 VII; Q5 VII; Q6 V
K	Topsoil	L5 IX; Q5 XXXII; QR VII; Q6 IX; P5 XIX; O5 XX
	Unclassified	L5 V; Q5, IX, X, XI, XII, XIV, XV; Q5 VIII, XXV, XXVI, XXVIII; QR I, III, IV; Q6 IV, V; P5 VI, VIII, XI, XIII, XV; O5 III, IV, VIII, XII, XV, XVI, XVII, XVIII

[a]Upper reds immediately above or adjacent to walls.

POST-DEPOSITIONAL ALTERATION OF ARCHAEOLOGICAL SEDIMENTS

Following deposition, the sediments were subjected to various forms of post-depositional change. On the Paralia, considerable human disturbance operated during the settlement's occupation, probably until ca. 3000 b.c. Natural processes, including biological activity (activity of insects, earthworms, plant roots, etc.) and soil formation (pedogenesis) have operated over a broad span of time: about 7000, 6500, and 5000 years, since the close of the Early, Middle, and Final Neolithic, respectively.

The excavation of pits and burials or wall-robbing and wall-building episodes have led to gross disturbance of the sediments. These activities are all considered to be part of the site "archaeology" and are treated elsewhere (e.g., Jacobsen and Cullen 1981; Cullen and Cook, forthcoming). Where evidence of post-depositional disturbance has been found, it is cited in the stratigraphic catalogue (Appendix B).

It was suggested during the excavations that some Paralia walls may have bounded small cultivation plots. Inspection of the most cultivable soils, namely the stone-free silt loams in grid squares L and Q showed, however, that the only post-depositional disturbance was by worms or plant roots. In both excavated areas many horizontal potsherds were evident in the soils, and in L5 (Units 37 and 50; see Figure 34 and Jacobsen and Farrand 1987:Plate 44), two thin, red-hued layers were also present. They had not been disrupted by cultivation, although they were permeated by worm holes.

During the field description of the sediments, occasional worm holes and common-to-abundant worm casts were noted in the upper 75 cm of all grid squares except Q6. During excavation in May 1974, worms were rare. They were absent from Q6 and Q5, and only a few were reported from Q4. Those in P5 were already curled up in a position of estivation by May, and only in L5, at the highest elevation, were they seen to be active. There they occurred at 80–100 cm below the surface and were clearly approaching estivation. Worm action was evidently greatest in the cool, moist winter months and appears to have been limited to the upper meter or so of the soil. Those trenches closest to present sea level showed least evidence of modern worm activity, perhaps because of slight soil salinity within 2 m of sea level. Therefore, before the sea attained its present height, worm action might have been greater even in the lowest archaeological levels, which at that time must have been beyond the influence of salinity.

Worm activity has clearly been a significant agency in sediment mixing and can probably be blamed, at least partly, for the very diffuse interfaces noted during section drawing. It is not certain whether worm action also caused the pulverization of charcoal on the Paralia. The presence of relatively large pieces of charcoal beneath stones and sherds, where the soil was slightly cemented by calcium carbonate, contrasts with the main body of rather homogenized gray sediments observed elsewhere. Large charcoal pieces were especially evident beneath stones in square Q6. Their presence might suggest that worm mixing was less in these positions, but the evidence is weak.

Concretions of calcium carbonate occurred in many places within the archaeological deposits. Carbonates frequently occurred as single concretions that were loose within their surrounding sediment matrix. Such concretions did not appear to have been formed in situ, and good examples of this type occurred within the upper reds, where they can be plausibly explained as having originated elsewhere, perhaps developing in an older soil formation.

Post-occupational accumulation of calcium carbonate was present in at least two forms:

1. off-white to very pale brown carbonate concretions forming a nodular plaster-like covering along the base of walls, a particular case being Wall Q in square P5 (Figure 25).
2. filaments and sheets of hard, off-white carbonate, especially beneath sherds and stones. These were thickest (ca. 2 mm) where sherds were horizontal, and they were clearly formed in situ since the Middle Neolithic. Although present throughout Paralia sediments, they were specially noted in the class E, dark gray stony clay loams. Their exact mode of formation is unclear, but they are important in demonstrating that significant accumulations of carbonate were taking place in specific localities within Paralia sediments. Detailed studies by Israeli

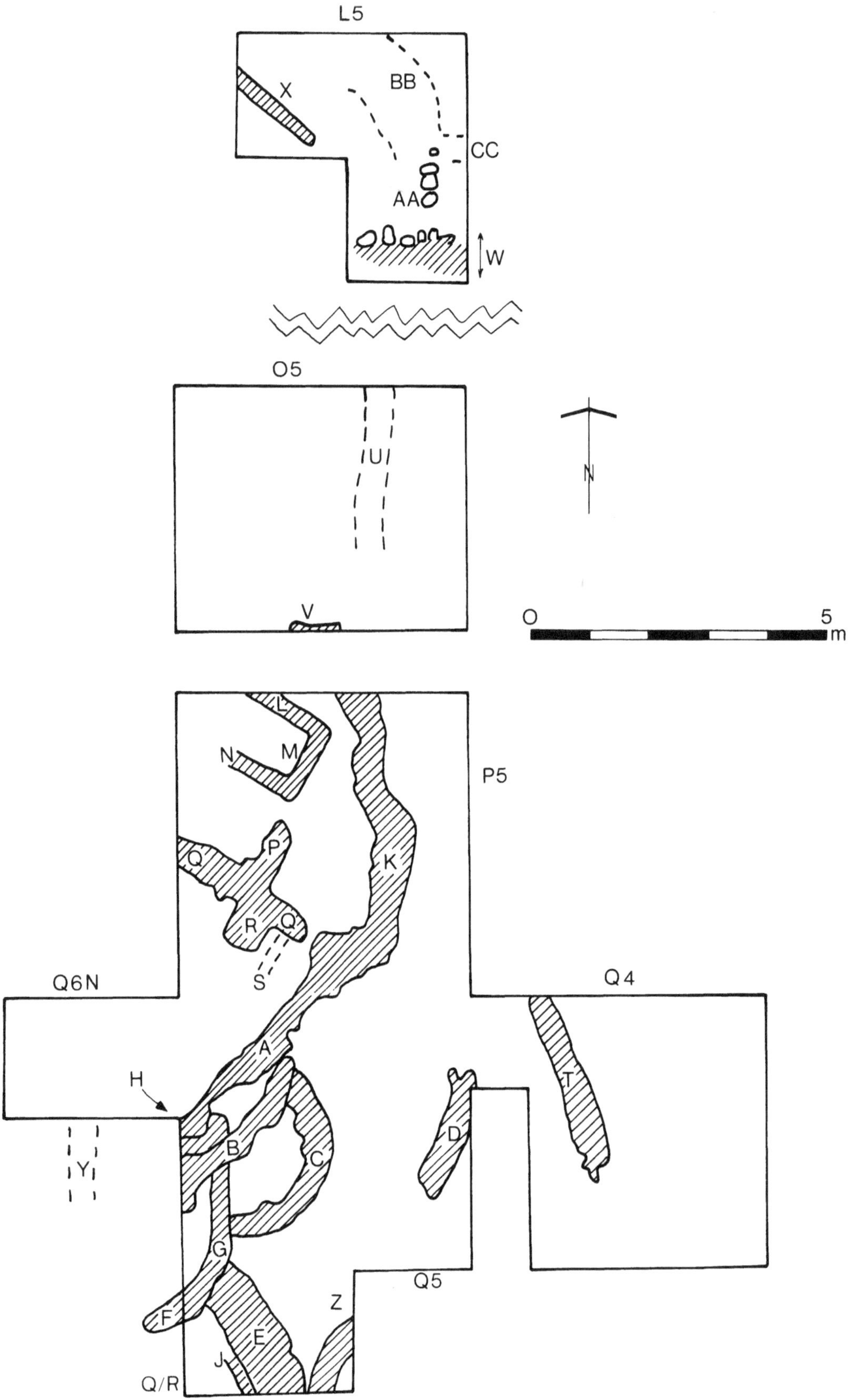

Figure 25. Schematic plan of Paralia walls lettered according to the system used in the text. Broken lines indicate possible walls. For suggested phases, see Appendix A and Figure 33.

scientists show that in the Negev desert, soils beneath stones can have relatively high moisture contents compared with adjacent soils, even in the driest season (Evenari et al. 1982). Such a phenomenon may affect the selective deposition of carbonate in similar localities on the Paralia.

A useful indication of sediment reworking is provided by evidence of rolled, worn, or battered potsherds.[2] As would be expected, the greatest quantity of worn sherds was from the upper stony loam and talus deposits (classes F and G). Those within the true talus appeared to be less worn than those in the upper stony loams, probably because active talus gravels, where aggrading, cover sherds fairly rapidly, whereas the upper stony loams, being relatively more stable, exposed sherds on the surface for longer periods. In addition to the upper stony loams, other deposits yielding worn and battered sherds were the following strata: L5 VII, a possible wall-robbing trench; L5 VI, a stratigraphically high layer that might have included worn sherds from upslope; various upper reds, e.g., Q6N:21, 22, and 27; certain upper portions of the class E stony clay loams, e.g., P5 XVIII and Q5 XXII, XXIII, and XXIV. None of these contexts could be diagnosed as mixed, reworked, or disturbed on the basis of pottery evidence alone, and only in the upper stony loams, talus, and topsoils (classes F, G, and K) were sherds consistently rolled. Larger unrolled sherds were present in the class B and C deposits in square L (L III and L IV) and in Q6 VII (among others).

In square Q4, a group of sherds in Units 3, 6, and 8 are quite anomalous (Jacobsen and Farrand 1987:Plate 56). They include unabraded Early Neolithic sherds, some abraded Middle Neolithic and later sherds, and they overlie deposits containing worn Final Neolithic pottery (K. D. Vitelli, personal communication). Their presence might be evidence of downslope movement of a soil mass (soil creep) in which abrasion of the Early Neolithic sherds did not take place. In contrast, rock creep of individual rock particles would entail the abrasion of all pottery. In this case, a mass of sediment deposited upslope during the Early Neolithic could have moved downslope, either suddenly or by progressive creep, and could have remained in one mass throughout. Such mass movement would result in only localized mixing with adjacent deposits.

Following the abandonment of the settlement, the occupational deposits were covered by a complex of stony deposits mainly of classes F, G, and K. Although these deposits exhibit abundant evidence of worm activity, no thick deposit of "vegetable mould" (Darwin 1945) was formed, probably because talus stones occasionally arrived from upslope. This rather mixed sediment, although subject to rock and soil creep, was sufficiently stable to form an incipient soil with an organic enriched A horizon and a weak B horizon (see profile Q, samples 1–5, Chapter 2). No well-developed B horizon, however, or horizon of carbonate accumulation has developed during the past five or six thousand years. In contrast, pedogenic carbonates in part of the Pikrodhafni alluvium in the Kiladha valley yielded a uranium-series date of 4000 ± 2000 B.P. (Pope et al. 1984).

CHAPTER FIVE

The Stratigraphic Succession

In this chapter, the *stratum*, as defined in Chapter 3, forms the basis of the stratigraphic succession. Because sedimentation is not simultaneous at all points within a single stratum, the result is, to a certain extent, diachronous. Within the context of Paralia stratigraphy, however, unless stated otherwise (e.g., in the case of P5 IIIa and IIIb), the deposition of the sediments contained within a given stratum is considered to be approximately synchronous. Although this approach might appear to lack precision, it is the only workable solution for erecting an independent chronological sequence for the Franchthi Paralia, and the problems inherent in this assumption are far less than those posed by sedimentary discontinuities, wall-robbing, cross-cutting during excavation, and reworked pottery.

Excavation was conducted by means of units numbered sequentially from top to bottom within trenches. Units were excavated in ''passes'' of up to 5–10 cm so as to be within a given sediment type. They usually provide a finer subdivision of the strata, and, where possible, these units are indicated by arabic numerals on the section drawings (Jacobsen and Farrand 1987).

The strata have been ordered in accordance with the principle of superposition to give a stratigraphic sequence for each grid square. Successive strata are indicated by roman numerals I, II, III, etc., but because of lensing, interdigitation of strata, and the intercession of walls of boulders which disrupt the sequence, it has not been possible to produce a *single* succession ordered from I, the earliest, to the latest stratum. Instead, a sequence of ''mini-sequences'' is given where appropriate, but the numeration, which consists of one set of roman numerals per trench, has been kept as orderly as possible.

Because strata of apparently identical physical properties can occur in different chronological positions, they have not been correlated on the basis of physical properties alone. Consequently, within a given grid square, two strata with the same number are physically connected at some point. Correlation between grid squares was made according to the principle that strata possessing the same physical attributes, occurring in the same relative succession, and/or at the same depth below ground level can be correlated. In such cases, the strata are equated as follows: Q6 VII = Q5 XXII. Such was the complexity of the stratigraphy, however, that correlation was possible only between immediately adjacent sections.

The succession for each vertical sequence within each trench is summarized in the following section. The strata are then ordered more formally in the flow diagrams (Figures 26–31). For a variety of reasons, it was not possible to erect a full Harris matrix (Harris 1979) for the site; the flow diagrams employ a simplified approach based upon strata identified in the sections. Furthermore, because of lateral variations within the sedimentary sequence, it has not been possible to assemble one master flow diagram showing the entire relative sequence for the Paralia. Instead, smaller flow diagrams have been compiled to clarify intertrench relationships, especially in the vicinity of grid square Q5. In the flow charts, a solid vertical line indicates either direct physical

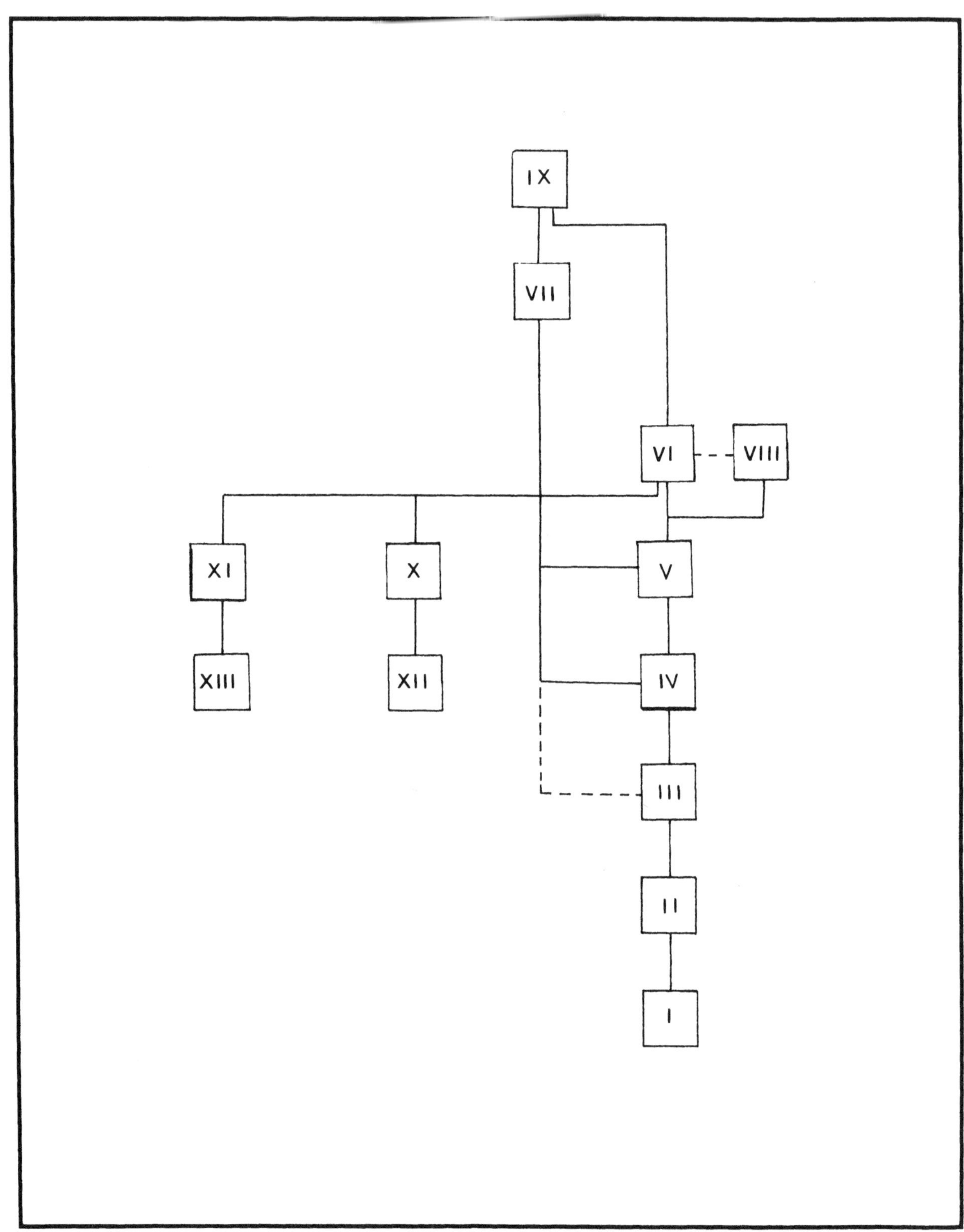

Figure 26. Stratigraphic flow diagram: L5.

superposition or that the stratum beneath has been cut by a feature containing the upper stratum. If one stratum overlies two or more strata, this is indicated by a solid line bent through a right angle, as in, for example, stratum XXXI over strata VI and XIV in Q5 (Figure 29). Horizontal solid lines indicate strata possessing the same stratigraphic position, while horizontal dashed lines link strata possibly occupying the same stratigraphic position.

Because stratigraphic positions are only relative to overlying or underlying strata, it is difficult to prove that strata occupying the same stratigraphic position are in fact contemporaneous. The illustrated sequences are most reliable where superposed strata are evident in section. Where there is a lateral component to the stratigraphy, e.g., to the east and west of Wall A in Q5 (Jacobsen and Farrand 1987:Plate 56) or to the north and south of Wall Q in P5 (Jacobsen and Farrand 1987:Plate 55), evidence from ceramic or lithic sequences may modify parts of the flow diagrams. Moreover, where excavators failed to recognize pits or cross-cut stratigraphy, artifactual sequences will not accord with the stratigraphic sequences. The stratigraphic nomenclature, however, should still provide the most reliable anchor points for the erection of a final archaeological sequence of the Franchthi Paralia.

The various sequences must not be viewed as continuous successions. On the contrary, gaps in the succession will occur any time the slope is not actually blocked by a wall, boulder, or some other barrier. Major hiatuses are indicated in the following, and more detailed descriptions of layer interfaces (Harris 1979) are given in the stratigraphic catalogue (Appendix B). The walls, lettered according to the system used in the text, are illustrated in Figure 25.

SUMMARY OF STRATIGRAPHIC SEQUENCE

Grid Square L5 (Figure 26)

Strata I-VII form a stratigraphic sequence from earliest to latest. Cuts and major stratigraphic breaks in the sequence are indicated. Stratigraphic relationships between strata I-VII and X-XIII are uncertain, but X-XIII are all overlain by VI.

I Stony red colluvium (A).[3]

II Talus with yellowish red loam matrix. Some occupation in vicinity.

III Dark brown stony loam (B), probably aggraded behind a barrier or wall.

IV Dark brown silt loam (C). Continues accretion of III, but a minor break at Unit 37 might be a floor.

V Red-hued clay loam to north, becoming very stony, almost talus-like to south. This appears to include material introduced from elsewhere, but slumping from upslope cannot be discounted.

VI Very pale-colored silt loam rich in smectite (H). Apparently cut by VII. This deposit also filled pits in L5NW.

VII Soft brown loam (J) bounded by an edge which cut IV, V, and VI, and probably III. Either a pit or a trench with disturbed fill. Possibly a stone-robbing trench and, if so, wall (BB) was probably contemporary with IV or V.

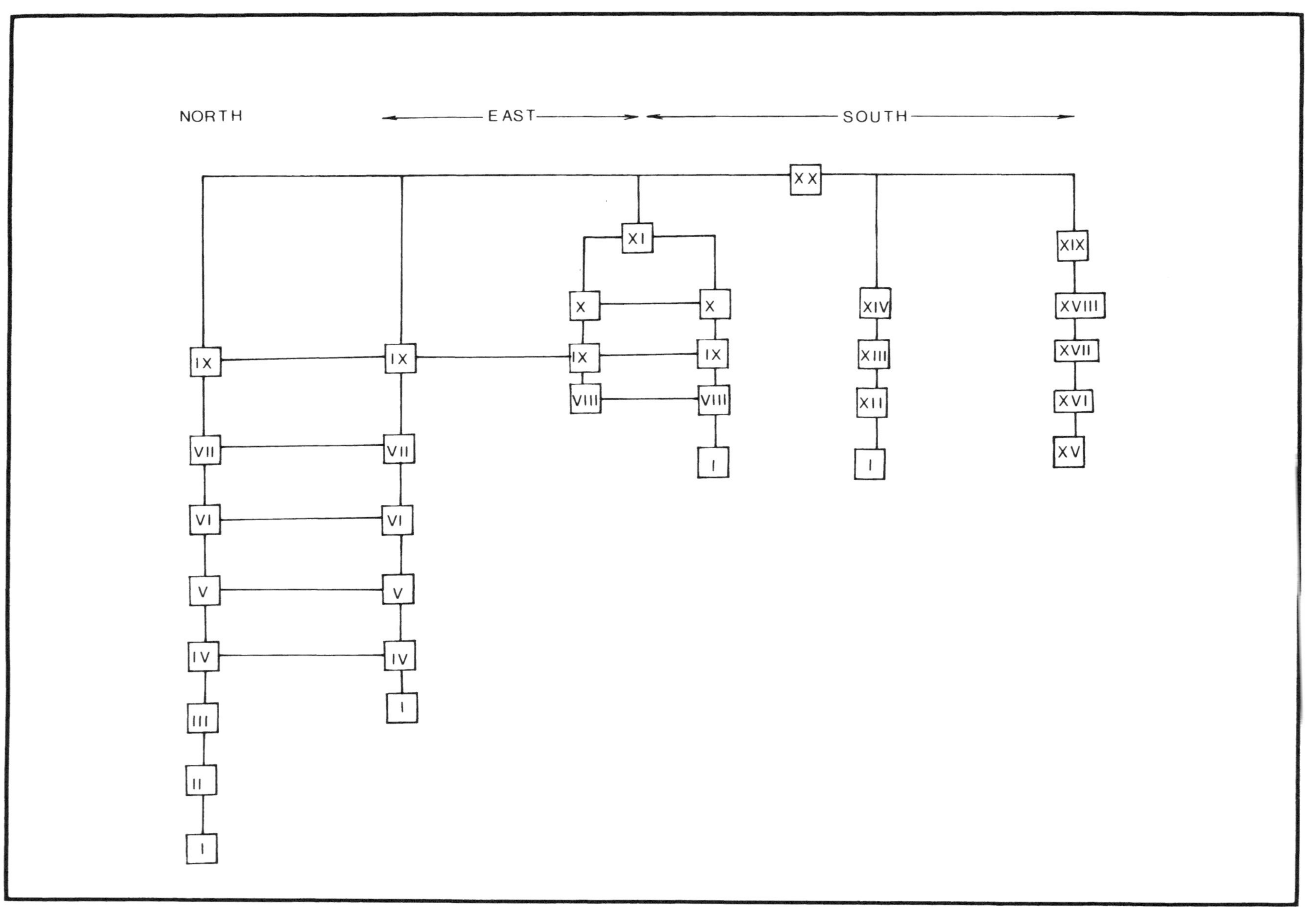

Figure 27. Stratigraphic flow diagram: O5.

VIII Brown stony loam (F) which merges laterally into VI but is partly separated from it by (collapsed) Wall CC. Probably contemporary with VI.

IX Topsoil.

Sequence in northwest corner of square:[4]

XII Stony brown deposit, similar to the red colluvium but not culturally sterile.

X Brown stone-free loam, accumulated against and above Wall X.

Second sequence:

XIII Similar to XII but below XI.

XI Brown stony loam, below VI, exposed in west section.

Grid Square O5 (Figure 27)

I Stony red colluvium. (A)

II Very pale brown loam, common stones.

III Soft reddish yellow loam with common stones and some $CaCO_3$ concretions. Resembles sediment class A, not D.

IV Soft, reddish yellow and light yellowish brown gravelly silt loam. Resembles talus.

Strata I-IV accumulated on a rather steep (31°) paleoslope. The sequence includes red colluvium (III). The presence of a complete pot and inter-unit sherd joins imply a rapid rate of deposition. For further discussion, see Appendix B.

V Light yellowish brown silt loam with occasional stones.

VI Grayish brown silt loam with occasional stones. Dark gray color probably derives from high content of pulverized charcoal.

VII Very pale brown silt loam.

Strata V, VI, and VII accumulated on horizontal surfaces. Stratum VI may contain much pulverized charcoal; strata V and VII possibly contain ash.

This sequence appears to have accumulated rapidly on subhorizontal surfaces, probably immediately after the accumulation of strata II-IV. This may represent an area of ash dumping, but the field and sedimentary evidence is inconclusive.

VIII Brown silt loam.

IX Reddish yellow sandy clay loam. Few stones, except in the northeast where they are abundant. Stones are larger than normal talus stones and may have come from pre-existing collapsed walls. Matrix was probably introduced (i.e., class D) for use in wall construction.

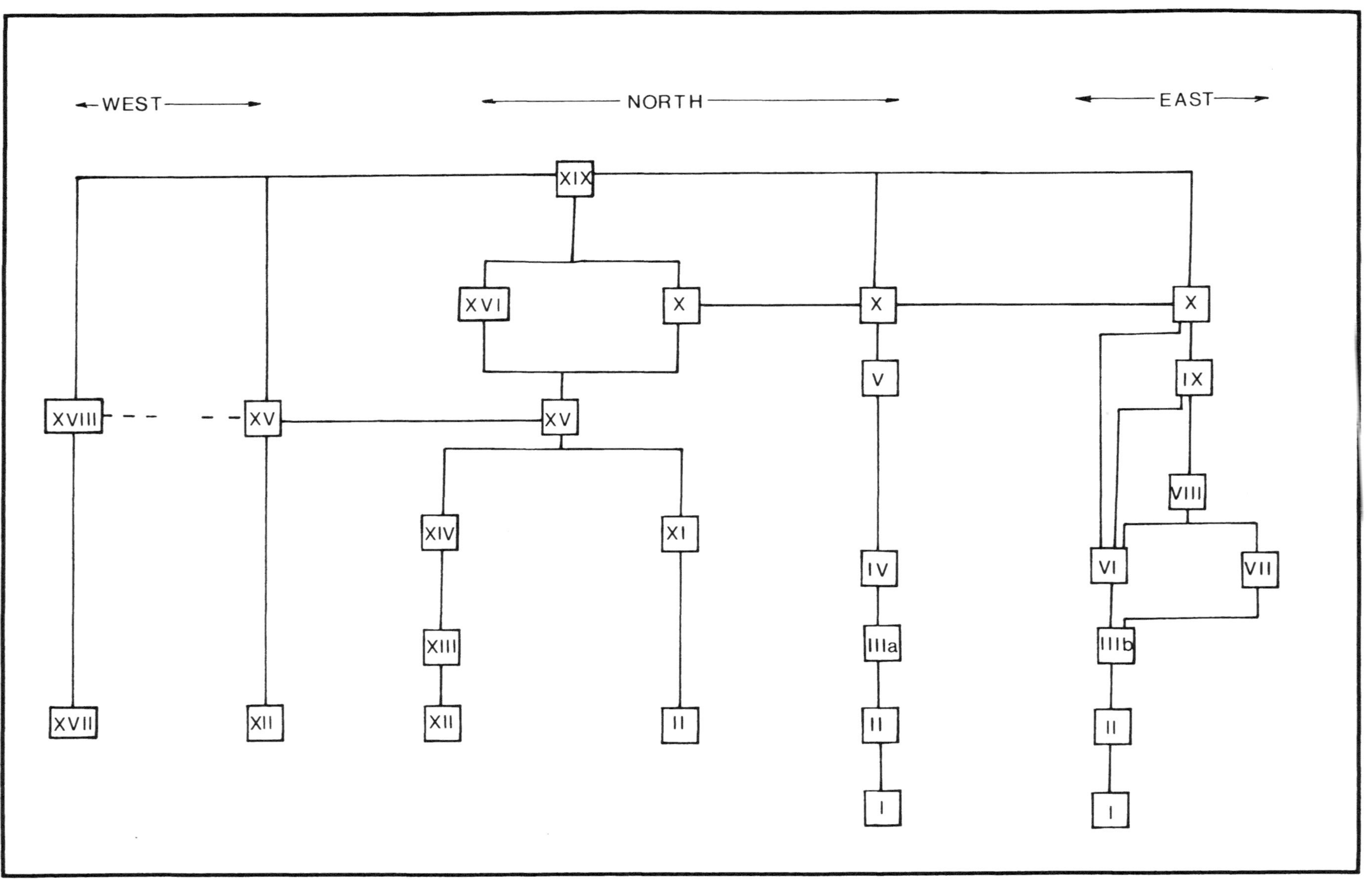

Figure 28. Stratigraphic flow diagram: P5.

X Talus gravel (G) contained in light yellowish brown matrix. Fills in trough formed by stratum IX.

XI Light gray silt, calcareous (H). Similar to L5 VI. See also catalogue of strata (Appendix B) for a discussion of these sediments.

XII Reddish yellow and light yellowish brown silty clay loam, few stones (D). Probably introduced for wall construction.

XIII Light yellowish brown loam with abundant stones. Talus accumulated upslope behind Wall K, same as P5 III and IV (G).

XIV Brown silt loam (C) with occasional stones. Probably accumulated in lee of boulder as for P5 V.

The above sequence, in the eastern half of O5, seems to have commenced with rapid aggradation in the northeast. The reddish layer, IX, which overlies this sequence may have been associated with a construction phase and may have accumulated during its destruction. The attenuated pre-IX sequence in the southeast of the square contrasts with that in the northeast. It resembles the attenuated sequence in the northeast of P5, which resulted from free talus movement (or at least non-deposition). The resultant trough then became filled with talus gravel. Deposit XI may not indicate a cessation in talus movement, but merely an increase in the rate of fine sediment accumulation.

XV Soft, pale brown loam with occasional stones.

XVI Thick accumulation south of Wall V and equivalent to P5 XI.

XVII Thick accumulation south of Wall V and equivalent to P5 XI.

XVIII Light brown clay loam (= P5 XV). Probably accumulated downslope of a wall which then collapsed on top of it.

XIX Yellowish brown loam which forms the matrix of what appears to be a collapsed wall.

XX Topsoil.

Strata XV-XIX can be correlated with equivalent deposits in P5. Like P5, the western half of O5 is dissimilar to the eastern half, and correlation between the two halves is tenuous at best.

Grid Square P5 (Figure 28)

I Stony red colluvium (A). Exposed in north and east sections.

II Reddish yellow sandy clay loam. Although in places this may form the upper part of the paleosol, i.e., part of stratum I, elsewhere it exhibits characteristics of an introduced sediment (class D) brought in for wall construction.

III Dark yellowish brown silt loam. Stony in north section, becoming less stony to the south where it continues as IIIa up to the boulder located in the center of P5, north section. Stratum IIIb extends to the south of the same boulder; the lower part is of class B, grading up to class C in the upper part. Stratum IIIb is correlated with Q5 V, but it is not necessarily contemporary with IIIa, which falls within an attenuated sequence.

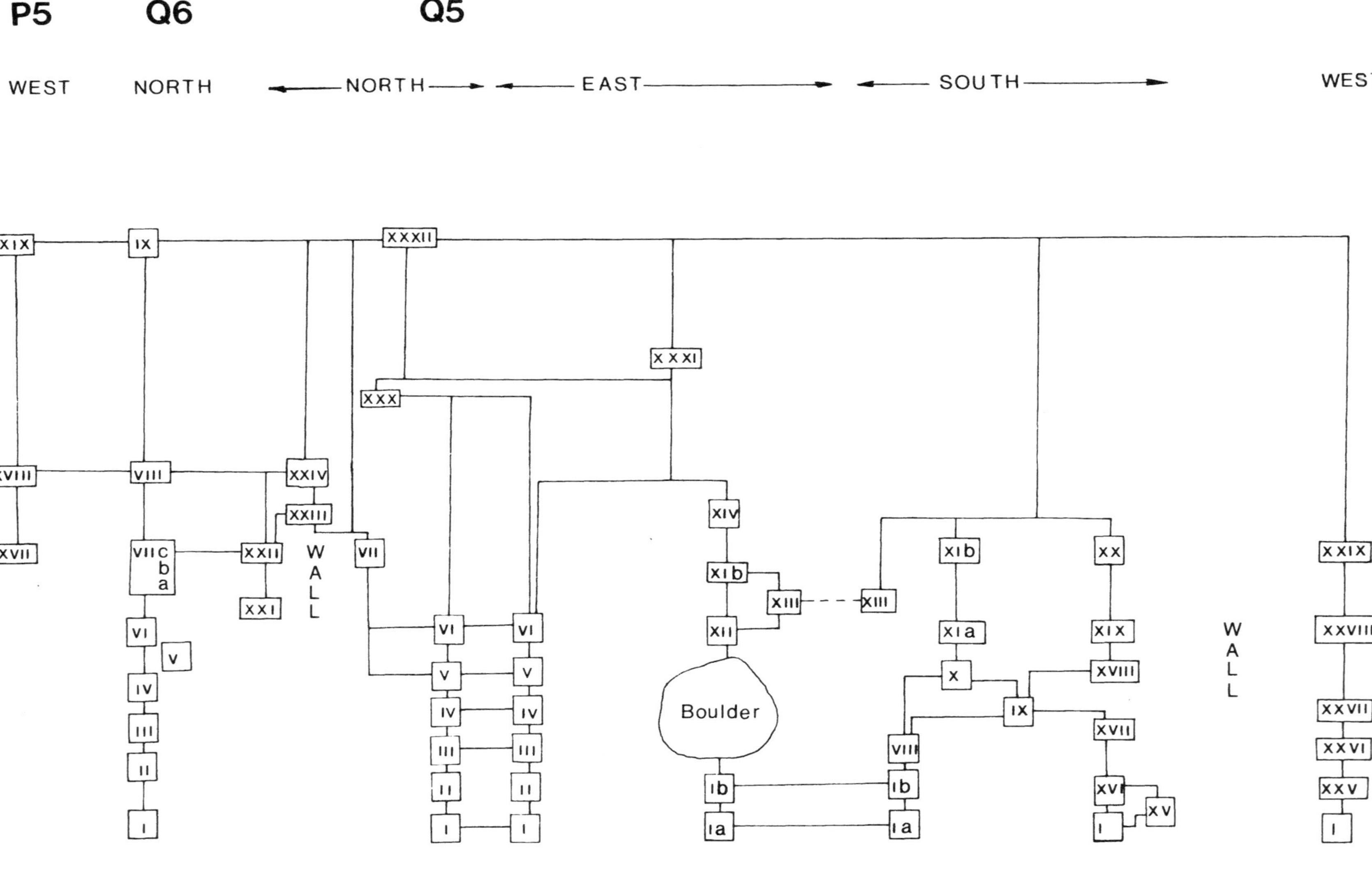

Figure 29. Stratigraphic flow diagram: P5-Q6-Q5.

IV Light yellowish brown loam containing weakly bedded talus gravel (G). Talus accumulated behind Wall K.

V Brown loam with occasional stones. Class C sediment, but probably only a localized development in the lee of a boulder on the slope.

VI Lens of brown loam with occasional stones. Occupies a trough between talus lobes.

VII Pale brown loam with abundant gravel (G). Talus accumulation behind Wall K.

VIII Gray-brown silt loam with few stones. Accumulated in trough between two talus lobes or in lee of boulder.

IX Very pale brown silt loam with common stones (F). Accretion on slope with some talus accumulation.

X Extensive horizon of light yellowish brown clay loam. A soil B horizon that developed on a relatively stable slope.

In the southeastern corner of the trench, an early aggradation of silt loam (IIIb) corresponds to a similar aggradational phase in Q5: strata III, IV, and V (Figure 29). In the northeastern quadrant, stratum IIIa is of uncertain status and cannot be correlated with IIIb because of an intervening boulder. Free talus movement appears to have continued in the northeast until Wall K was built, after which talus accumulated on the slope as illustrated in the north section (see Jacobsen and Farrand 1987:Plate 48). These sediments are poorly defined, but they almost certainly include much reworked material from upslope.

The following succession in the western half of the trench is separated from the eastern sequence (I-X) by Wall K. Direct correlation between them is impossible except near the top of the succession (X).

XI Dark yellowish brown loam with occasional stones. Occupies space between Walls K, L, and M and may result from spillage over Wall K.

XII Thin reddish clay loam (D) between Walls K and L. Possibly a floor or floor foundation.

XIII Dark brown loam above XII. Probably either a floor or post-occupational debris accumulated upon a floor.

XIV Sediment class D, similar to XII. An introduced sediment, probably for wall construction; later collapsed and disintegrated.

XV Dark brown loam, occasional stones. Gently dipping layer above Walls L, N, and Q. Accretion on slope after abandonment of building.

XVI Brown stony loam (F). May be a continuation of stratum X. Includes soil B horizon.

Strata XVII and XVIII cannot be directly correlated with the other strata in P5, but they are directly correlated with class E deposits in grid squares Q5 and Q6 (e.g., Q6N VIII and VII).

XVII Dark gray brown clay loam with common stones. Includes a surface related to the building level of Wall Q, i.e., this is probably the level upon which Wall Q was built. Correlates approximately with Q5 XXII and Q6 VIIc.

XVIII Similar to stratum XVII, but it is above the building level of Q and had accumulated against Wall Q. It therefore postdates this wall.

Grid Square Q5 (Figure 29)[5]

Few section-to-section correlations can be made within square Q5. Each sequence is considered independently in the following order: north section, east section, south section, and west section. Where layers can be followed from section to section, they carry the same number.

Q5, North Section

I Stony red colluvium (A).

II Yellowish red stony talus. Archaeologically sterile.

III Brown, stony loam (B). Aggrading talus with abundant cultural material; occupation in vicinity. Accumulated behind barrier.

IV Light brownish gray silt loam, common stones (B). Continued the aggradation of stratum III.

V Light brownish gray loam, few stones (C). Continued aggradation of stratum IV, but sedimentation ceased abruptly at V/VI interface, where there was a hiatus.

VI Red-hued loam (D). An introduced sediment. It is unclear to which structure this might have been related. Cut by wall trench of VII.

VII Mixed fill (J) containing many stones, apparently inserted to support adjacent wall. Wall trench and fill, dug to accommodate Wall A, cuts V and VI.

The relationship between strata I-VII and XXI-XXIV was established by reference to Wall A. Wall A was constructed immediately after the excavation of VII; XXIII overlies Wall A.

XXI Close to foot of Wall A. Reddish clay loam (D).

XXII Brown clay loam (E). Q5 XXII = Q6 VIIc.

XXIII Brown clay loam (E), accumulated against Wall A.

XXIV Brown clay loam with common stones accumulated against Wall A. Q5 XXIV = Q6 VIII.

X Thin stony horizon, possibly a soil B horizon (F).

XXXII Topsoil.

Q5, East Section

The sequence in the northern part of the east section is similar to that of the north section. Stratum VI allows the underlying layers to be equated with those of Q5 north section. Only XXXI can be followed further to the south; therefore the southern sequence cannot be confidently correlated to the main sequence in Q5 north.

Ia Stony red colluvium (A).

Ib Thin layer, strong brown in color, few stones. Localized talus development in vicinity of paleosol; some occupation in vicinity.

XII Pale brown silt loam with common stones; above boulder. Possibly correlated with XIa in south section.

XIII Brown loam with occasional stones (D). An introduced sediment probably related to Wall D to the south. Tentatively correlated to stratum XIII in south section, but the layer is not continuous.

XIb Pale brown silt loam with occasional stones. Continues into south section.

XIV Light yellowish brown loam with few stones.

XXXI Above the hiatus in the sequence. Yellowish brown gravelly loam (G). Talus which accumulated behind Wall D after an erosional interlude.

The above sequence is punctuated by several hiatuses: Ib/XII; above and below XIII; XIV/XXXI. The sediments probably include much material reworked from upslope, and the sequence is poorly related to those in the north and south sections.

Q5, South Section

I Stony red colluvium (A).

Ib Dark brown loam with abundant gravel. Approximately the top of the paleosol; some talus development. Some occupation in vicinity.

VIII Soft, light brownish gray silt loam, abundant gravel. Talus (B), possibly aggraded behind a barrier on the slope.

IX Yellowish brown gravelly loam, poorly defined towards east.

X Pale brown silt loam with common stones. The unusual steep and oblique boundary with IX may relate to a pre-existing wall.

XI Pale brown silt loam. Poorly defined but visible as two layers in east section. This was not the case in the south section, but it has been arbitrarily subdivided to accommodate XIII in accordance with the relationships in the east section.

XIII Reddish loam, apparently the same as XIII in east section. This layer may have related to a wall now represented by stones above Unit 148 in section (a collapsed wall?).

Q5, South Section, Western Sequence

I Stony red colluvium (A).

XV Yellowish red stony deposit alongside Wall E. Possibly the fill of a foundation cut.

XVI Yellowish brown silt loam with occasional stones (B), merged into XV. Accumulated upslope behind Walls C and E and postdates them.

XVII Yellowish red sandy clay loam (D). Probably a surface laid deliberately against Wall E and possibly also Wall C.

IX As above. See stratum IX, south section.

XVIII Above a possible surface represented by IX/XVIII interface. Description as of IX.

XIX Light yellowish brown clay loam, common gravel (F).

XX Similar to XIX but fewer stones. Overlies Wall E.

XXXII Topsoil.

In the south sequence, only strata I, Ia, Ib, VIII, XV, XVI, and XVII are uncontaminated, well-sealed stratigraphic units. Strata XIX, XX, and XXXII probably contain much re-sorted material. Strata IX, X, XI, XIII, and XVIII, although of some archaeological value, probably include much material rolled from upslope. They may also include cross-cut units. The complex of Walls C, E, and G severs all direct relationships between the south and west sections.

Q5, West Section

A vertical sequence, with hiatuses, between Walls F and H.

I Stony red colluvium (A).

XXV Brown to yellowish red loam with occasional stones.

XXVI Yellowish brown loam. Possibly the fill of a foundation cut for Wall F to south.

XXVII Reddish yellow silty clay loam with serpentinite pebbles and $CaCO_3$ nodules (D). Appears to be a floor built between Walls F and H.

XXVIII Pink silt loam with many large stones. Layer of fill accumulated between walls.

XXIX Reddish loam. In the north, where it links to Q6 VIIb, it appears to have been on top of Wall H, possibly as the wall superstructure. Wall A may have been cut into XXIX. The upper stony accumulation may represent a reactivation of talus movement on the slope.

XXXII Topsoil. Wall B was related to Units 94 and 95, although the exact relationship is unclear.

Above XXVIII, the layers are poorly defined with merging interfaces.

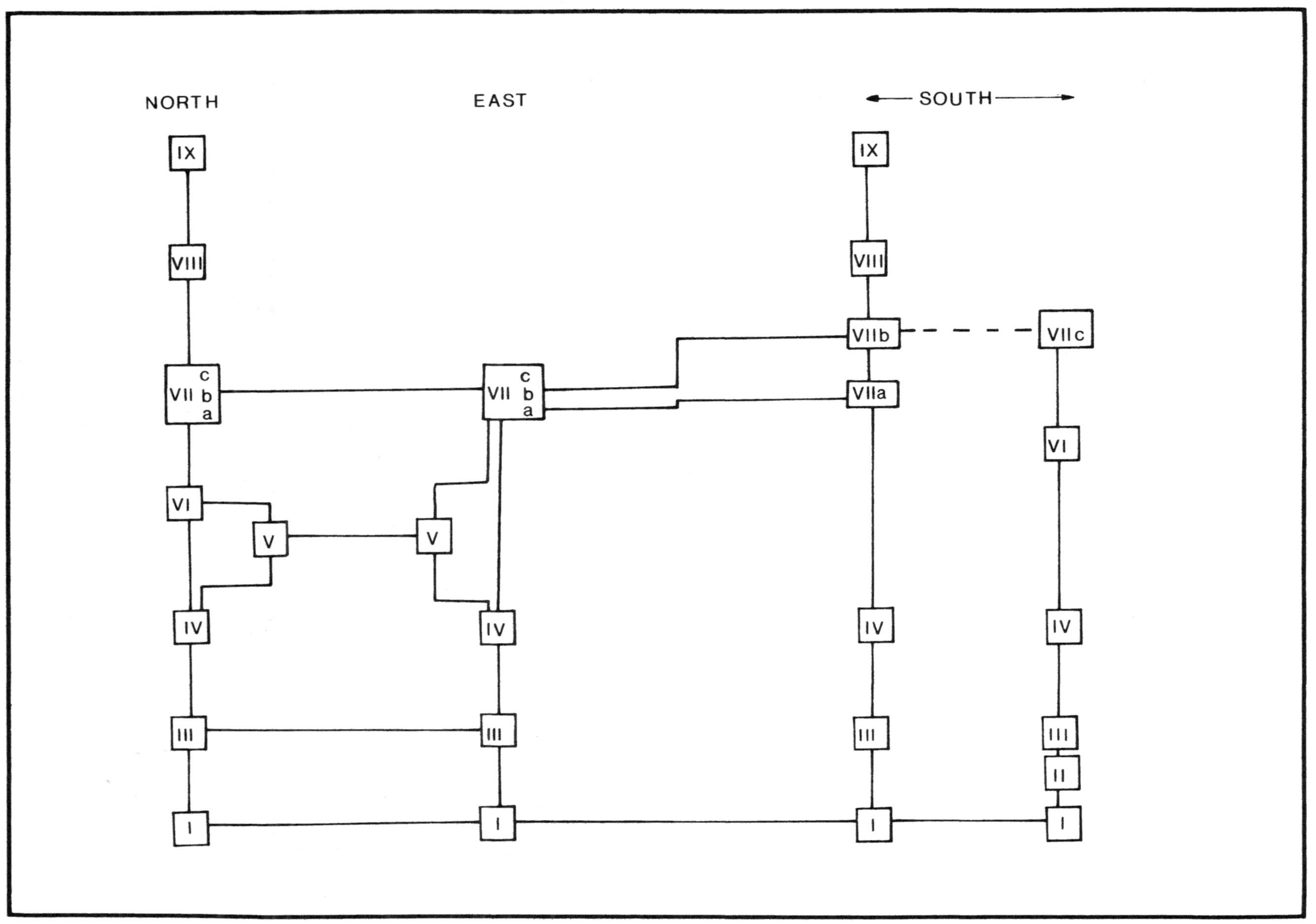

Figure 30. Stratigraphic flow diagram: Q6N.

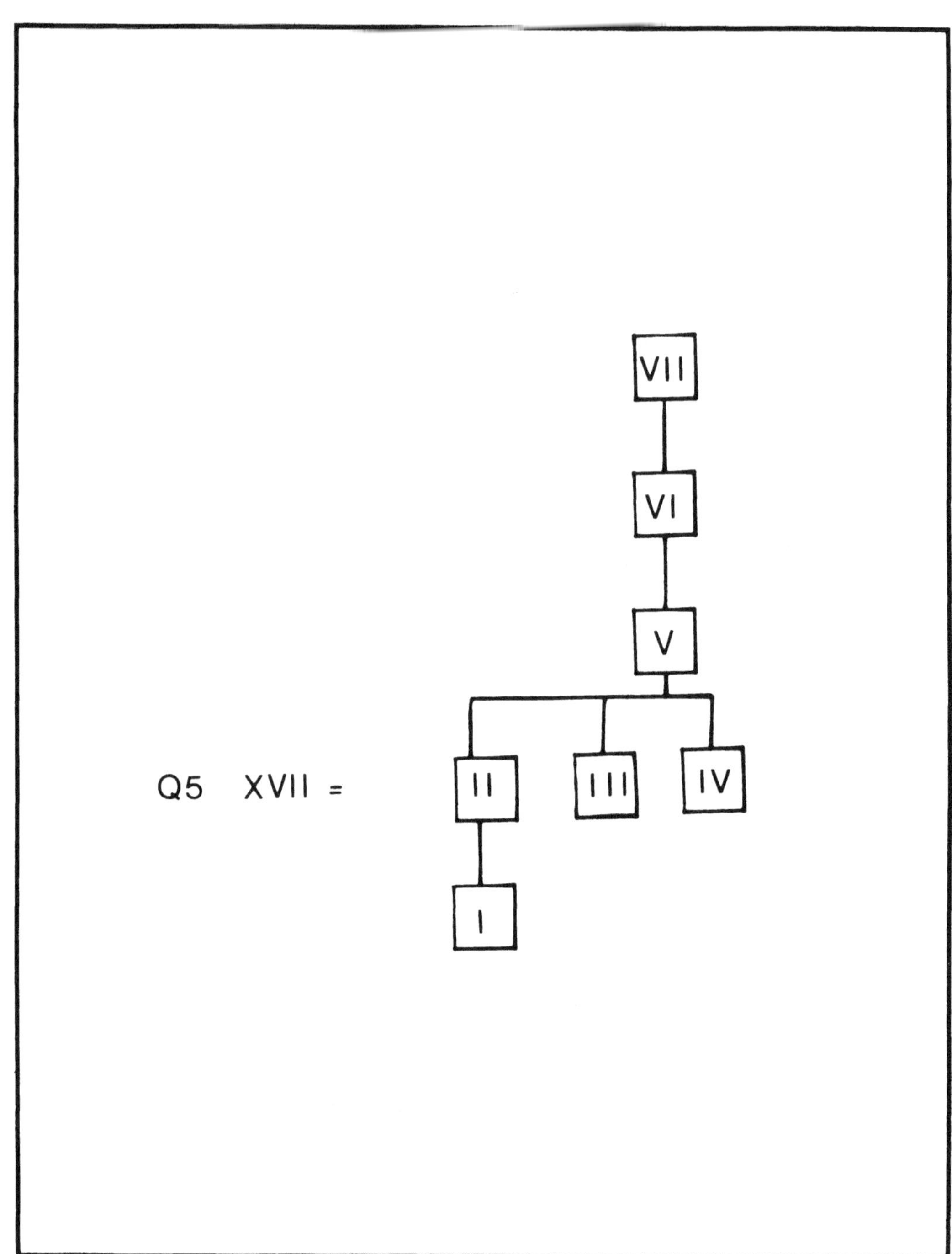

Figure 31. Stratigraphic flow diagram: QR5.

Grid Square Q6N (Figure 30)

I	Stony red colluvium (A).
II	Small patch of grayish clay loam visible only in south section.
III	Brown clay loam. Presence of high organic carbon in soil profile S suggests that this is a paleosol A horizon (IIA1 horizon).
IV	Light brownish gray loam with common stones. Gradual accretion up to the level of VI.
V	Brown stony silt loam, lower interface of which may represent a feature or disturbance. Cuts stratum IV. Similar feature also visible in south section.
VI	Light brown (7.5YR) stony loam (D), best developed in north section. Formed a subhorizontal, possible occupation surface.
VIIa, c	Gray-brown clay loam, locally very stony, with dipping or horizontal sherds as described in text (sediment class E). Thick, complex layer, probably aggraded first on a horizontal surface, then with progressively steeper dips. Fairly rapid accumulation.
VIIb	Lens of reddish clay loam contained within main body of VII. Visible only in east section. Possibly collapsed from Wall H.
VIII	Like VIIa, c. Can be traced into Q5 XXIV.
IX	Topsoil, only a small patch of which remains.

Although the above layers can usually be traced from the north section into the east and south sections, there appeared to be a very rapid change towards pinker, siltier soils in the southeast. The acute problem of lensing and interfingering of deposits is illustrated (in reverse) in the drawing of the east section (Jacobsen and Farrand 1987:Plate 53).

Grid Square QR 5 (Figure 31)

I	Light brown loam, occasional stones. Gradual accretion behind Wall E. Probably same layer as Q5 XVI. Stony red colluvium was not reached.
II	Reddish yellow loam with rare stones (D). QR II = Q5 XVII.
III	Brown loam. Possibly part of built Wall Z.
IV	Pale brown loam, accumulated against Walls E and J.
V	Light brown loam with some talus lenses. Accumulation of class F deposits behind, then above Wall E.
VI	Dark brown loam with locally developed talus lenses and possibly also a weakly developed soil B horizon.
VII	Topsoil.

CHAPTER SIX

Discussion and Conclusions

GENERAL DISCUSSION OF THE PARALIA SEDIMENTS

Probably the simplest way to generalize the sedimentary processes and stratigraphy of the Paralia is by means of a block diagram (Figure 32, top). This diagram of a hypothetical slope shows how different successions of strata will accumulate at different locations. In the following discussion, the sedimentary classes described in Chapter 3 are indicated in parentheses.

In the foreground, talus creep, the predominant process of the midslope, has operated continuously from at least the early Holocene up to the present day. In Figure 32 (top), this is represented by deposit 2, which lies upon deposit 1, the stony red colluvium. Aggradation has been slight, and consequently there has been a continuous downslope movement of debris. This process could introduce early artifacts from upslope into footslope contexts, thus providing misleading dating evidence.

In the midground, a wall (3) has been constructed across the slope and has caused the aggradation of deposits 4 and 5 (sediment classes B and C). This process is as described for the fining-up sequence in Chapter 4 (Figure 24). Meanwhile downslope, on the lee side of the wall, relatively little accumulation will take place unless there has been some dumping or building collapse. To conform with the evidence from Q6N, allowance has been made for this (deposit 6), and the overall result is that the ground surface is now stepped.

Subsequently, as a result of building, dumping, localized collapse of structures, and movement of sediment from upslope, a suite of sediments, deposit 7 (class E), has accumulated in the area downslope of the wall. At the same time, more accumulation may have occurred on top of stratum 5, but, because the space behind the barrier has been filled, this will probably be slight. During this phase lateral stratigraphy develops, with early deposits being upslope and later deposits downslope.

In the background, a building phase (8) has now developed upon the platform created by deposit 7. This is shown to be of similar construction technique and context to those of Walls L, M, and N in grid square P5. The wall superstructure may have been of pisé—in grid square P5 and Q5, a reddish clay loam of sediment class D. Similar sediments are contained as lenses within the underlying accumulation of deposit 7 (hatched, Figure 32, top), and they have probably made a significant contribution to this phase of buildup.

This construction (8) formed a barrier across the slope, and another aggradational phase has accumulated behind it (10). In this case, it is less stony than deposit 4 because few stones will roll across the relatively gentle slope and traverse the entire bench (see Chapter 4 and Figure 24). At approximately the same time, a sediment accumulated within the building (9). Stratum 10 can be seen to overlie deposits 7, 5, *and* 2.

Building phase 8 and its associated sediment have in turn been built upon by another wall (11). Stony deposits (12, class G) have accumulated upslope, and later deposits (13) have ac-

Figure 32. Top: Block diagram showing hypothetical sediment sequence discussed in text. The relative chronological sequence is indicated at the left. Flow diagrams, however, would vary depending on which sequence is viewed or exposed. Bottom: Hypothetical section at right angles to the slope showing talus accumulation over a moderately long period (C and D) and aggradation behind a wall (E). A and B horizons of soil profile are developed within the pre-existing slope deposits. Note: Most phases of the site's history are absent or only fleetingly developed in the sequence at C and D.

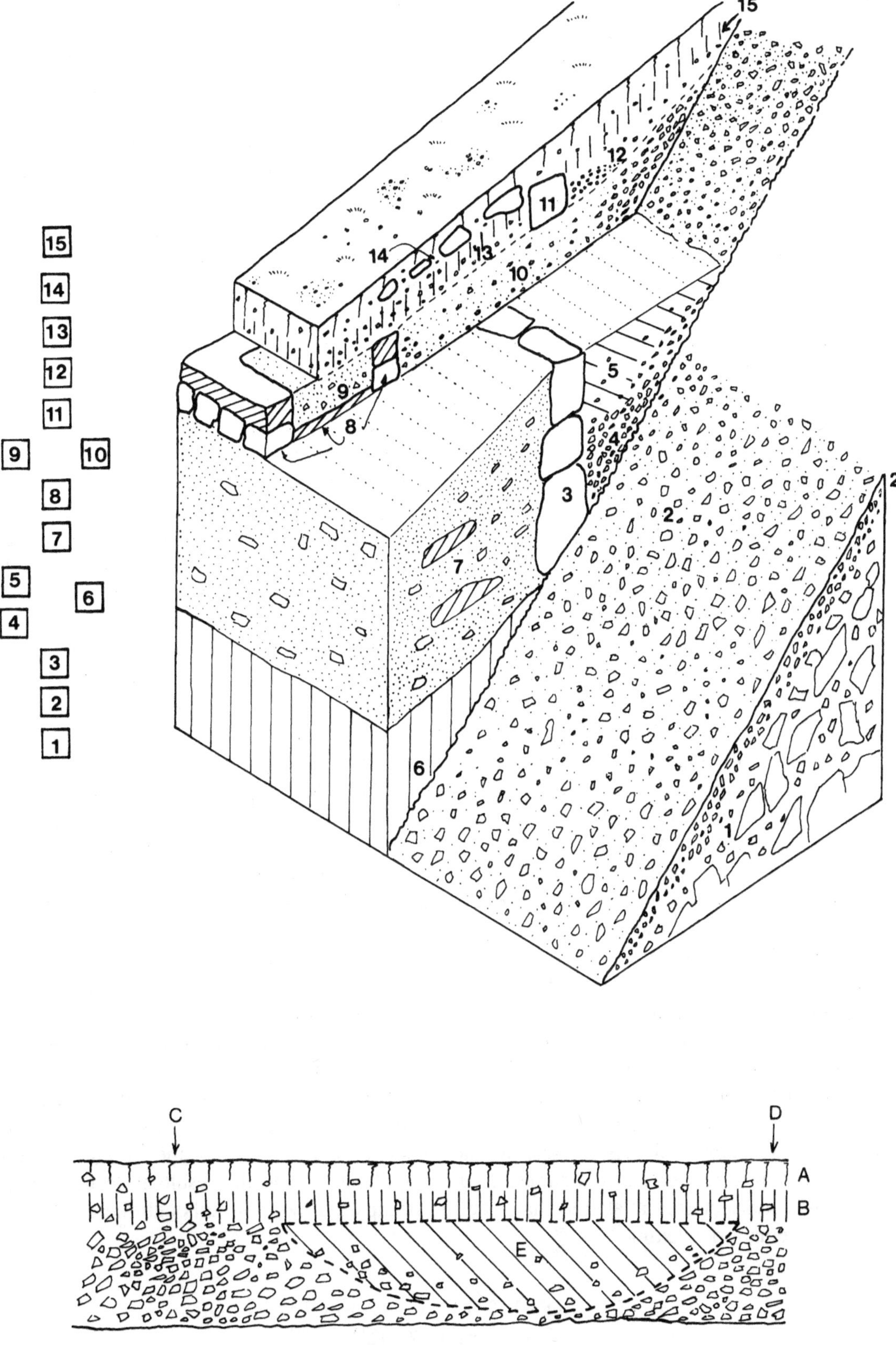

Figure 32.

cumulated downslope. The wall then collapsed and became incorporated in the slope deposits (14). The resultant trail of stones is all that remains of the original wall; for similar examples, see O5, south section, and Q5, south section, upslope of Unit 46 (Jacobsen and Farrand 1987:Plates 47 and 50). During this phase, the talus slope has become relatively stable, and little new material is being introduced for building. Finally, during this stable phase, a weak soil B horizon has developed (15, see Chapter 2). This has developed *within* the pre-existing stratum 14 and is therefore not sedimentary.

All artifacts arriving on the surface during this late phase will remain on the surface for a relatively long time. Consequently, sherds from these stony upper strata (class F) tend to be well rolled.

Although complicated, the sequence illustrated is decipherable. Unfortunately, no such complete succession exists at any single location on Paralia. A similar succession to that illustrated in Figure 32 (top) was found in squares P5, Q5, and Q6, but it was not possible to demonstrate a complete sequence. As is quite evident, if by chance an excavated section missed the deepest succession, a much shorter sequence would result. The configuration of early sediments upslope and later sediments downslope was common, however, being present in squares L5, O5, P5, and Q5.

The problem of missing stratigraphic components is aggravated in sections at right angles to the slope (north-south sections, see Figure 32, bottom). The sequence exposed is very dependent upon the location of the section line, and, again, chronologically late sediments can be directly superimposed upon rather early surfaces. Furthermore, because aggrading sequences upslope of walls taper laterally over short distances, their use for correlation over long distances is weakened.

As if the above problems were not enough to contend with, pits, later walls, robbed walls, burials, and other disturbances have all complicated the record. For example, in an apparently simple situation such as Q5N, where an aggrading sequence is upslope of a wall (Wall A, Jacobsen and Farrand 1987:Plate 56), the sediments have apparently accumulated upslope of a different wall (Wall C, represented only by two stones below Wall A [Jacobsen and Farrand 1987: Plate 56]). Wall A was quite clearly placed in a later cut filled with stratum VII. The real relationship between sediment and Wall C was visible only in the south section of Q5N (not illustrated).

Stratigraphic complications obviously affect the interpretation of the cultural remains. For example, deposits 10 and 12 will include much material rolled from upslope. This will be especially true if, for example, a wall and its associated deposits have collapsed and released early artifacts into the sediment transport system. Alternatively, deposits which include introduced sediments such as 7 and 9 may contain an admixture of early sherds if, as appears to have been the case on the Paralia, these introduced sediments themselves contained sherds. Fortunately, the opposite case (e.g., later material being introduced into early contexts as a result of pit excavation or robber trenches) usually appears to have been isolated by the excavators.

The prevalence of phases of non-deposition is therefore more important than has often been recognized and, for the Early Neolithic at least, *only* where walls were built will we find an aggraded archaeological deposit. During later phases, especially during the Middle Neolithic, introduced materials probably assumed greater significance, and the resultant accumulation is apparently more closely related to that found in occupation mounds, although the details (e.g., in Q6N) remain perplexing.

THE CHRONOLOGICAL DEVELOPMENT OF SEDIMENTARY DEPOSITS

The complex range of sedimentary environments outlined above virtually precludes the establishment of a stratigraphic sequence comparable to that produced for Franchthi Cave (Farrand,

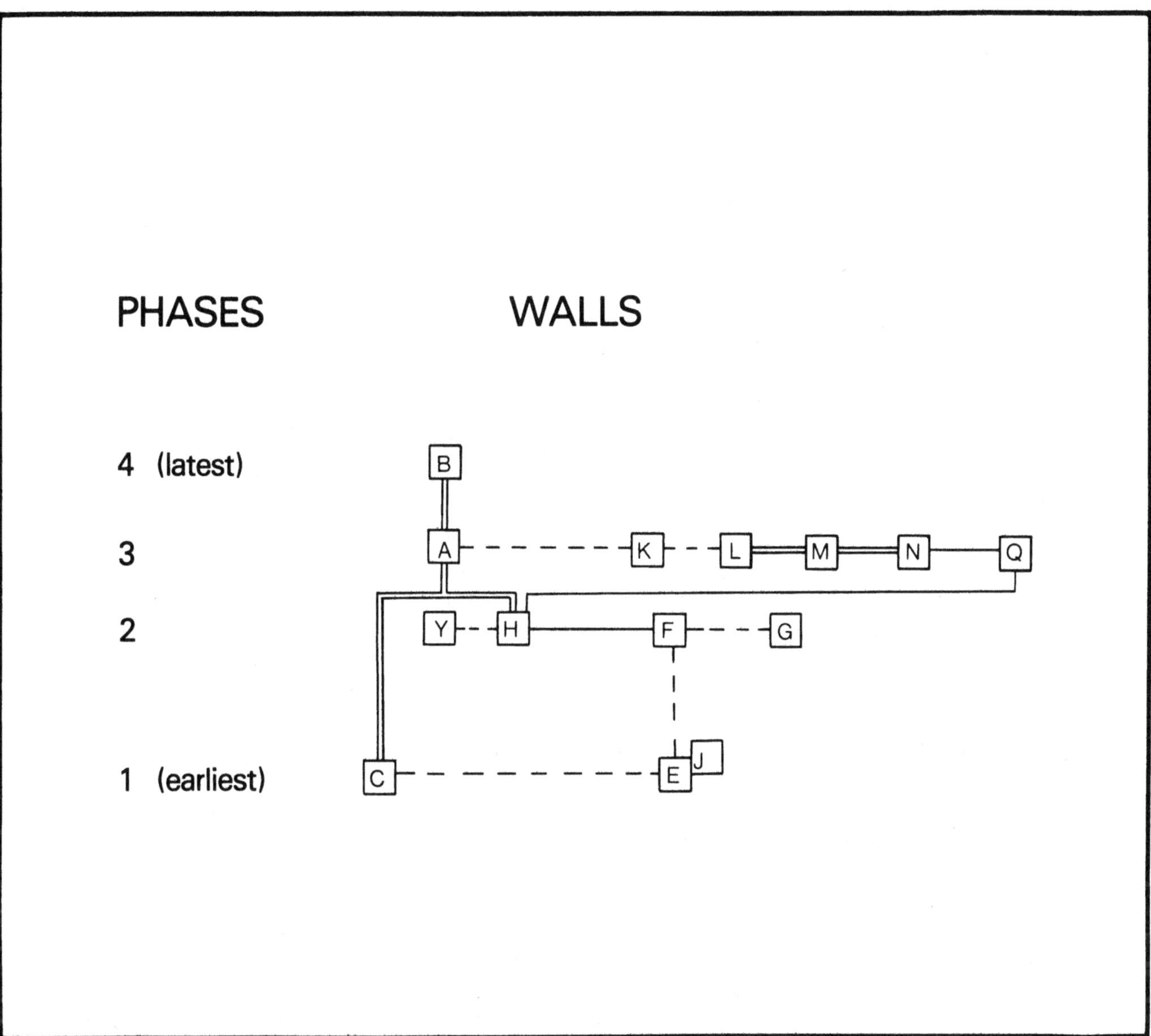

Figure 33. Main Neolithic wall phases in grid squares Q5, P5, Q6, and QR5. Stratigraphic relationships: double line = good; single line = quite good; broken line = possible.

forthcoming). This problem is accentuated by the lack of radiocarbon dates from the Paralia deposits, suitable material for dating being virtually absent. As a result, all dates in the following discussion are based on comparison of ceramics from Paralia contexts with those from the dated sequence within the cave. Greater resolution of time than is implied in the four subdivisions of the Neolithic (see Figure 33) has been undertaken by K. D. Vitelli (forthcoming a-b), but it is not attempted in this report.

The sequence as excavated appears to consist of a series of sedimentary accumulations upslope of walls and in other favorable environments on the slope, separated by hiatuses of unknown duration. The end result is an area of low mounding near the base of the debris slopes. Because of the considerable problem posed by hiatuses and lateral changes in sedimentary accumulation, up and down, as well as across the slope, only key major depositional episodes are identified in the following outline.

The earliest human settlement on the Paralia occurred during Early Neolithic times. Artifacts of this date are contained within sediments which immediately overlie the paleosol. In some cases, notably in grid squares L5 and Q6, potsherds are found mixed in the upper part of the paleosol; otherwise, artifacts are scarce or absent in the paleosol. In addition, some of the walls of the Paralia settlement appear to be founded on the paleosol. For these reasons, the original settlement is interpreted to have taken place at a time when the now-buried paleosol constituted the land surface. Settlement probably commenced about 8000 years B.P., at or near the beginning of the Early Neolithic period (Figure 33), and it follows that the paleosol must have formed at this location prior to that time. The time of the beginning of soil formation can only be estimated. Within the cave, sediments of reddish hue (2.5-5 YR) dominated the deposits from the lowermost levels until the Mesolithic period. Radiocarbon dates from charcoal in these deposits range from about 22,000 years B.P. to about 10,000 years B.P. (Jacobsen and Farrand 1987:Plate 71). This deposition is therefore late Pleistocene. A date for the Paralia paleosol of pre-8000 B.P. (i.e., early Holocene) is only slightly later than for the reddish cave sediments, but a closer dating is not possible.

The land surface on which the Paralia paleosol formed must have remained relatively stable throughout the period of soil formation. This land surface cannot be directly traced away from the Paralia, since it is bounded by limestone outcrops on the north, east, and south, and by the sea on the west. A recent seismic study has, however, recognized a strong reflecting surface veneered by younger deposits, beneath the waters of Kiladha Bay (van Andel et al. 1980; van Andel and Sutton 1987). This reflector has been joined with a buried land surface at the southern end of Kiladha Bay and is reasonably regarded as equivalent to the paleo-land surface recognized at the base of the Paralia excavations.

During the Neolithic occupation of the Paralia, sediments accumulated on the hillslope. Much of this deposition occurred upslope of several walls running across the slope in grid squares Q5 and P5. The brownish gray and pale brown silt loams in profile Q (strata III, IV, and V, north section of Q5, Jacobsen and Farrand 1987:Plate 56) belong to this group. Contemporary deposits occur in grid square Q4 and probably in P5 and QR as well. It may be that the Neolithic stone walls acted as retaining walls and allowed the accumulation of these sediments upslope as described in Chapter 4. In contrast, downslope, sedimentary accumulations appear to have been attenuated.

The pale brown silt loams in profile L (strata III and IV, east section of L5, Figure 35) are also in large part Early Neolithic, although the upper part may be transitional to Middle Neolithic. The relatively high levels of organic carbon and the pulverized charcoal in the silt-sized fraction are probably a direct result of the Early Neolithic occupation.

The mineralogy of these deposits, which is comparable to the other sediments on Paralia (excepting the smectite in stratum VI in L5), suggests that these occupation deposits are derived largely from the same sources. These possible sources include residuum from the underlying bedrock, slope wash and debris from upslope, windblown sediments, sediments deposited by the sea, and additions by the prehistoric inhabitants as described in Chapters 3 and 4.

The possible contribution of residuum from the underlying bedrock cannot be evaluated since the nature of the bedrock and the depth at which it lies are unknown. Slope wash and debris from upslope are considered a major source since many limestone fragments, ranging in size from large boulders to sand, litter the slope and are ubiquitous throughout the deposits, from the paleosol to the surface. The deposits probably include some windblown additions, especially as more extensive tracts of lowland must have been exposed before the sea attained its present level. Such a source may account for some of the finer serpentinite fraction observed, but the relative importance of aeolian additions is difficult to estimate.

During the period 8500–7000 B.P., the shoreline is estimated to have been one or two kilometers farther out from its present position immediately adjacent to the Paralia (van Andel et al. 1980; van Andel and Lianos 1984). If that reconstruction is accurate, sediments deposited by the sea are probably not a significant source. The human occupants were probably responsible for minor additions of obsidian, chert, sandstone, and serpentinite since all were used as raw materials for artifacts.

The duration of the Early Neolithic occupation of Paralia is uncertain. Radiocarbon dates from deposits of Early Neolithic age in the cave range from nearly 8000 years B.P. to about 7000 years B.P. If the Early Neolithic settlement on Paralia is fully contemporaneous, the deposits span about 1000 (radiocarbon) years.

The transition to Middle Neolithic may occur within the upper part of the grayish silt loams in profiles L and Q (upper stratum IV in L5, upper stratum V in Q5 North). Above these, the reddish loams and clay loams (sediment class D: stratum V in L5 and VI in Q5 North) are certainly of Middle Neolithic age (ca. 7000–6500 B.P.). Other deposits of sediment class D are strata XXVII in Q5 West, XII and XIV in P5, and within VII in Q6 North. These reddish sediments are poor in organic carbon, high in iron oxide, and have relatively low CECs: properties similar to those of the buried B horizon (see Chapter 3). It is suggested, on the basis of the presence of certain exotic stones and other properties that such "upper red" sediments were transported to the site by the Middle Neolithic inhabitants (see Chapter 3).

Other Middle Neolithic deposits are recognized above early Middle Neolithic deposits in grid square Q6N (stratum VII). The division between Early and Middle Neolithic probably occurs within strata IV and V in Q6N, i.e., within the C horizon of the ground soil in profiles R and S. These Middle Neolithic sediments (class E in Chapter 3) are silty, organic-rich, and vary in color from brown to brownish gray, with lenses of reddish hue. Pulverized charcoal is also present. The properties are similar to those observed in the Early Neolithic deposits in profiles Q and L, and similar intensive alteration by human occupation is regarded as the cause. Such Middle Neolithic deposits, however, may have been redeposited from their original site of deposition as described in Chapter 3.

The deposits overlying the paleosol in Q6N (stratum III) may have been disturbed or redeposited during the Neolithic since burials were found near the northeast corner of Q6N and nearby in Q5. The Q6N burials are thought to be Early Neolithic, whereas that in Q5 is securely assigned to the Middle Neolithic (Jacobsen 1979).

The duration of the Middle Neolithic in the cave is about 500 (radiocarbon) years, and a similar timespan is assumed for the Paralia occupation. Over much of the Paralia excavation, the Middle Neolithic is the last period of prehistoric occupation. Late Neolithic artifacts, which are represented in late seventh millenium B.P. deposits in the cave, have not been found outside the cave.

Artifactual evidence for the latest period of Neolithic occupation on Paralia, the Final Neolithic (ca. 6000–5000 B.P.), is restricted in its occurrence. Sediments with associated Final Neolithic pottery occur in surficial deposits in grid square Q4 and in a few other near-surface locations in other trenches, but the most extensive area of activities of the Final Neolithic period as excavated is in L5 (stratum VI, L5 north and east). These deposits are unique on Paralia in two respects: high values for calcium carbonate and the dominating presence of smectite in the clay-sized fraction.

The whitened, highly calcareous deposits fill, in several cases, distinct pits, one of which showed traces of burning. In a few cases, the carbonate nodules appear to line the pits. In all cases, the carbonate-rich material is associated with Final Neolithic artifacts, which include a number of grinding stones. Although the exact nature of activity represented by the pits and their deposits is unknown, it is thought that they were associated with the production of lime, either as a deliberate product, or as a waste product, possibly associated with the production of clay vessels, as noted in Chapter 3.

The Final Neolithic is the last prehistoric occupation on Paralia. Only a few Final Neolithic dates, falling about 5200 years B.P., are available from the cave. They are not sufficient evidence for estimating the duration of occupation on Paralia.

Following the abandonment of the site, the slope stabilized and the Holocene ground soil formed within the upper part of the Neolithic deposits. This produced the weak B horizon within the upper stony loams and talus (stratum X and XVI in P5) over the approximately 5000-year time span since the site was abandoned.

MAXIMUM EXTENT OF THE PARALIA SETTLEMENT

Both the slope morphology of the dry land site and the results of submarine work conducted in Kiladha Bay have indicated that the Paralia settlement originally occupied a larger area than is now visible onshore. It is evident from the steeply beveled footslopes that the site has been truncated by marine erosion both during and since the Holocene transgression. This is especially clear in the north section of square Q6N (Jacobsen and Farrand 1987:Plate 56). In addition, geophysical survey and coring undertaken by van Andel, Gifford, and their colleagues have provided a much clearer view of the geomorphology and former occupation of the nearshore zone (van Andel et al. 1980; Gifford 1983; Chapter 7, this volume). As a result of this work, some 70 cm of sediment containing Neolithic cultural material has been intercepted at several locations on the floor of the bay up to some 200 m west of the site (Chapter 7).

Figure 34 shows the modern slope profile, the depth of occupation deposits, the original slope profile, the present sea floor, and the probable position of the early Holocene land surface below sea level. These data have been used in concert to estimate the former extent of occupation deposits. This estimate is of course only a little better than speculation, but it is hoped that at least some idea of the original site morphology may result from it.

The following elements have been extrapolated from the modern ground surface and that of the original slope profile:

1. The profile of the modern ground surface. As described in Chapter 1, the Paralia slope comprises a limestone backwall, a midslope, and a colluvial footslope. The footslope deposits have been truncated by marine action, which, by cutting the base of the slope, produced an over-steepened slope face immediately upslope. It is possible, however, to extrapolate geometrically the uneroded footslope profile into the bay to produce an estimate of the original

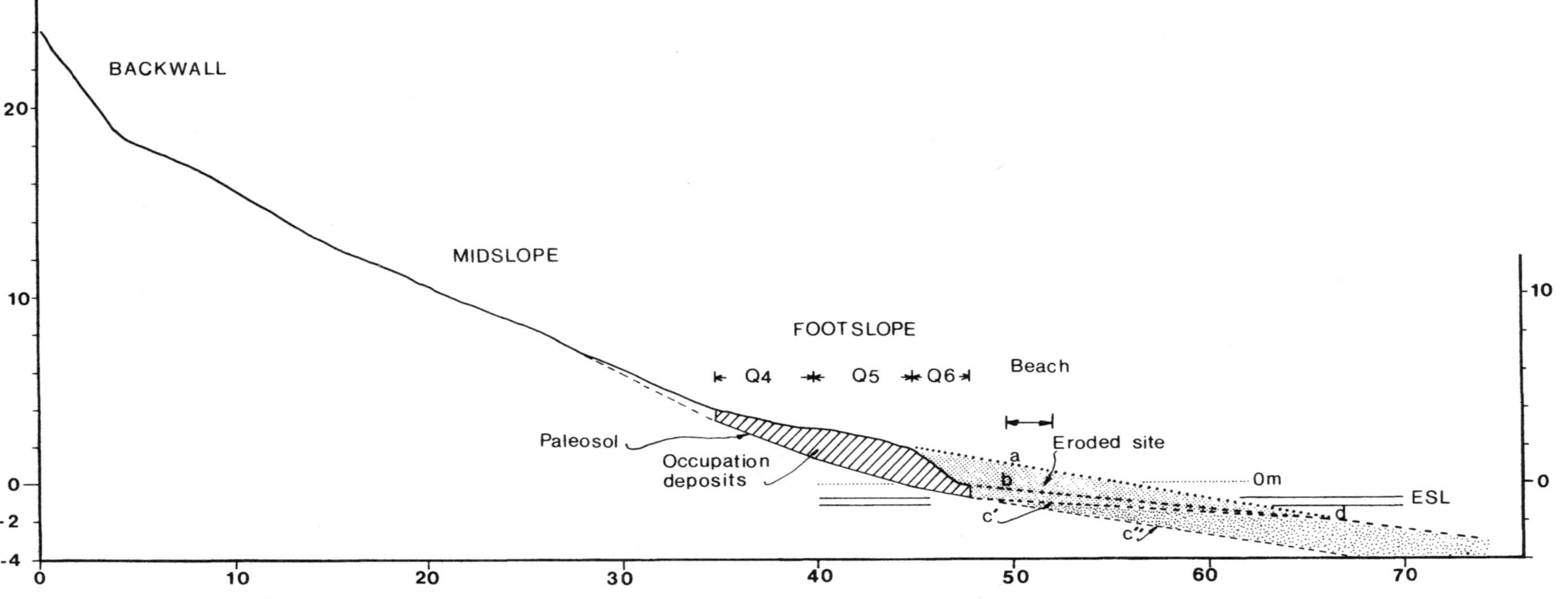

Figure 34. Slope profile through grid squares Q4-Q6, extended into Kiladha Bay in order to estimate the original extent of occupation deposits. a-d, see text; ESL = estimated sea level showing the approximate tidal range; 0m=0 meters according to the Greek datum. Scales are in meters.

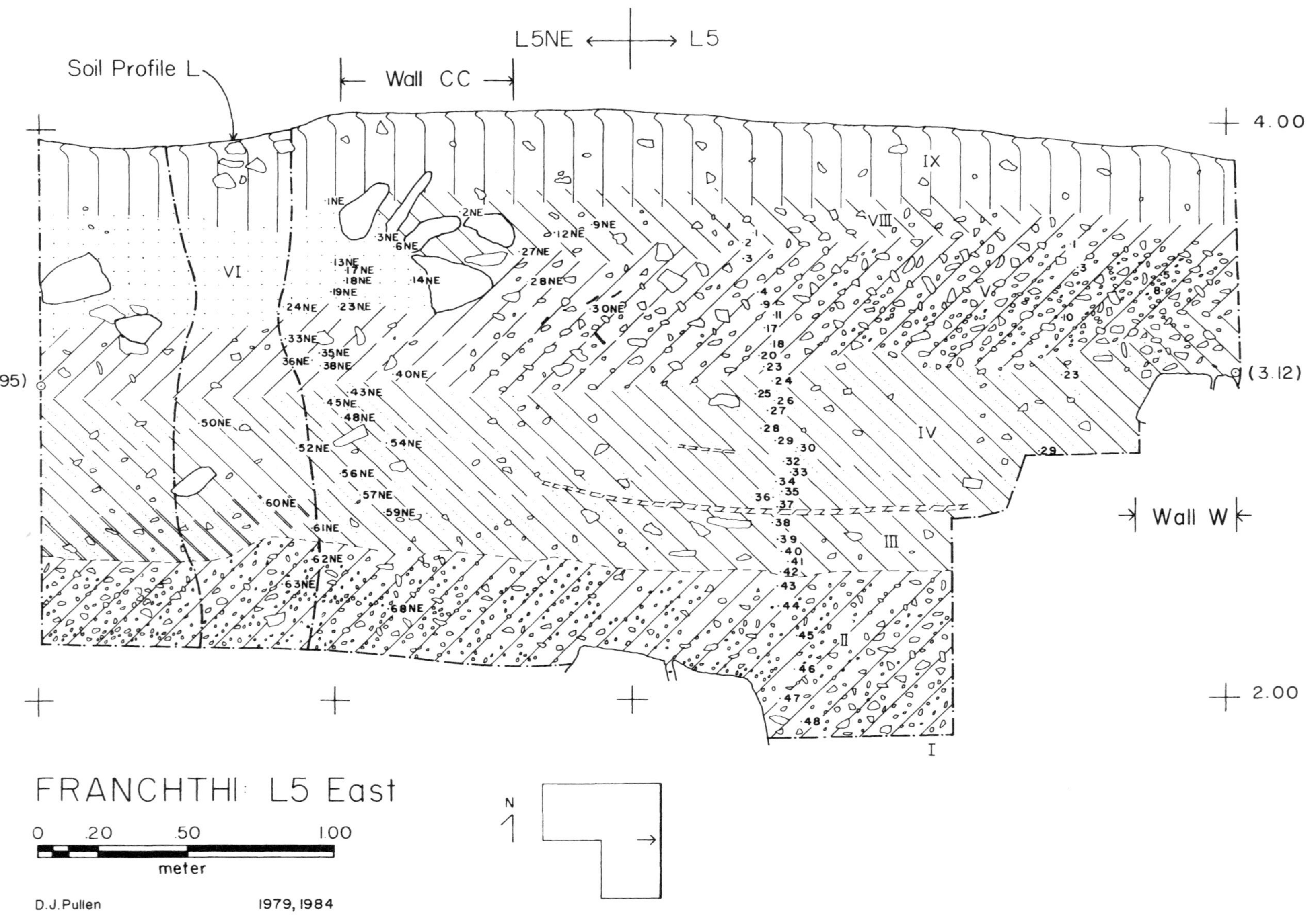

Figure 35. Master section drawing of L5 East.

ground surface (line *a*, Figure 34). No attempt has been made at this stage to extrapolate using mathematically derived curves, although this might be possible at a later stage of analysis. Line *a* meets the sea bed (*c*′) at point *d* and is approximately parallel to the sea-bed gradient (*c*″).

2. The truncated element of the modern ground surface in square Q6N (line *b*, Figure 34). This is a cut surface and reflects erosional processes operating *since* the accumulation of the archaeological sediments.
3. The paleosol developed on the stony red colluvium. This is the buried land surface and is equivalent to the early Holocene surface encountered by van Andel and others within the bay. It exhibits a smooth, concave-up profile, similar to the lower part of many hillslopes in temperate regions.

   This surface can simply be extrapolated by continuing the paleosol surface along the sea floor (line *c*′) on the assumption that the sea floor is a bench eroded in stony red colluvium. This links with line *a* at *d* to produce the shaded wedge of sediments indicated.

The above reconstruction can be questioned on two grounds. First, profile *c*′ is not a controlled extrapolation of the paleosol surface; it is debatable whether it is more realistic to extrapolate the straight-line surface from Q6N or to allow for a progressive decrease in the slope angle. Second, no allowance has been made for the accumulation of marine sediments on the early Holocene land surface. Both van Andel (van Andel et al. 1980) and Gifford (1983) have demonstrated that the firm, early Holocene land surface has been blanketed by softer marine deposits. Van Andel has shown that, at a distance of some 50 m offshore, approximately 5 m of Holocene marine sediments have accumulated since the transgression (van Andel et al. 1980:Figure 9). An extension of this line, line *c*″, is depicted on Figure 34 and the assumed depth of marine sediments is stippled above it. Although approximate,[6] this in fact coincides with the extrapolation of the paleosol surface on Q6N. More recent work by Gifford shows a pre-transgression land surface between lines *c*′ and *c*″ (Chapter 7).

The extrapolation *c*″, which is probably more realistic than *c*′ when viewed in conjunction with line *a*, extends the site indefinitely. Although only general statements can be made at this stage, it would appear that the Paralia settlement must have extended considerably farther than the present exposure. A conservative estimate, employing lines *a* and *c*′, predicts that the site formed a wedge extending some 18 m west of the present limit. The second model, using *a* and *c*″, allows the possibility of a much larger site. Finally, the evidence presented by Gifford in Chapter 7 allows for an extension of the site at least 28 m to the west. Whichever reconstruction is preferred, there is no evidence that the deposits were ever any deeper than has been recorded in the deepest parts of grid squares Q5 and Q6 (2.2 m).

To conclude, it is evident that the extant Neolithic settlement of Franchthi Paralia may represent only the edge of a much more extensive former settlement. This appears to have developed on the lower colluvial footslopes (now submerged below Kiladha Bay) between the excavated site and the probable course of an early Holocene river (van Andel et al 1980: Figure 10). According to the results of the coring noted above, such a settlement may have spread over 1-2 ha or more, although unequivocal evidence is still lacking. The presence of such a settlement area therefore raises the possibility that the excavated site, rather than being within the core of the occupied area, was in fact in a more marginal location at the base of only sparsely inhabited stony debris slopes.

PART II

The Offshore Investigations

John A. Gifford

Sytze Bottema

CHAPTER SEVEN

*Analysis of Submarine Sediments off Paralia**

John A. Gifford

INTRODUCTION

Prehistoric sites submerged in the shallow waters around Greece have been known for some three decades (Leatham and Hood 1959; Harding et al. 1969), though they have been seldom excavated. With the realization in recent years that prehistoric terrestrial sites submerged on the world's continental shelves may still preserve some contextual information, sites at present sea level became candidates for investigation since they might have some component or activity area submerged and yet preserved in the nearshore zone. Paralia is an example of this category of site, and early on the excavators suggested that it could represent just the edge of a Neolithic activity area, perhaps a settlement, that had been inundated by the post-glacial rise of world sea level (Jacobsen 1976:84, 1979:279-280).

Van Andel (1987:34-49) has reconstructed the paleogeography of the landscape around the Franchthi embayment, and particularly the immediate vicinity of the Paralia site, as it evolved from a terrestrial to the present marine setting during the post-glacial eustatic sea-level rise. Here we present further detail to his reconstruction, we test the Paralia excavators' idea of a partly submerged site, and we assess the degree of post-depositional transformation that Neolithic cultural deposits would have experienced during and since their submersion.

Franchthi Cave is a solution feature developed in the Franchthi Limestone, a gray-to-black, massively bedded limestone of early Cretaceous age (Vitaliano 1987:14). The headland of the same name dominates the north side of Kiladha Bay.

*We thank T.W. Jacobsen (Indiana University) and Tj. H. van Andel (Cambridge University) for their encouragement and assistance in planning this project and in discussion of its results. The Ephoria Enalion Arkhaiotiton (Underwater Branch of the Greek Archaeological Service) granted the necessary permission for both seasons of field work. Assistance from the American School of Classical Studies in Athens was kindly provided by its directors, Henry Immerwahr in 1981 and Stephen Miller in 1985.

Participating in the 1981 fieldwork were T. Cullen, K. Pope, V. Arvanitopoulos, and N. Lianos; we thank them all for their crucial assistance in the underwater coring. In addition, R.K. Vincent served as land and underwater photographer. Contributing substantively to the success of the 1985 fieldwork were: J. McK. Camp II (diver and underwater photographer), N. Lianos (diver), M. Jacobsen (surveyor), S. Diamant (logistical assistance), F. Cooper (surveying assistance), and K.D. Vitelli (examination of the pottery from the bulk basal core samples). Grain-size analyses of the core sediment samples were performed at the Archaeometry Laboratory (University of Minnesota) by C.L. Hill in 1981 and by A. Ollendorf in 1985. J. Gennett undertook the pilot study of pollen in the 1981 cores.

This project was funded by grants from the Committee for Research and Exploration of the National Geographic Society.

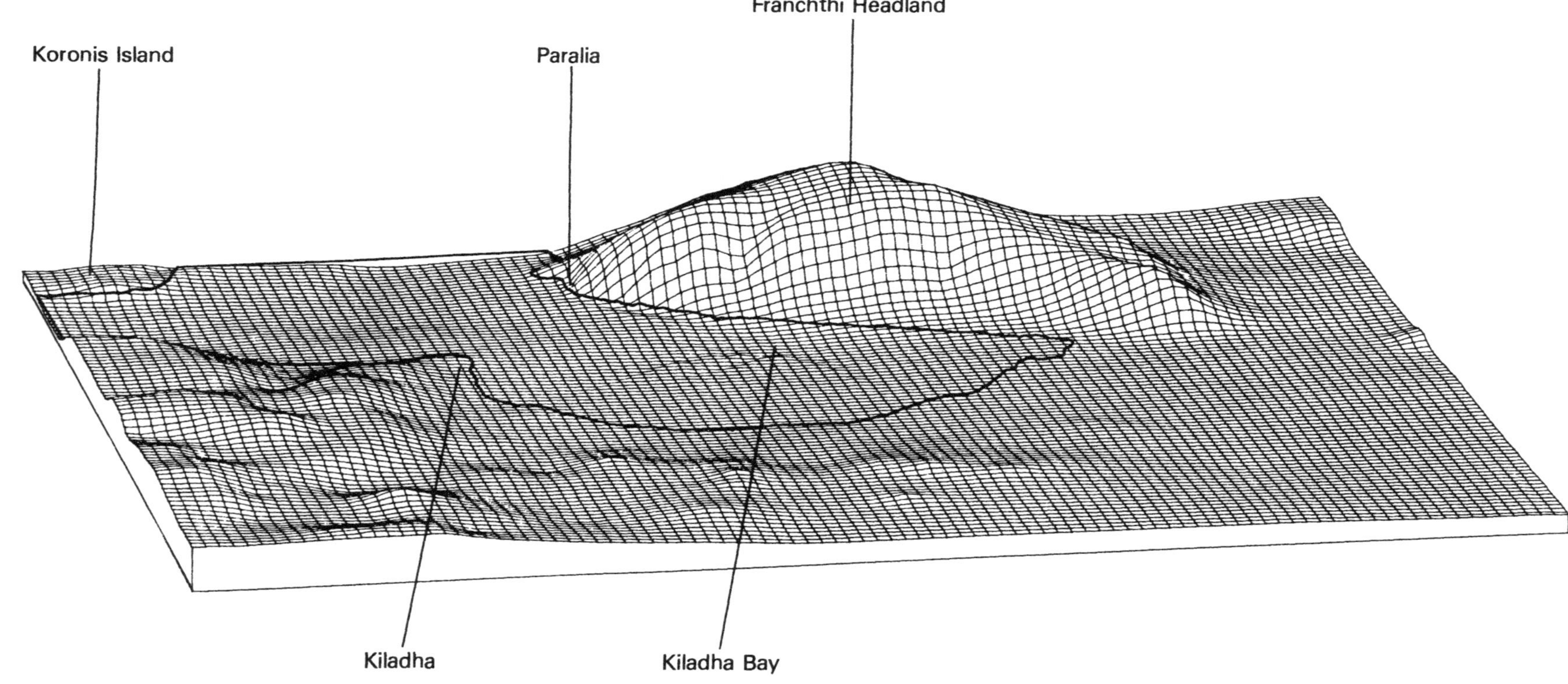

Figure 36. A computer-generated perspective block diagram of the Kiladha Bay area, as seen from an elevation of 15° above the horizon and looking north. Vertical exaggeration is 8.5x. The heavy line shows the position of present sea level. Base map: Greek Army Map Service, Sheet 73097 (1:5000).

Besides the main work undertaken in the 1970s within Franchthi Cave itself, excavations were carried out along the shore, at elevations of only 1-3 m above the present sea level, of a small, structurally controlled cove formed in the Franchthi Limestone. The excavated area, called Paralia, is some 75 m in horizontal distance and 15 m lower than the Franchthi Cave entrance. Figure 36 shows the location of Paralia relative to the Franchthi headland and the present shore of Kiladha Bay.

Traces of stone structures, probably walls or wall foundations, were uncovered in several of the Paralia grid squares, but the stratigraphy was complex and discontinuous (see above, Part I) partly as a result of the steep slope on which the structures were built during the Neolithic period.

A marine geophysical survey of the seabed off Paralia (termed outer Kiladha Bay), undertaken in 1979 as part of a larger reconnaissance of the Franchthi embayment, produced reconstructions of the area's mid-to-late Holocene paleogeography that supported the possibility of a submerged extension of the Paralia site (van Andel et al. 1980). The project described in this chapter was designed to test directly the hypothesis, by coring the sedimentary sequence and recovering samples of both the post-transgression marine sediments and the pre-transgression land surface assumed to underlie them. Sediments from the submerged land surface would be analyzed for microscopic traces of cultural activity as well as for paleoenvironmental indicators.

In 1981, our immediate objective was to determine the nature of the sediment sequence and if it could be cored successfully. After discovering Neolithic pottery sherds at the bottom of both cores recovered, the 1985 field work sought to determine the areal distribution, age, and density of cultural material below the marine sediments. Fourteen cores were recovered during the second field season.

The photograph reproduced as Plate 3 was taken from near the entrance to Franchthi Cave and shows a general view of outer Kiladha Bay, where field work took place during both seasons. The surface position of 1981 core site FC 2 is indicated by the small boat at the left of the photograph.

METHODOLOGY

From studies of the submarine sedimentary sequence off the Franchthi headland by van Andel et al. (1980) it was apparent that, depending on the locality, some 3-6 m of marine muds would have to be penetrated in order to reach any cultural material at or near the mid-Holocene land surface. Present water depths between Franchthi headland and Koronis Island range from 2 m to 10 m. The total water/sediment-column depth range of 5-16 m is somewhat too deep for hand coring from a surface-moored platform (especially in open-water conditions), but it is too shallow for effective piston or gravity coring using standard oceanographic equipment. A compromise was found in a hand-operated incremental coring system using a cased hole. Although the equipment was designed for terrestrial use in water-saturated sediments, in this project it was operated successfully by two divers standing on the bay bottom at each core location.

Plate 4 illustrates the coring system's components. The corer itself is a small (75 cm long x 4 cm outside diameter) stainless-steel piston-type device fitted with quick-disconnect couplings and meter-long extension rods for incremental coring to a sediment depth of 7 m. To prevent hole collapse between removal of the core sections, a casing of thick-walled, 7-cm (inside diameter) plastic tubes equipped with a steel bit is manually pushed into the bottom, around and ahead of the corer. Additional meter-long casing sections are joined as needed to the top of the string by means of internal threads on each plastic tube section. The corer only partially removes all the sediment within the casing due to the disparity in their diameters; therefore, an open-ended stainless-steel tube (the bailer), 6 cm in outside diameter and fitted with a one-way flapper valve at its lower end, is inserted into the cased hole alternatively with the corer to churn up the excess sediment and remove it from the casing before the next-deeper core section is recovered. In this way almost no core contamination from slumping can occur (Plates 5 and 6). This describes the procedure for continuous coring. In 1985 most of our samples were obtained without continuous coring, as explained below.

We made several modifications to the standard terrestrial coring procedure necessitated by the different working conditions. During both field seasons we immediately extruded each core section underwater, using as a receptacle a pre-labeled plastic tube section of suitable length and inside diameter (Plate 4). After capping, these tubes prevented damage to or contamination of the core sections.

In 1985, two further improvements were made to our underwater procedures: (1) prior to coring at each location, we laid on the bay bottom a circular plate of thin steel, 1.5 m in diameter and having a hole 20 cm in diameter at its center, as a solid platform that distributed the divers' weights so they could move and work without sinking into the soft bay-bottom sediments; and (2) after taking each core, we marked its location by sinking a rod 3 m long, either of copper or (at four locations) of stainless steel, into the bottom next to the core hole. Only some 15 cm of the rod were left protruding above the sediment. All the core holes thus might be relocated if necessary, though local searching with an induction metal detector would be required.

The 1981 project indicated that use of surface-supplied air for the diving operations would be more efficient than SCUBA. Thus in 1985, a low pressure air compressor powered by a small gasoline engine was purchased in the U.S. and temporarily imported into Greece. Again, as in 1981, mechanical problems with the compressor severely limited the actual diving time and therefore the total number of cores collected. During both field seasons, the coring proceeded very slowly due to conditions of zero visibility that developed soon after the excess muddy sediment was bailed from the core hole. Each pair of divers generally spent 60-90 minutes working on the bottom before being relieved by another team.

As mentioned above, in 1981 the marine sediment cover off Paralia was cored at two localities (FC 1 and FC 2) between the Franchthi headland and Koronis Island to the west. The sediment sequence observed in both cores was a dark gray (Munsell color N 4), slightly pebbly, sandy mud with carbonate bioclastics (mostly shell fragments) distributed unevenly down the length of the cores. At the base of core FC 1, 5.5 m below the present bottom of outer Kiladha Bay and in a water depth of 4.5 m, a stratum rich in mollusc shell fragments and subangular limestone pebbles was found to rest on a hard surface that stopped the corer. From this coarse stratum over 30 pottery sherds were recovered from inside the core casing. Almost all were undiagnostic, but the exceptions showed fabrics characteristic of Neolithic wares.

In addition to the sherds, a number of ecological indicators of cultural activity were found in the basal sediments of both cores: many charcoal fragments (one of *Ficus* sp.), several carbonized *Triticum* sp. caryopses, several small fish vertebrae, mud plaster fragments (Plate 7), and microscopic flakes of oxidized copper were recovered.

In 1985 fourteen cores were taken in the same general area west of Paralia (Table 2 and Figures 37 and 38). All core locations were triangulated from transit stations located on a Franchthi excavation datum (station S-1+000), a bench mark on Koronis Island (HAGS monument 68; cf. Cooper 1987:12), and a known location along the shore at Kiladha village. Core locations were plotted on a 1:1000 base map. Table 2 summarizes the cores' characteristics. Although the 1981 cores FC 1 and FC 2 were located only by underwater taping from shore, we believe that the former lies within a 10-m radius of OK85/1 and the latter within a 20-m radius of OK85/2.

TABLE 2

SUMMARY OF 1985 ORMOS KILADHA (OK) CORES

Date Obtained	*Core Number*	*Coordinates*[a]	*Water Depth*	*Sediment Thickness*	*Total Depth Below MSL*[b]
18-20 May	OK85/1	19090/14293	4.0 m	5.3 m	9.3 m
20-21 May	OK85/2	19106/14198	5.5 m	4.7 m	10.2 m
22-23 May	OK85/3	19193/14278	4.2 m	4.6 m	8.8 m
23 May	OK85/4	19002/14311	4.0 m	4.25 m	8.25 m
23-24 May	OK85/5	19300/14267	5.25 m	4.6 m	9.85 m
24 May	OK85/6A	19054/14300	4.3 m	4.7 m	9.0 m
26 May	OK85/1A	19106/14295	4.1 m	5.1 m	9.2 m
27 May	OK85/7	19150/14296	3.95 m	5.05 m	9.0 m
27 May	OK85/8	19101/14338	3.0 m	2.4 m	5.4 m
28-30 May	OK85/9A	19101/14219	5.1 m	5.9 m	11.0 m
30 May	OK85/10	19102/14084	9.1 m	1.5 m	10.6 m
31 May-1 June	OK85/11	18957/19311	10.2 m	4.5 m	14.7 m
3 June	OK85/1B	19107/14295	4.1 m	4.7 m	8.8 m
4 June	OK85/12	19077/14326	3.6 m	2.9 m	6.5 m

[a]Greek plane coordinate system (Cooper 1987:12).
[b]MSL = mean sea level, not corrected for estimated tidal range of 0.4 m (cf. Note 6).

At each core location, water depths were measured by means of a metal sounding chain and are considered precise to ±0.05 m. Core depths were taken from measured lengths of casing tubes down the core hole and are equally precise. In the several cases of cores with the same number but an alphabetic suffix, we obtained a duplicate core within 1 m of the original hole, necessitated by the presence of buried stones at those localities. The exception is OK85/1, where the bottom marker was accidentally pulled up and could not be relocated in exactly the same position; thus OK85/1B may not be within 1 m of the original location.

Some of the 1985 core locations are shown in Figure 37, a computer-generated perspective view (looking north-northeast at an angle of 30°) of outer Kiladha Bay between the Franchthi headland and Koronis Island. Also shown (in the lower left foreground) is the shore of the mainland at Kiladha village. (Only small sections of all three of these shorelines are included.) The bathymetry of Figure 37 is based on Figure 5 of van Andel et al. (1980), as modified by our soundings at each core location. We discovered that the depth contours given in Figure 5 of van Andel et al. (1980) should be increased by 1-2 m. The revised bathymetry as well as selected core locations are also shown in Figure 38, a map of the same area. Because the 1981 work was limited to points 100 m and 200 m west of Paralia, in the 1985 season we established a transect oriented approximately north-south and centered on the location of core OK85/1 (Figure 38). That core was relocated in the general vicinity of the 1981 core FC 1, 100 m due west of Paralia. Cores OK85/3, 4, 5, and 6A were located on the north-south transect, at 50-m intervals. Most of the cultural material was recovered from cores north of the OK85/1 locale.

Cores OK85/2 and OK85/10 were located, respectively, 200 m and 300 m west of Paralia. OK85/11 was cored through the sediments of the drowned river channel discovered by sub-bottom

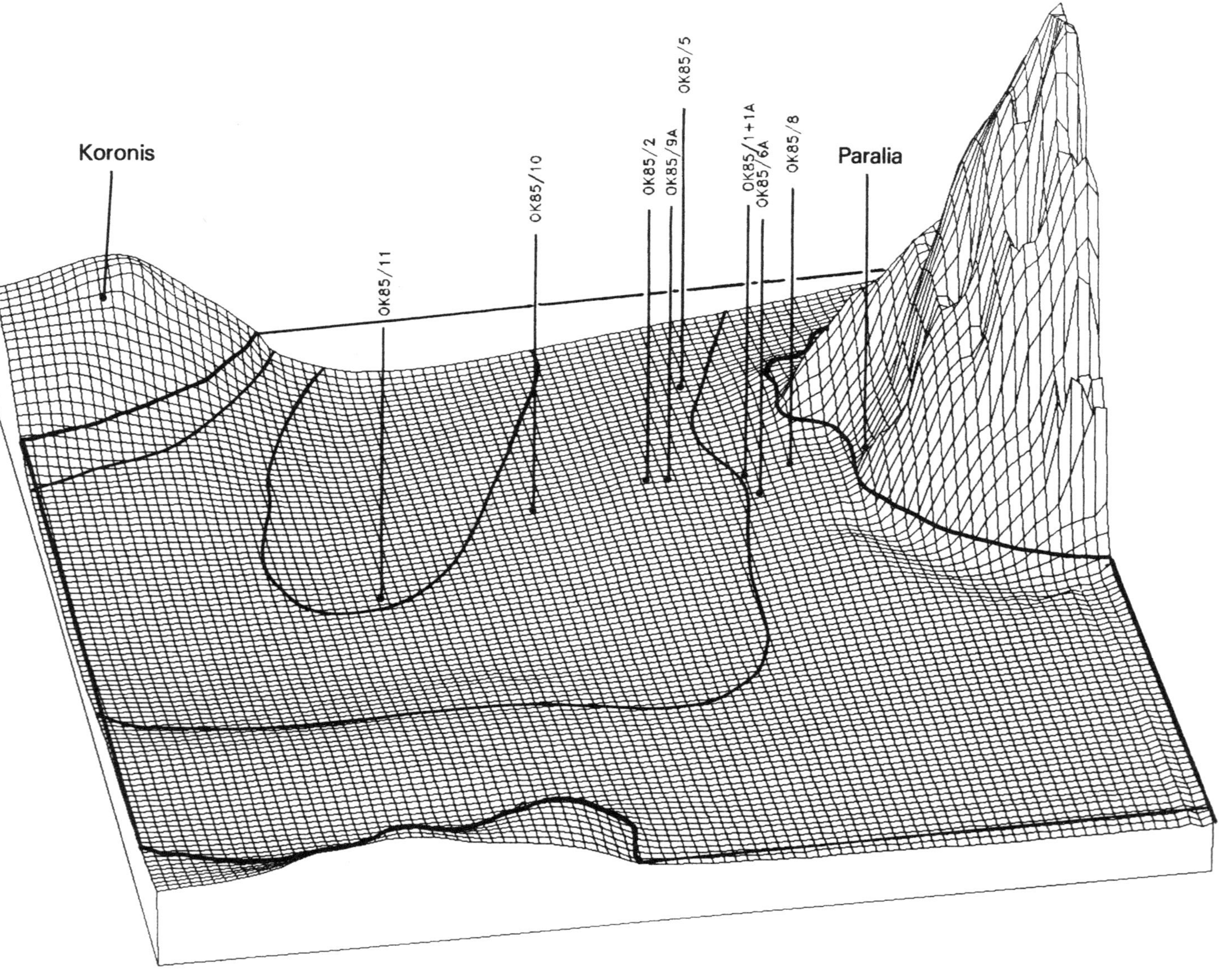

Figure 37. Perspective view of outer Kiladha Bay, showing bathymetry and selected 1985 core locations (looking north-northeast at an angle above the horizon of 30°). Bathymetric contour interval is 4 m. Vertical exaggeration: 40x. Map sources: van Andel et al. 1980 (Figure 5); 1:1000 topographic map of Paralia area (with offshore core locations) prepared by M. Jacobsen.

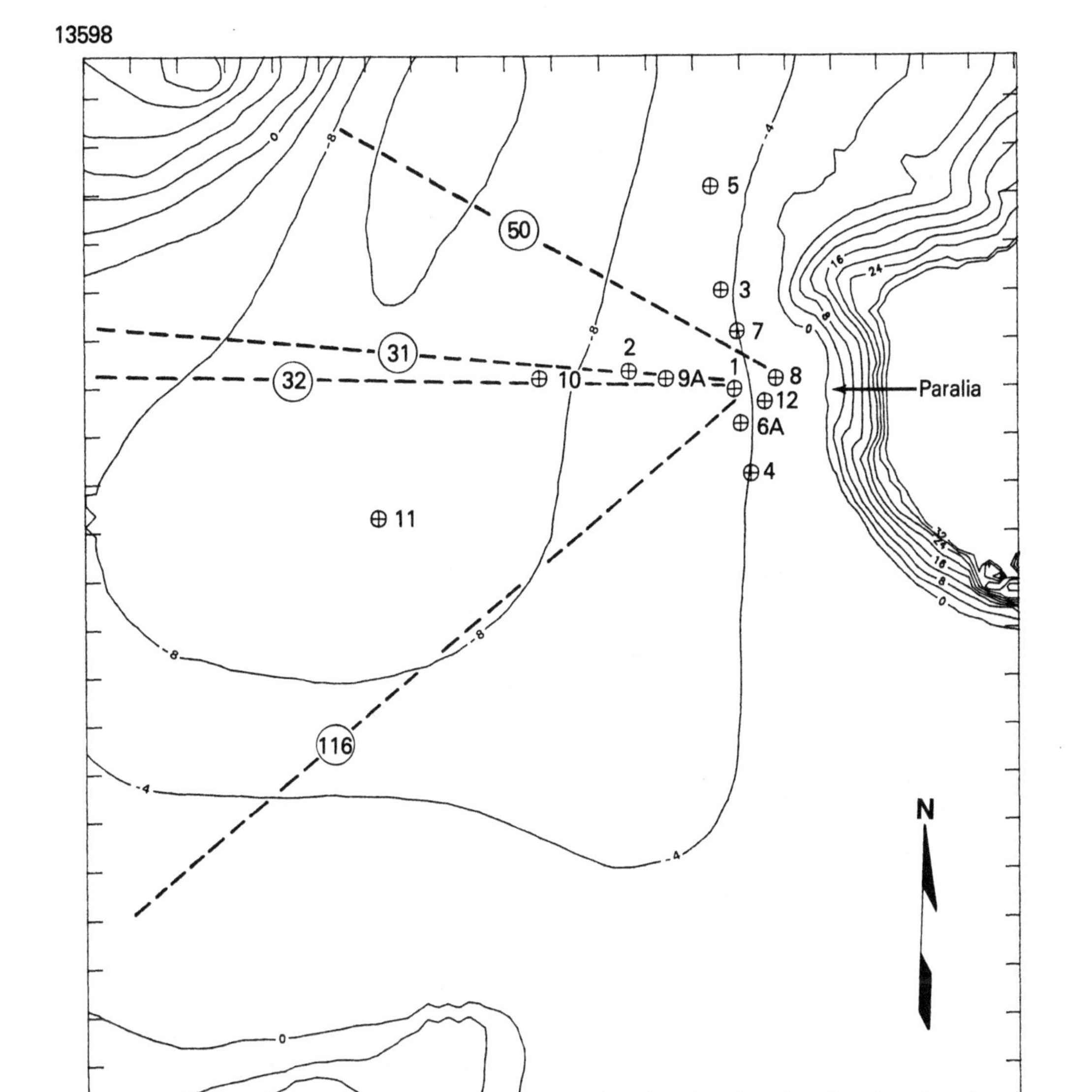

Figure 38. Index map showing the locations of 12 of the 14 cores taken in 1985. The contour interval (above and below sea level) is 4 m; only contours below 32 m are shown on Franchthi headland. Broken lines represent the locations of bottom-penetrating sonar profiles 50, 31, 32, and 116 shown in Figure 18 of van Andel (1987).

profiling just southeast of Koronis island (van Andel et al. 1980:Figures 6 and 11, cross-section B), specifically for recovering pollen from the marine sediment section (see Chapter 8).

All our cores bottomed on hard surfaces that could not be penetrated by the hand-operated equipment. In most cases the obstructions seemed to be large stones rather than bedrock surfaces, based on the slightly different feel of the drill string hitting one or the other surface. At this lowest level in each core we recovered anywhere from one to three liters of water-saturated sediment by trapping it in the core bailer, pulling up the string of extension rods, and emptying the bailer into a 20-liter plastic container on the bottom next to the core hole. These samples are referred to here as *bulk basal sediments*.

As collected, the samples consisted of a seawater-sediment slurry; they were processed at the end of each diving session (late morning and afternoon) in the following way. First, fresh water was directed through the slurry in the container at high pressure to suspend the fine sediment fractions of silt and clay, as well as organic fragments. The muddy wash water was poured from the container through a 1-mm plastic mesh screen that trapped the charcoal fragments and other organics (predominantly small fragments of the marine grass *Poseidonia*) but allowed the mud suspension to pass through. This simple flotation process was repeated until all mud was flushed from the sample, the wash water ran clear, and only material coarser than coarse sand size remained in the 20-liter container.

This washed coarse material was next passed through 4-mm and 2-mm plastic sieves to produce three size fractions. The finest fraction was discarded. The coarsest material, consisting of limestone and other rock fragments, mollusc shells and shell fragments, and (occasionally) ceramic sherds, was described and selectively retained. The fraction between 4-mm and 2-mm diameter was split in half (by volume), with half being curated at the Navplion Museum. The half returned to the United States was further subdivided by passing it through a 2.83-mm diameter sieve, thereby producing the two size fractions whose binocular microscopic identification is described below.

With two exceptions, only bulk sediment samples were collected from the lowest 30-40 cm section at each 1985 coring location. Considerations of time and efficiency dictated this approach, rather than the considerably slower procedure of piston coring and sampling each sediment sequence, but it seemed reasonable given that the project was aimed at investigating the contact between the marine sediment and the underlying pre-transgression land surface. The two exceptions are OK85/11, piston cored and sampled continuously at 5-cm intervals for pollen analysis, and OK85/1B, sampled at 10-cm and 20-cm intervals for sediment-grain-size analysis. The results of analyses of these samples, as well as the bulk basal sediment samples, are given in the next several sections.

Cultural material in the form of pottery sherds was found in bulk basal samples from cores FC 1, FC 2, OK85/1, OK85/1A, OK85/3, OK85/5, OK85/7, and OK85/8 (Plate 8). These sherds were deposited with other Franchthi excavation materials at the Navplion Museum, where they were briefly examined by Dr. K.D. Vitelli (see discussion below). Half of each of the bulk samples was deposited at the Navplion Museum, primarily for subsequent mollusc identification, accomplished in the summer of 1987 by Reese.

LABORATORY ANALYSES

In an approximate analogy with terrestrial excavation techniques, we are basing our interpretations of the pre-transgressive environment west of Paralia on 16 "sondages" some 4-5 m deep and 7.5 cm in diameter. While the vertical (stratigraphic) control within each sondage is good, all contextual relationships that existed among the cultural materials and environmental indicators at the bottom of each sondage were lost in the recovery process. The sample sizes themselves are relatively small and doubtless do not accurately reflect the actual distribution of buried artifactual and environmental material. Nevertheless, information on local vegetation, the paleoecology of local marine habitats, and sedimentary depositional environments can be extracted from the sediment samples.

Radiocarbon Dating

As noted in the preliminary report on this project (Gifford 1983), sufficient charcoal fragments were recovered from the basal bulk sediment samples of both 1981 cores to allow their dating by the AMS technique. The 540-560 cm interval of Core FC 1 yielded 28 mg of wood charcoal fragments, 1-3 mm in maximum dimensions, hand-picked in the field from a 1-mm-mesh screen. All of the sample was sent to the University of Arizona Accelerator Dating Facility (Tucson) in January 1982.

Core FC 2's 545-565 cm interval yielded 28 wood charcoal fragments, 5-6 mm in maximum dimension, as well as one *Triticum* caryopsis and an unidentified seed. The four largest wood charcoal fragments were hand-picked and also sent to the Arizona Accelerator facility.

The 1985 bulk basal sediment samples produced three additional radiocarbon dates. Just enough material was found to allow assay by conventional techniques, but each received extended counting time to minimize the standard deviation of the counting error. The following samples were sent to Beta Analytic (Miami) in February, 1986:

OK85/1: charcoal fragments, hand-picked from 1-mm-mesh screen during water separation in the field; from base of core, 5.3 m below bottom, in 4 m of water;

OK85/1A: charcoal fragments, hand-picked from 1-mm-mesh screen during water separation in the field; from base of core, 5.1 m below bottom, in 4.1 m of water;

OK85/1B: charcoal fragments, hand-picked from 1-mm-mesh screen during water separation in the field; from base of core, 4.7 m below bottom, in 4.1 m of water.

All five of the dated samples represent stratigraphically undisturbed material not contaminated by younger charcoal or plant remains. Their curation was well documented from the time of collection to the time of analysis. Table 3 summarizes the results of the analyses.

TABLE 3

RADIOCARBON AGE DETERMINATIONS (UNCORRECTED) ON OK CORE SAMPLES[a]

Lab No.	*Core Sample (Depth in cm)*	*C-14 Age*	*Sample Size*	*Sedimentation Rate*
AA-31	FC 1:540-560	6220 ± 130 B.P.	(0.03 g C)	0.88 mm/yr
AA-32	FC 2:545-565	7610 ± 150 B.P.	(0.11 g C)	0.73 mm/yr
Beta-15612	OK85/1:510-530	6600 ± 250 B.P.	(0.35 g C)	0.79 mm/yr
Beta-15613	OK85/1B:440-470	6860 ± 120 B.P.	(0.75 g C)	0.66 mm/yr
Beta-15614	OK85/1A:490-510	6720 ± 100 B.P.	(0.60 g C)	0.74 mm/yr

[a]Cf. Jacobsen and Farrand 1987:Plate 71.

Sedimentological Analyses

The Kiladha Bay coring project was planned around the laboratory investigation of relatively small volumes of sediment recovered from the bottom of a cased core hole. Because these samples are fundamentally different from those collected during the course of a terrestrial excavation, their analysis was undertaken in a different manner. No possibility existed of studying important characteristics such as sedimentary structure or texture in situ, as they were destroyed in the sampling process. Thus the information presented here is of a purely granulometric nature, concerning the distribution of particle sizes in the sediments and variations in grain composition. This limitation holds for both the bulk basal sediment samples and the sediment samples from OK/1B.

Due to the nature of our core samples and the available analytical techniques, only the second level of data analysis of putative submerged sites—the micro-sedimentary characteristics of the cultural deposits as defined by Gagliano et al. (1982:14)—could be studied. Ideally, we should have characterized known sediment samples taken from in-situ contexts in the Paralia excavations by means of the same grain-size analytical techniques applied to the basal bulk core samples, but such samples were not obtainable.

Table 4 presents the results of binocular microscope identification of particle types in two size fractions of the bulk basal samples: the coarse granule size (-2 to -1.5 ϕ, or between 4 and 2.8 mm diameter) and the fine granule size (-1.5 to -1.0 ϕ, or from 2.8 to 2.0 mm in diameter). (The Phi grain-size scale used here and in most North American sedimentological research equals the negative logarithm to the base 2 of the grain diameter expressed in mm; it simplifies the calculation and comparison of grain size parameters.) For each of the two size fractions, all particles in the size fraction were counted for a weighed volume of sample (usually 10-15 g) and assigned to one of six combined categories: (1) lithic fragments, (2) intact juvenile mollusc shells, (3) marine fauna skeletal fragments, (4) vertebrate bone fragments, (5) charcoal fragments, and (6) cultural material.

Several of these six are composites of 16 categories actually used in the counting procedure, combined here for ease of presentation. For example, the category "lithic fragments" is the sum of all limestone, quartz, serpentinite, and unidentified rock fragments, while "marine fauna skeletal fragments" includes ostracode and foraminifera tests, bryozoa fragments, echinoid spine and shell fragments, and crab carapace fragments.

Considering the intact juvenile mollusc shells as sedimentary particles (rather than for their faunal information, as below), it should be noted that they are generally in excellent condition, unlike some shell material described by Shackleton and van Andel (1986:138). Mollusc shell from the cores has been protected from post-depositional modification by its cover of sediment. The mollusc shells and other marine faunal skeletal fragments from the cores doubtless represent a mixture of several local nearshore environments. It was hoped by separating intact juvenile forms from the fragments that some indication of energy of the depositional environment could be discovered, but no pattern was clear in the variation between the two.

Cultural material includes microsherds, microdebitage, mud plaster fragments, and lime plaster fragments. The microsherds were identifiable with certainty as ceramic fragments, but all were too worn to permit more precise classification. Microdebitage has proved to be a useful indicator of cultural activity (Fladmark 1982) and also bears on the question of post-depositional site modification, as discussed below. Plate 7 shows an example of the observed mud plaster fragments; they are distinguishable from lime plaster fragments by their color, texture, and reaction to dilute acid. Finally, it should be noted that the charcoal fragments tallied in Table 4 are in addition to the larger fragments that had already been recovered during the preliminary sample-washing procedure for identification by Hansen.

TABLE 4

PARTICLES/GRAM IN THE COARSE AND FINE GRANULE FRACTIONS OF OK85 BASAL SEDIMENTS

-2 to -1.5 ϕ (Coarse): Particles/g of Size Fraction[a]

	(1)	*(2)*	*(3)*	*(2)+(3)*	*(4)*	*(5)*	*(6)*
OK85/1	7.0	0.2	5.8	6.0	0.3	0.1	2.4
OK85/3	10.0	1.6	10.0	11.6	0	0	0.7
OK85/4	7.0	4.0	16.0	20.0	0	0.3	0.1
OK85/5	4.8	2.2	23.6	25.8	0	0	0
OK85/6A	9.9	2.8	12.0	14.8	0	0	0.1
OK85/7	2.0	7.3	24.3	31.6	0	0	0.1
OK85/8	8.6	1.6	11.3	12.9	0.1	0.1	0.1
OK85/9A	6.3	5.8	31.2	37.0	0.1	0.2	0.1[b]
OK85/10	5.3	1.4	17.0	18.3	0	0	0
OK85/12	7.4	5.2	10.1	15.3	0	0	0.1

-1.5 to -1.0 ϕ (Fine): Particles/g of Size Fraction

	(1)	*(2)+(3)*	*(4)*	*(5)*	*(6)*
OK85/1	15.0	63.0	0.8	1.5	10.7
OK85/3	22.7	37.6	0.1	0.1	1.9
OK85/4	17.6	59.6	0.1	0.6	0.1
OK85/5	9.6	63.7	0	0.1	0
OK85/6A	24.4	40.1	0.1	0.4	0.3
OK85/7	7.9	78.3	0	0	0
OK85/8	16.3	40.4	0	0.1	0
OK85/9A	9.7	63.3	0.3	0.3	0.3[b]
OK85/10	12.4	48.7	0.1	0	0.1
OK85/12	22.0	38.1	0.2	0	0.1

[a]Particle categories: (1) lithic fragments, (2) unbroken juvenile mollusc shells, (3) marine fauna skeletal fragments, (4) bone fragments, (5) charcoal fragments, (6) cultural material (including, microsherds, microdebitage, mud plaster fragments, and lime plaster fragments).

[b]Includes one obsidian microdebitage flake.

Because *all* particles in a weighed sample of the size fraction were counted, counts in Table 4 may be presented as particles per gram of that sample's size fraction. As this is an absolute measure of the particle type rather than a percentage, it allows independent comparisons among core samples.

Composite categories 4, 5, and 6 are the clearest indicators of cultural activity. The coarse-granule fractions of three basal core samples, OK85/1, OK85/8, and OK85/9A, contained particles of all three categories, while that fraction of OK85/4 contained particles of charcoal and cultural material. In the fine-granule fraction, five basal samples (cores OK85/1, 3, 4, 6, 9A) produced particles of all three categories, while OK85/10 and 12 contained bone and cultural material only. Two obsidian microdebitage flakes were recorded in the basal sample from OK85/9A, one in each of the size fractions counted. The other microdebitage flakes were identified in the coarse-granule fraction of cores OK85/1, OK85/3, OK85/4, OK85/6 + 6A, OK85/10, and OK85/12; they include the chocolate brown and light-colored chert types derived from the ophiolite complex, as mentioned by van Andel and Vitaliano (1987:20).

Only the basal samples from OK85/1 and OK85/9A produced material of particle-type categories 4, 5, and 6 in both their coarse- and fine-granule fractions. In the coarsest fraction (>-2 ϕ) of the OK85/1 bulk basal sample 25 sherds were recovered, including several fragments of unburnished ware having a dark paste with white angular temper fragments, presumably the type called Lime Monochrome Ware (Vitelli, forthcoming a). In addition, K.D. Vitelli identified from the >-2 ϕ mesh fraction of the basal sediment of cores OK85/3 and OK85/5 worn sherds of Andesite Unburnished (Pink), characteristic of Franchthi Ceramic Phase 2, approximately of Middle Neolithic age (personal communication, August 1985; see Plate 8).

While charcoal, bone, and cultural material represent the three particle types most directly associated with human activity, some of the exotic rock types of the lithic fragments category indirectly suggest the same thing. As Wilkinson and Duhon (see above) note for the Paralia site, all lithic fragments included in the basal stony red colluvium are limestone, and any other rock types recovered from overlying sediment strata must have been artificially introduced. In particular, they note that their class D sediments (the upper reds) commonly contain well-rounded granule- to pebble-size serpentinite fragments, some with secondary carbonate concretions. Serpentinite fragments of this description were noted in the >-2 ϕ and the -2 to -1.5 ϕ fractions of bulk basal sediment from core OK85/1. Fragments of other exotic rock types such as sandstone and marlstone were also identified in this bulk basal sample.

Whereas the bulk basal samples inform us about the areal distribution of particle types at the bottom of the cores, they reveal nothing about the variation in particle types through the sediment section, which is a time-dependent function of depositional and erosional processes. To obtain this sort of information, core OK85/1B, taken in 4.1 m of water, was sampled continuously at 10-cm and 20-cm intervals for detailed grain-size analysis. The macroscopic sediment type is a shelly, slightly pebbly dark gray sandy mud, identical to the sediment type noted in the 1981 cores (Gifford 1983:Table 1). In addition to the sediment samples of core OK85/1B, the basal sample (450 cm) of OK85/11 was chosen for grain-size analysis because it was observed to be a reddish-brown clayey mud quite different from the overlying gray sandy mud.

Grain-size analysis of 24 samples of core OK85/1B and the one sample of OK85/11 was done at the Archaeometry Laboratory (University of Minnesota, Duluth) following the technique described in Gifford et al. (1982:66). This same technique was used for the samples of the 1981 cores FC 1 and FC 2 described in Gifford (1983). Once the various grain-size fractions were obtained, the 0-0.5 ϕ fraction (coarse sand) of 16 of the OK85/1B samples was weighed and studied under a binocular microscope to identify and count the particle types present, using the same classification scheme employed for the coarser fractions of the bulk basal samples. The results are summarized in Figure 43 and discussed below.

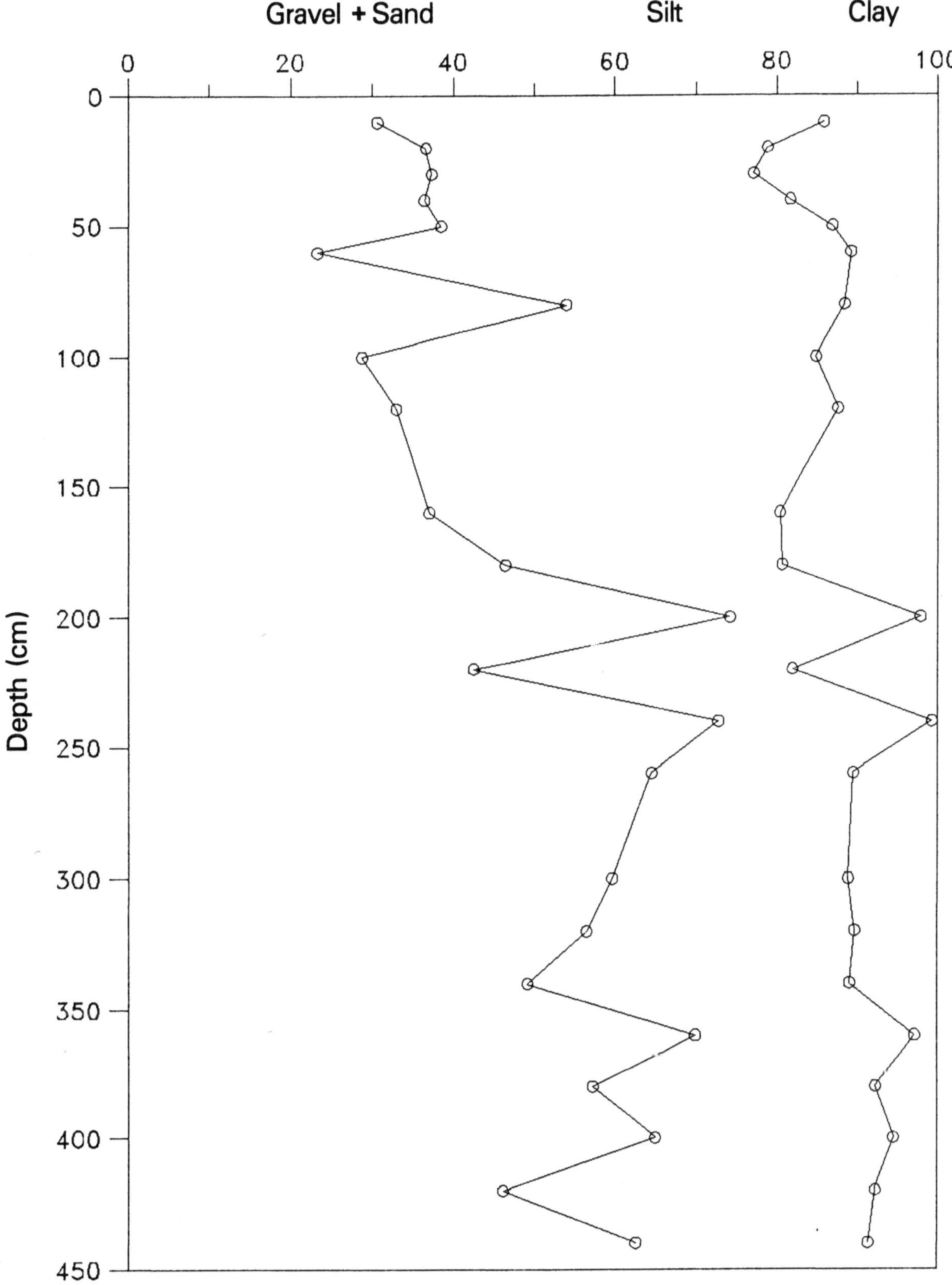

Figure 39. Variation with depth of three grain-size fractions (gravel+sand, silt, clay) in samples of core OK85/1B.

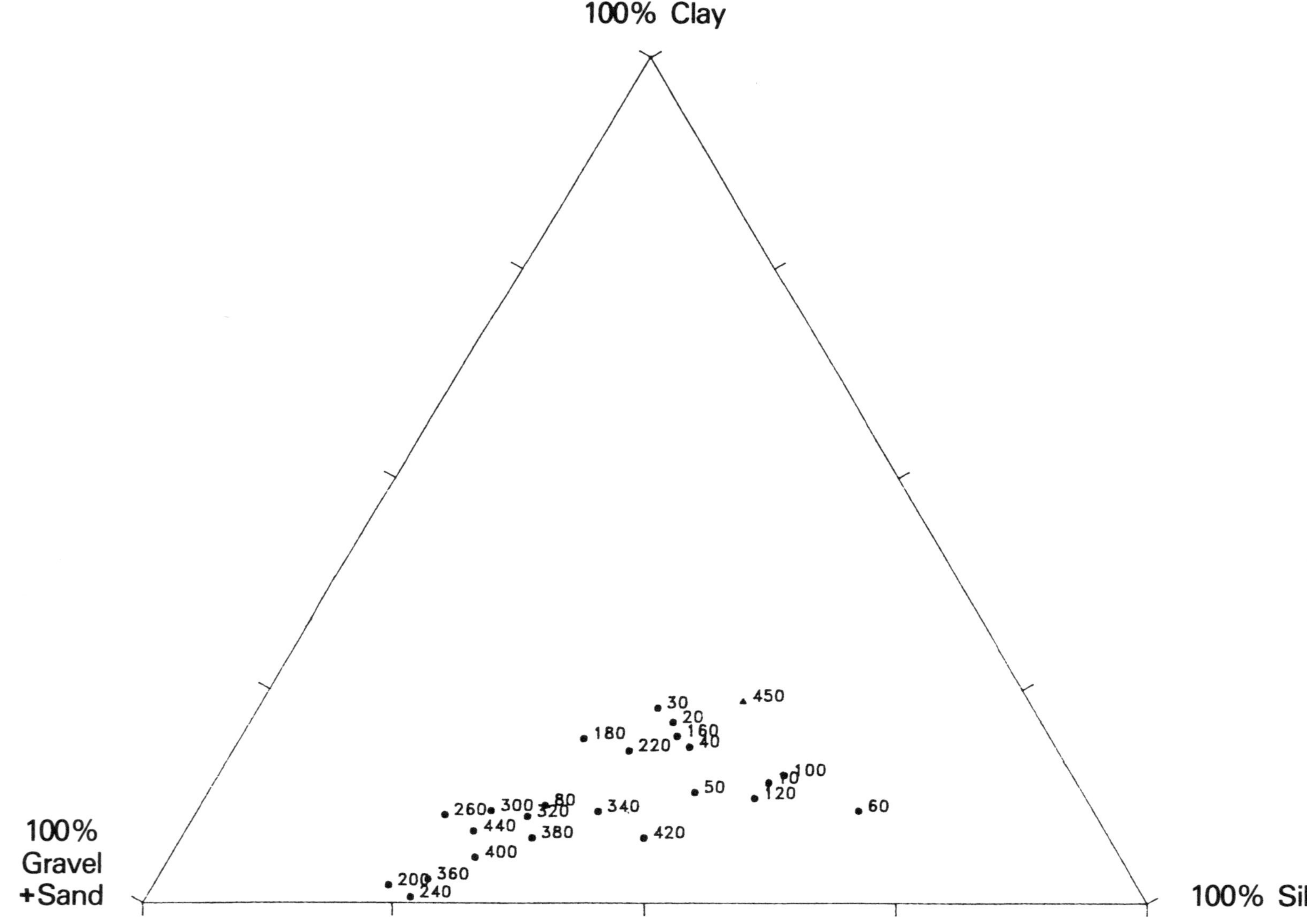

Figure 40. Triangle plot showing distribution of three grain-size fractions (gravel+sand, silt, clay) in samples of core OK85/1B (circles) and the basal sample (450) from core OK85/11 (triangle).

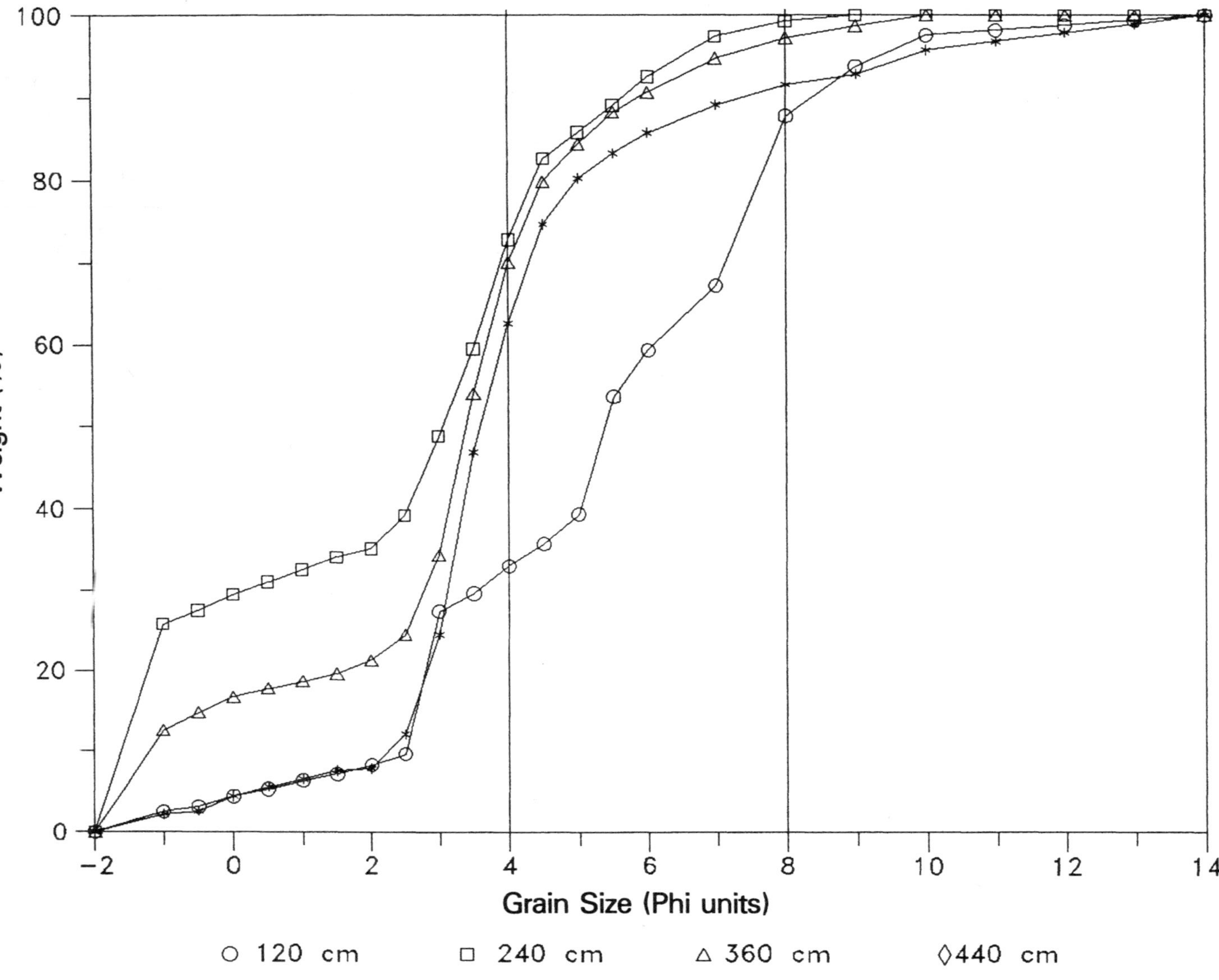

Figure 41. Cumulative grain-size plots of four samples from core OK85/1B.

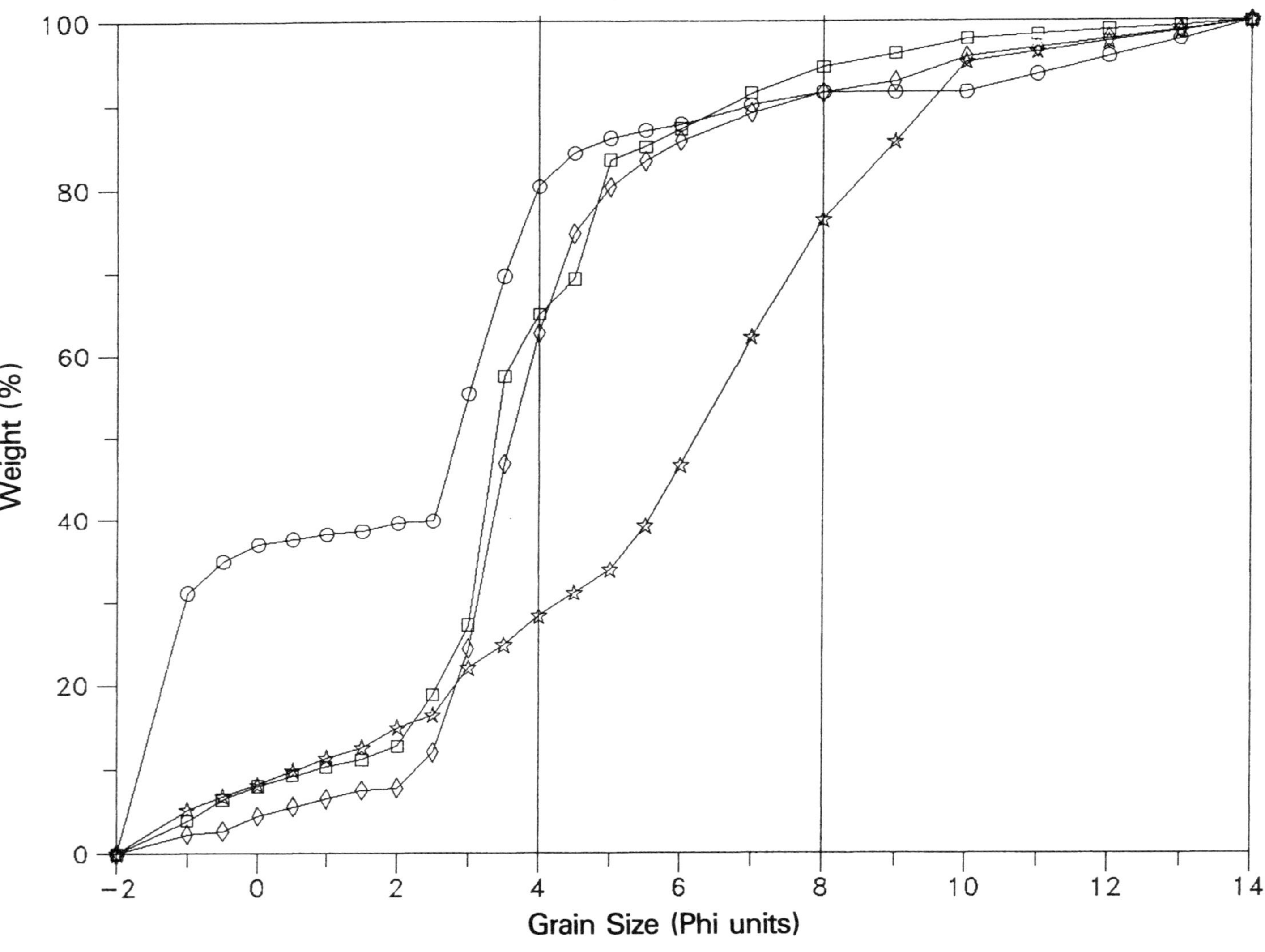

Figure 42. Cumulative grain-size plots of basal sediment samples from cores FC 1, OK85/1B, and OK85/11.

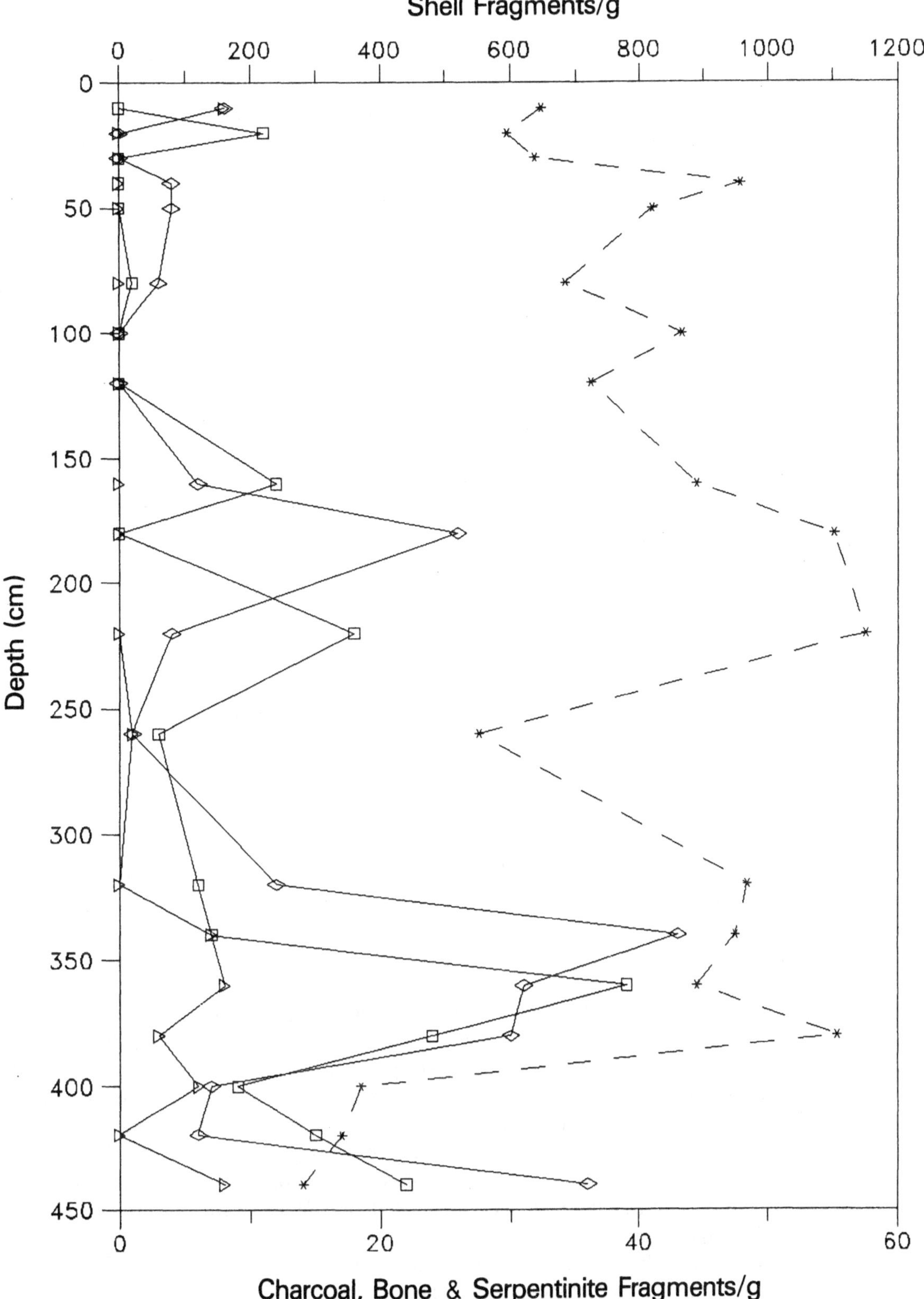

Figure 43. Variation with depth of four components of the 0-0.5ϕ grain-size fraction of core OK85/1B: shell fragments/gram of sediment and charcoal, bone, and serpentinite fragments/gram of sediment. Note different x-axis scales.

Considering first the overall distribution of grain sizes, the results for OK85/1B are presented in two different forms in Figures 39 and 40. In Figure 39 the percentage variations of the three most general size components—gravel + sand, silt, and clay—are graphed against sample depth in centimeters. The most notable variations occur at depths of 200, 240, and 360 cm below the top of the core; all three samples are significantly coarser in overall texture (and contain no clay) than the sediments above and below. This graph may be directly compared to Figure 2 of the preliminary report (Gifford 1983), in which the same information is plotted for core FC 1. Coarse layers were identified at 210 and 350 cm below the top of that core. In both cores, which lie within approximately 10 m of one another, these coarse horizons represent finely comminuted mollusc shell fragments (shell hash) that were visible as distinct layers in the split core sections prior to sampling. This indicates at least local continuity of the layers.

The same data are replotted in Figure 40 on a triangle diagram, where each apex represents one of the three size categories just specified. The three coarsest samples are clustered toward the 100% gravel + sand apex, and the samples with the most clay-size grains are seen to be at 20 cm and 30 cm below the top of core OK85/1B. Also plotted here is the one sample from OK85/11 (450 cm); it contains more clay than any of the OK85/1B samples.

Plots of variation in gravel + sand-silt-clay give only a summary impression of grain-size change. Figure 41 gives, for four samples, a more detailed plot of variation over the entire size range analyzed (-2 to 14 ϕ) in the form of a cumulative-weight-percent graph. Here sediment grain size increases from gravel and sand on the left, through silt, to fine clay on the extreme right; the vertical lines at 4 ϕ (0.0625 mm) and 8 ϕ (0.0039 mm) are the boundaries of the central silt-size class. Because each sample curve is cumulative, large fractions produce steep curve segments; the relatively coarse shell material in the 240-cm sample is thus apparent at the toe of that sample's cumulative curve. In contrast to the other four samples shown in the figure, the 120-cm sample is seen to contain more silt and less coarse sediment, a fact also generally indicated in Figure 40.

Figure 42, the second cumulative grain-size graph, plots basal sediment samples from three different cores: 1981 core FC 1 (550 cm), and 1985 cores OK85/1B (400 cm and 440 cm) and OK85/11 (450 cm). The basal sample from FC 1 contains a relatively large percentage of coarse grain sizes (also evident in Figure 2 of Gifford 1983), but its fine sand and mud fractions are rather similar to the two samples from OK85/1B. In contrast, the 450-cm sample from OK85/11 has a different grain-size distribution entirely, indicating a different kind of sediment at the base of that core.

It is informative to compare the variation in gross sediment texture described above with the variation in particle types of the 0-0.5 ϕ fraction (coarse sand size) downcore in OK85/1B, which is summarized in Figure 43. Four particle types are graphed: mollusc shell fragments/g of the size fraction (upper X-axis), and charcoal, bone, and serpentinite fragments/g of the size fraction (lower X-axis). As was true for the bulk basal samples, these curves reflect absolute changes in the particle concentrations from top to bottom of the core. This graph may be directly compared to Figure 39, which shows the same core's gross grain-size variation on an identical vertical axis. However, it should be kept in mind that in Figure 43 only a single size fraction, finer than those studied for the bulk basal samples, is plotted.

High values of shell fragments per gram of the size fraction are evident at 200 cm and 360 cm below the top of the core. As could be expected, these represent the layers of shell hash visible in the gross particle-size variations of Figure 39. Interestingly, the coarse layers contain, in addition to shell fragments, two of the other three particle types—charcoal and serpentinite fragments. High values of all three occur in the 160-220 cm and 320-380 cm intervals.

Two other correlations are also evident: a large number of serpentinite and charcoal fragments occurs at the base of the core (440 cm) in the absence of large numbers of shell fragments, and

10-30 cm below the top of the core smaller peaks of bone, charcoal, and serpentinite fragments co-occur with average concentrations of shell fragments. All these distributions will be considered in the final section.

Pollen Analysis

Splits of sediment samples from core FC 1 were used in a pilot study of the quantity and degree of preservation of pollen grains in the 1981 cores. Counts of 50-100 grains per slide were obtained for most of the FC1 core samples, but no diagram was produced since it was felt that the 20-cm sampling interval was too coarse for this purpose.

In 1985, core OK85/11 was obtained specifically for pollen analysis. It was located in 10.2 m of water, closer to Koronis Island than to Paralia (Figures 37 and 38). In this general area is the thalweg of the drowned and buried river channel reconstructed by van Andel et al. (1980), and we hoped to penetrate a thicker, more continuous section of marine sediments in the channel fill. This was accomplished, and 68 sediment samples, averaging 10 g each (wet weight), were taken at 5-cm intervals from the nearly continuous core section recovered. Some intervals could not be sampled due to loss in coring, despite exceptional care taken in recovery.

All samples were sent to S. Bottema of the Biologisch-Archaeologisch Instituut (Groningen) in September 1985. The objective of this palynological study was to expand upon the work of Sheehan (1979) by analyzing a depositional sequence geographically much closer to Franchthi than Sheehan had been able to sample. The resulting pollen diagram is discussed in Chapter 8.

Analysis of Shell Material (D.S. Reese)

Basal samples from twelve 1985 cores (OK85/1A, 2, 3, 4, 5, 6A, 7, 8, 9, 9A, 10, and 12) produced samples of marine invertebrates, as did the two cores taken in 1981 (Gifford 1983). The 1985 basal core samples did not all produce the same quantity of marine invertebrate remains. Samples from cores OK85/1A, 2, 4, and 12 produced one small plastic bag (the unit) sample; cores OK85/3, 5, 6A, 7, and 10, three-fourths of a unit; core OK85/9A, one half of a unit; and core OK85/8, one-quarter of a unit. All core samples contain basically the same species of marine invertebrates, which are identified in Table 5. Many of them are juveniles, a fact which in some cases makes specific identification difficult. Their relative numbers are described as either *common* or *rare*.

Comments. Most of the species present in the bulk basal core samples are found on or buried in sand and/or mud bottoms. A few (*Cerithium*, *Murex*, *Arca*, and *Chlamys*) are found associated with both sand/mud and rocky shores and bottoms. Several rarely found species are found only on rocky shores and bottoms (*Patella*, *Gibbula*, *Bittium*, *Mytilus/Modiolus*, *Spondylus*, *Ostrea*, and *Chama*).

The faunal collection contains very little that is unexpected in a natural beach sample originating largely from a marine fauna buried in sand/mud. However, a single mammal tooth fragment (OK85/6A) and burnt shell fragments (*Murex* in OK85/1A and 10, *Cerithium* in OK85/2) are likely the result of human activity. The eight *Cerithium* with broken lips (OK85/6A, 7, 10, 12 [four examples]) may have been broken when the meat was extracted for consumption, as is known from other archaeological sites.

Many of the species present in the basal cores have also been found in the excavations at Franchthi Cave (J. Shackleton 1988a, 1988b; J. Shackleton and van Andel 1980, 1986; Jacobsen 1973b:257-58; N. Shackleton 1969). The species not previously reported as found in the cave are: vermetid, *Crepidula*, naticid, cf. *Sphaeronassa*, *Nucula*, *Loripes*, *Chama*, *Cardita*, *Parvicardium*, *Gastrana*, *Tellina*, *Psammobia* and crab.

TABLE 5

MARINE INVERTEBRATES IDENTIFIED FROM
THE 1985 BULK BASAL CORE SAMPLES

CLASS GASTROPODA (Snails)
- Family Patellidae (Limpets)
  - *Patella* sp.: OK85/3; rare
- Family Trochidae (Top shells)
  - *Gibbula* sp.: OK85/7, 8, 10; rare
- Family Vermiculariidae (Worm tubes)
  - Unidentified vermetid: OK85/3, 4; rare
- Family Cerithiidae (Needle or Horn shells)
  - *Cerithium vulgatum* Bruguière, 1792: OK85/1A, 2, 3, 5, 6A, 7, 8, 9A, 10, 12; common
  - *Bittium reticulatum* (Da Costa, 1778): OK85/1A, 2, 3, 4, 9A, 10, 12; rare
- Family Calyptraeidae (Slipper clams)
  - *Crepidula unguiformis* Lamarck, 1822: OK85/3, 4, 8, 10; rare
- Family Naticidae (Moon shells)
  - Unidentified naticid: OK85/1A; rare
- Family Muricidae (Murex shells)
  - *Murex trunculus* (Linnaeus, 1758): OK85/1A, 2, 4, 5, 6A, 7, 9A, 10, 12; rare
- Family Nassariidae (Nassa or Basket shells)
  - *Cyclope* (=*Neritea*) *neritea* (Linnaeus, 1758): OK85/1A, 2, 3, 4, 12; rare
  - Probably *Sphaeronassa mutabilis* (Linnaeus, 1758): OK85/6A; rare
- Family Conidae (Cone shells)
  - *Conus mediterraneus* "Hwass" Bruguière, 1792: OK85/10, 12; rare
- Family Bullidae (Bubble shells)
  - *Bulla striata* Bruguière, 1792: OK85/1A, 2, 3, 5, 6A, 7, 8, 10; rare

CLASS SCAPHOPODA (Tusk or Tooth shells)
- Family Dentaliidae
  - *Dentalium* sp. (at least two species): OK85/1A, 2, 4, 5, 6A, 7, 9A, 10, 12; rare

CLASS BIVALVA (Clams, Mussels, Oysters)
- Family Nuculidae (Nut clams)
  - *Nucula nucleus* (Linnaeus, 1758): OK85/3, 4, 5, 7, 8, 9A, 12; common
- Family Arcidae (Ark shells)
  - *Arca noae* Linnaeus, 1758: OK85/5, 8, 9A, 10; rare
  - *Arca barbata* Linnaeus, 1758: OK85/9A, 12; rare
- Family Mytilidae (Mussels)
  - *Mytilus galloprovincialis* Lamarck, 1819 and
    Modiolus barbatus (Linnaeus, 1758): OK85/5, 8, 12; rare

Family Pinnidae (Pen or Fan shells)

Pinna nobilis Linnaeus, 1758: OK85/10; rare

Family Pectinidae (Scallop shells)

Chlamys varia (Linnaeus, 1758): OK85/2, 4, 5, 7, 8, 9A, 10, 12; rare

Family Spondylidae (Spiny oysters)

Spondylus gaederopus (Linnaeus, 1758): OK85/12; rare

Family Ostreidae (Oysters)

Ostrea edulis (Linnaeus, 1758): OK85/4, 8, 10; rare

Family Lucinidae

Loripes lacteus (Linnaeus, 1758): OK85/1A, 2, 3, 4, 5, 6A, 7, 8, 9A,10, 12; common

Family Chamidae (Hoof shells)

Chama gryphoides Linnaeus, 1758: OK85/8; rare

Family Carditidae (Heart clams)

Cardita sulcata Bruguière, 1792: OK85/1A, 4; rare

Family Cardiidae (Cockles)

Parvicardium exiguum (Gmelin, 1790): OK85/1A, 2, 3, 4, 5, 6A, 7, 8, 9A, 10, 12; common

Cerastoderma glaucum (Bruguière, 1789): OK85/1A, 3, 6A, 7, 9A; rare

Families Solenidae and Cultellidae (Razor clams)

Solen sp./*Ensis* sp.: OK85/3, 4; rare

Family Tellinidae (Tellin shells)

Gastrana fragilis (Linnaeus, 1758): OK85/1A, 2, 3, 4, 5, 6A, 9A, 10, 12; common

Tellina fabuloides (Monterosato, 1884): OK85/1A, 2, 7; rare

Tellina pulchella Lamarck, 1818: OK85/1A, 4; rare

Families Donacidae and Mesodesmatidae (Wedge shells)

Donax trunculus Linnaeus, 1758 and

Donacilla cornea (Poli, 1795): OK85/2, 4, 5, 6A, 7, 8, 9A, 10, 12; common

Family Sanguinolariidae

Psammobia faroensis Gmelin, 1790: OK85/6A, 12; rare

Family Veneridae

Tapes (=*Venerupis*) *decussatus* (Linnaeus, 1758) (Carpet shells) and

Tapes (=*Venerupis*) *aurea* (Gmelin, 1790): OK85/2, 4, 5, 7, 8, 9A, 12; common

Venus verrucosa Linnaeus, 1758 (Venus shells): OK85/8, 9A, 10; rare

CLASS CRUSTACEA

Order Decapoda (Crabs): OK85/3, 4, 7, 10, 12; rare

The forms not previously reported are mainly small species or juvenile individuals, and are often fragmentary. Such small forms have not yet been systematically studied from the cave (Shackleton 1988b:65).

Analysis of Botanical Remains (J. M. Hansen)

Carbonized material was recovered as described above. Nine samples of carbonized plant remains were sorted for identifiable fragments. After analysis, some of the carbonized fragments were radiocarbon dated, also described above.

Each sample was sorted under low power (8x-10x) magnification using a Zeiss stereoscopic microscope. Wood charcoal fragments were broken by hand to provide a clean transverse section and were compared to modern charred samples for identification. Table 6 summarizes the results of study of the botanical remains from nine bulk basal core samples.

Discussion. The presence of fig (*Ficus carica*) in these samples adds a new species to the plant remains from the Franchthi excavations, as no fig was recovered from the water-sieved trenches inside the cave (Hansen 1980 and forthcoming). The fig seeds recovered from the cores are not carbonized, but rather are fragile, hollow shells that appear to be mineralized. Because these seeds come from the basal levels of the cores it seems unlikely that they represent modern contamination, though this possibility cannot be ruled out. Neolithic remains of fig have been found at Rachmani, Sesklo, and Dimini in Thessaly, and Olynthos in Macedonia (Renfrew 1973), as well as Early Helladic Lerna (Hopf 1964) and Late Helladic Tiryns (Kroll 1982) in the Argolid. Only at the latter site are large quantities of uncarbonized as well as carbonized seeds found. In Britain, mineralized fig seeds have been found in cess pits and latrine contexts where high levels of calcium phosphate in the deposits have resulted in mineralization (Green 1979). Whether the areas in the bay struck by the corer represent latrine deposits, it is impossible to say; but it is interesting that fig seeds, which are not digestible by humans, do not occur in the excavated cave deposits.

The next most abundant find from these core samples is the barley (*Hordeum* sp.) rachis fragments. It is uncertain whether these are from two-row or six-row barley. A number of wheat (*Triticum* sp.) spikelet forks as well as culm fragments were also found. Such chaff remains are fairly common from Neolithic levels inside the cave, where numerous wheat and barley grains were also recovered. No domestic grains were identified from the 1985 core samples, although wheat grains were found in the cores taken in the bay in 1981 (Gifford 1983). One small wild barley grain (*Hordeum* cf. *murinum*) was also identified. Other finds include lentil fragments, pistachio nutlets, almond fragments, and one poppy seed.

With the exception of the fig seeds, all these remains were also found in the water-sieved levels of Franchthi Cave. Lentils, almonds, and pistachios were present from the Upper Palaeolithic (ca. 13,000 B.P.) onward, but the presence in the core samples of both wheat and barley chaff fragments indicates that we are dealing here with Neolithic material. The radiocarbon measurements seem to indicate a Middle Neolithic date.

Most of the wood charcoal fragments were quite small and, so far, difficult to section for identification. Further work on them is planned for the future when the remaining wood samples from the cave excavations are examined in detail. A preliminary analysis has revealed the presence of almond (*Prunus amygdalus*), kermes oak (*Quercus coccifera/trojana*) and possibly strawberry tree (*Arbutus* sp.). Kermes oak is fairly common in the area today, while wild almond and strawberry trees occur only rarely. The plant assemblages from the Neolithic levels in the cave suggest that the vegetation of the area at that time was probably similar to that of today, with possibly more arboreal species. The species so far identified from the cores do not indicate a different interpretation.

TABLE 6

IDENTIFICATION OF BOTANICAL REMAINS FROM OK85 CORES

Sample	*Number of Fragments*
OK85/1: charcoal ?	
cf. *Prunus amygdalus* (mineralized)	1
Prunus amygdalus (shell fragments)	2
OK85/1: wood charcoal	
Prunus amygdalus	1
cf. *Arbutus andrachne*	1
OK85/1A: charcoal	
Prunus amygdalus (shell fragments)	2
Pistacia sp. (fragment)	1
Gramineae sp. indet. (fragment)	1
OK85/1A: wood charcoal	
Quercus coccifera/trojana	1
OK85/1A: organics, 1-2 mm	
Ficus carica	43
Prunus amygdalus (shell fragment)	1
Pistacia sp. (fragment)	1
Lens sp.	1/2
Hordeum cf. *murinum*	1
Hordeum sp. (rachis fragment)	10
Triticum sp. (spikelet forks)	11
Gramineae sp. indet.	1
Culm nodes indet.	2
Culm fragments indet.	3
OK85/1B: >1-mm organics	
Ficus carica	200 approx.
Lens sp.	1/2
Papaver sp.	1
Hordeum sp. (rachis fragments)	20
Triticum sp. (spikelet forks)	15
Gramineae sp. (rachis frags. indet.)	3
OK85/3: >1-mm, non-lithic bottom	
Ficus carica	50
Hordeum sp. (rachis fragments)	3
Triticum sp. (spikelet forks)	7
Gramineae sp. indet.	1
OK85/7: bottom organics	
Hordeum sp. (rachis fragments)	3
Triticum sp. (spikelet forks)	7
OK85/9A:	
Possible fecal material; plant fibers; possible fish bone and mollusc.	
OK85/12: charcoal ?	
Mud; no organics visible.	

The question of whether the sediment at the base of the cores represents in-situ material or slope wash is difficult to determine with certainty on the basis of the plant remains. The carbonized material is very well preserved and shows no sign of abrasion such as would be expected if the sediments had been transported any distance. This question is considered in the following section.

GENERAL DISCUSSION AND CONCLUSIONS

The geographic scale of this underwater investigation is one to two orders of magnitude smaller than those undertaken by van Andel and his co-workers (van Andel et al. 1980, van Andel and Lianos 1984). Our project had the specific goal of determining whether cultural material could be identified below the nearshore sediments west of Paralia and what this material indicated about human activity there. In this final section we consider these questions in the light of the sediment analyses just presented, under three general topics: (1) the nature of the sediment deposits west of Paralia, (2) the nature of the original context of cultural material recovered from several of the cores, and (3) how this context was affected by a marine transgression.

The Sediments off Paralia

In broad geological terms, the 1985 coring confirmed what the 1981 coring had indicated. A late Holocene transgressive marine unit overlies the presumed late Quaternary land surface west of Paralia, and that unit is heterogeneous, containing mollusc shell concentrations of uncertain depositional significance.

The 1979 geophysical survey of van Andel et al. (1980) penetrated this entire marine sedimentary section in outer Kiladha Bay with a 3.5 kHz acoustic profiler; the resolution of their seismic reflection records is on the order of 0.5 m. In particular, two of the seismic track lines from the 1979 survey (van Andel 1987:Figure 18)—nos. 31 and 32—run over or very close to our 1985 east-west core transect, as plotted in Figure 38 (along with two other 1979 survey track lines, nos. 50 and 116). Thus the transverse seismic reflection profiles 31 and 32 of van Andel (1987:Figure 19) may be considered to record remotely the section cored from OK85/8 to OK85/10 (Figure 38).

Van Andel et al. (1980:398) noted the presence in their seismic reflection profiles of a set of indistinct, local reflectors within the transgressive sediment sequence of outer Kiladha Bay (as shown in their Figures 6 and 11); they are relabeled reflectors *a* and *b* in van Andel 1987 (Figure 19) and are interpreted as defining the latest of a series of successive bay floors during the transgressive infilling of the bay. Based on the horizontal and vertical scales of Figure 19 of van Andel (1987), and given the 0.5 m resolution of the seismic records, there can be little doubt that reflectors *a* and *b* represent the layers of shell hash cored in 1981 and 1985, if only because the sediment section contains no other deposits with different acoustic properties. There is nothing but shelly, sandy marine mud above the basal sediments of all the 1981 and 1985 cores.

From the comments above on radiocarbon dating, one could calculate an average rate of sediment accumulation for the five cores whose basal sediments were dated. However, some assumption must be made regarding when the deposition of marine sediment actually began, which could have been a long time after the (sub-aerial) deposition of the dated charcoal. Assuming first that marine sediments were deposited immediately after the charcoal, the average sedimentation rate for the five samples is 0.76 mm/yr. This is on the low side for estuaries (Biggs 1978:Table 5), although Shackleton and van Andel (1986:135) note a low rate for Kiladha Bay that could be due to the prevalence of limestone bedrock in the surrounding drainage basins, which does not produce abundant clastic detritus.

Assuming instead that marine sediment deposition in the vicinity of the OK85/1 cores did not begin until ca. 3800 years B.P., when the transgressing sea level reached -9 m (van Andel 1987:Figure 10), then the 4.7-m-thick marine sediment section was deposited at an average rate of 1.24 mm/yr. For a small southern Greek bay such as Kiladha this is a rapid but not unreasonable rate, reflecting in large part the average suspended sediment load introduced. For the Lac de Tunis, Thornton et al. (1980:87) estimated a late Holocene sedimentation rate of 0.67-0.75 mm/yr, while the Main Salt Lake of southeastern Cyprus was filling at rates ranging from 1.3 to 2.2 mm/yr (Gifford 1978:136).

Further assuming the midpoints of the two reflectors *a* and *b* (van Andel 1987:Figure 19) to be represented by the shell fragment maxima of core OK85/1B (Figure 43) at ca. 200 cm and ca. 360 cm below the top of the core, then the calculated age of these two sub-bottom reflectors, using the faster of the two estimated sedimentation rates, would be 2480 and 4460 radiocarbon years B.P., respectively. (The same deposit is identified in van Andel et al. [1980:Figure 11] as a foreset complex dating to 3000-1500 B.P.) Given all the assumptions on which they rest, these new estimates can only be taken to indicate the layers' ages in the most general way.

Turning from the marine sediment section off Paralia to the pre-transgression land surface underlying it, we have some indication of its slope from cores OK85/8, OK85/1, and OK85/2. At OK85/8, approximately 50 m off Paralia, the total depth from sea level to the basal surface is 5.4 m (Table 2). Fifty meters further offshore, the total depth in the vicinity of OK85/1, 1A, and 1B (all within a few meters of each other) averages about 9 m while 50 m still further west the total at OK85/2 is 10.2 m. The calculated slope of the buried basal surface between the two inshore core locations is thus about 4.2°; the slope between the two outer cores is about 1.4°. There is apparently a slope break somewhere between OK85/8 and OK85/1, which could represent the toe of the late Pleistocene footslope reconstructed by Wilkinson and Duhon (see Chapter 6).

It is not possible to calculate the slope-break position more precisely due to the variability of the hard basal surface. The three cores taken at OK85/1 differ by 60 cm in their depths to the basal surface, and 1981 core FC 1, also in the vicinity, penetrated some 20 cm deeper yet. The scale of this variability points to a very irregular hard surface or surfaces at the base of these four cores. The variation of 0.5-1 m is at just about the resolution limit of the 1979 seismic reflection profiling of van Andel et al. and may be due largely to point-source reflectors such as boulders. Thus the precise nature of the surface's irregularities cannot be identified clearly in the records of the basal reflector off Paralia. A high-resolution sub-bottom survey along closely spaced track lines controlled by electronic positioning might reveal some patterning in the variation of the reflector's depth, suggesting an artificial origin such as stone wall foundations.

Besides the small-scale variability in the basal surface depth at a distance of ca. 100 m off Paralia, core OK85/10, located 300 m offshore in 9.1 m of water, unexpectedly bottomed in only 1.5 m of sediment on a basal surface of a definite bedrock "feel" (as opposed to the feel of surfaces below the inshore cores). While no bedrock knobs or protrusions were recorded in the seismic reflection profiles, it appears that either such a knob, or a very large boulder, exists at that particular location.

Based on the analysis of a sample of the late Quaternary sediment substrate underlying the Paralia excavations (the stony red colluvium of Wilkinson and Duhon), neither of the 1981 cores and only one of the 1985 cores—OK85/11—actually reached this unit. The 450-cm sample of that core differs from all other sediments analyzed in being the finest grained (Figures 40 and 42). In addition, its 0-1 ϕ grain-size fraction contained more lithic fragments by an order of magnitude than were counted in the same size fraction of OK85/1B; the predominant mineral types present are iron-oxide-stained translucent quartz and secondary carbonate aggregates, identical to the mineral types noted in a sample of the stony red colluvium (Gifford 1983:279). The sediment stratum at the bottom of OK85/11 is identified with confidence as stony red colluvium, sediment class A of Wilkinson and Duhon, and equivalent to the upper member of the Loutro alluvium as defined by Pope and van Andel (1984:Table 3).

Archaeological Context and Submerged Early Sites

Submerged sites are now known from many of the world's continental shelves (Flemming 1983a). Three studies relevant to the Kiladha Bay project have been reported from the Mediterranean coast of Israel, the north-central Gulf of Mexico continental shelf, and from the Sporadhes Islands of the northern Aegean Sea.

From one to several hundred meters off the coast of northern Israel, submerged prehistoric sites have been discovered through offshore dredging and removal of the sediment overburden by storm activity (Galili and Weinstein-Evron 1985). The geological setting of those sites is quite different from outer Kiladha Bay, being located in a north-south trough separating two Pleistocene eolianite ridges, but their age range of Pre-Pottery Neolithic B through early Chalcolithic encompasses the presumed age of Paralia. The maximum depth below sea level reported for the submerged Israeli sites of Neolithic age is 7 m, which is some 2 m shallower than off Paralia. However, the bottom slopes around the Israeli sites appear to be comparable with the low angles off Paralia.

Because wide areas of the submerged sites off northern Israel have been exposed through a combination of human and natural processes, their study has proceeded much as a land excavation. Structures such as stone house walls and stone-lined wells have been cleaned and mapped, demonstrating that features such as slab floors and hearths have survived the transgression. Little published information is available in English concerning the context of artifacts and paleoenvironmental indicators associated with the features, but at one site small burned fragments of bird bones, olive pits, potsherds, flint debitage, and probable straw fragments have been excavated from pit fills as deep as 2 m below the level of the surrounding bottom (Galili and Weinstein-Evron 1985:40). While the preservation of organic material at these sites is apparently good, some of the coarseware sherds recovered are reported to be poorly preserved, and some of the larger stone tools appear to have been abraded through rolling (in the surf zone?) before burial ca. 6000 B.P. or earlier below quartz-rich muddy calcareous sands. It must be noted that many uncertainties remain about the degree and timing of late Holocene tectonism along the Mediterranean coast of Israel during the late Holocene, which complicates interpretations of local sea level history and how it may have affected the preservation of submerged sites.

A closer parallel to the Kiladha Bay situation would involve locating and testing sites that are both submerged and buried by transgressive marine sediments. Gagliano et al. (1982) have reported an attempt to locate Archaic-stage shell middens submerged on the northern Gulf of Mexico continental shelf. The general locations of the sites had first to be predicted based on the identification of large-scale relict geomorphological features visible in sub-bottom seismic profiles. Whether a site actually exists at any given locality can be verified (or disproved) only by vibracoring through the overlying marine sedimentary cover and sampling the pre-transgression land surface believed to include cultural deposits in the form of shell middens. The sampling method is thus similar to ours.

Gagliano et al. (1982:14) identify four levels of data analysis at which core samples of submerged archaeological sites may be studied in order to verify the presence of cultural material in small-volume core samples. Proceeding from the simplest to the most complex analytical scale, they are:

1. gross lithology and minor sedimentary structures visible by megascopic examination (macro-sedimentary characteristics, in their terminology);
2. grain-size analysis of sediment samples, and point counting of the constituent particles of selected size fractions (micro-sedimentary characteristics);
3. geochemical analysis of selected on-site and off-site sediment samples to detect chemical indicators of cultural activity, such as elevated phosphorus concentrations;
4. in the case of ambiguous indications of submerged sites, evaluation of all three previous levels of analysis for consistency of interpretation.

Their study approached the identification of submerged and buried archaeological sites by means of type cores taken from known depositional environments (Gagliano et al. 1982:52), which is the method of analogy that has been applied for decades to the identification of, among other geological phenomena, sedimentary depositional environments (Kraft 1985).

Gagliano and his colleagues were interested in identifying any trace of human activity on the Texas-Louisiana continental shelf, in the absence of definitive onshore site indicators such as exist at Paralia. They were concerned with a different scale and type of context than off Paralia, where we strongly suspected prior to 1981, and knew after that time, that cultural material existed below the marine sediment cover of outer Kiladha Bay. In 1985 our objective was to determine the original, pre-transgression context of this cultural material: material in primary, use-related context would essentially confirm settlement or other activity in the area of the offshore cores, whereas material in any type of secondary, redeposited context would be ambiguous.

Closest to Paralia in space and time is the submerged Neolithic site described by Flemming (1983b; 1985) from the Sporadhes islands of the northern Aegean Sea. Off the islet of Aghios Petros (adjacent to Kyra Panaghia) Flemming and co-workers made a detailed marine geomorphological reconnaissance of the submerged portion of a known Neolithic land site, analogous to Paralia.

The cultural material, including Neolithic and Bronze Age ceramics, bones, obsidian, and flint, was found on a relatively steep (14°) rock slope with discontinuous sediment cover. Flemming assumes occupation of the site to a depth of 10 m below present sea level at 7000 B.P., comparable to the age and depth of Paralia. In his consideration of the sequence and effects of the late Holocene transgression on the now-submerged portion of the site, Flemming proposes that the cultural material was embedded in a terra rossa soil that was winnowed away by wave activity. The lag deposit of bedrock fragments and cultural material would then have settled onto the underlying bedrock surface and would have been mixed with marine transgressive sediments. This scenario is not applicable to Paralia, as explained below.

Flemming (1985:138) addresses the question of the context of the cultural remains off Aghios Petros: are they in situ or reworked by wave action? He rejects as an oversimplification the model of material settling vertically onto the bedrock surface, thereby preserving contextual relations, at least in two dimensions.

Flemming offers two alternative scenarios of site formation: (1) maximum disturbance, in which cultural material would have been transported orthogonally down the bedrock slope some 10-15 m, and all context lost; and (2) minimum disturbance, in which there was a segregation of cultural material as a function of size, with the larger fragments becoming embedded in pockets of marine sediment and only the smaller ones moving as much as 10-15 m downslope. "It is impossible," he notes, "to distinguish between these two models on the present evidence. In both cases stratigraphic vertical context has been destroyed, though in the second model assemblages might still preserve considerable relational context" (Flemming 1985:139).

Flemming's study also is relevant to ours because of the quantification of densities of submerged cultural material. In the underwater survey area, ca. 50 m x 35 m, Flemming estimated that about half the area was covered by a sediment thickness of 20 cm or more. It was the 1-m^2 test quadrats in the areas of relatively thick sediment that produced quantities of sherds, bone, and flint ranging as high as scores of large fragments per cubic decimeter of sediment. Flemming observes that this probably represents a concentration of material at the bedrock surface that originally had been distributed throughout a section of terrestrial sediment some 2 m thick.

Nothing approaching the density of cultural material observed by Flemming off Aghios Petros was seen in any of the cores taken in outer Kiladha Bay. This could either be due to (1) the absence of a cultural activity area off Paralia, so that the low densities of bone, charcoal, and cultural material reflect only the introduction, prior to late Holocene transgression, of reworked cultural material from the excavated structures through the mechanism of downslope movement of debris (see above, Part I); or (2) that our cores did not penetrate far (if at all) into dense, in-situ cultural deposits offshore. The latter scenario implies that such a deposit lies just at or below the level of the hard surface that stopped our coring operations.

The Late Holocene Marine Transgression off Paralia

Flemming's interpretation of the Neolithic cultural material off Aghios Petros as a lag deposit remaining after the washout of the terra rossa matrix is reasonable, given the local steep bedrock slope. The local geomorphology around Paralia is quite different, particularly in terms of (1) the low slope angle of the late Pleistocene land surface some 100 m offshore; (2) the elevation of this terrace-like surface; and (3) the evidence for moderate slope stability after occupation of Paralia (represented by the weakly developed topsoil, class K of Wilkinson and Duhon).

The question of context involves whether the cultural material (microsherds, microdebitage, bone, and charcoal) as well as possible indirect indicators of cultural activity (notably the serpentinite granules and pebbles from OK85/1) are secondary—derived from upslope around the known Paralia structures—or primary, and therefore derived from the immediate vicinity of the offshore cores. An obvious approach to answering this question is to consider both the density distribution and the preservation of the material.

Considering the distribution of particle types (Table 4) among the various core locations, almost all the cores show low concentrations of bone, charcoal, and cultural material. Figures 44 and 45 portray the distribution of these particle categories from the bulk basal core samples. Both figures are based on particle counts of the fine-granule-size fraction.

In Figure 44, the distribution of the combined counts of bone and charcoal is plotted with a contour interval of 0.1 particle/g of the sediment-size fraction. The vicinity of cores FC 1, OK85/1, 1A, and 1B is clearly the maximum of the distribution. In Figure 45, the high concentration of particles of cultural material (plotted with an interval of 1 particle/g of the size fraction) indicates the same conclusion: there is a quantitative difference in the nature of the basal sediments at this location compared with all the other locations cored.

It is interesting that even for other bulk basal samples showing some of these particles in the coarse- or fine-granule fractions, there is no good correlation between their concentration and the presence of larger ceramic sherds: core OK85/5, for instance, produced four large sherds (Plate 8) but almost no cultural material in either of the granule-size fractions. Yet the preservation of bone, charcoal, and botanical remains is very good in the bulk basal samples, which suggests these fragments have not been transported far, either downslope from primary deposits represented by the excavated area or across the terrace as it was submerged by the transgression.

We propose the following explanation for all the observations and data presented above. It is only one of several possibilities, and, although very much ad hoc, requires only a reasonable sequence of physical processes to occur during the late Holocene transgression, which is the prime mover of the hypothesis.

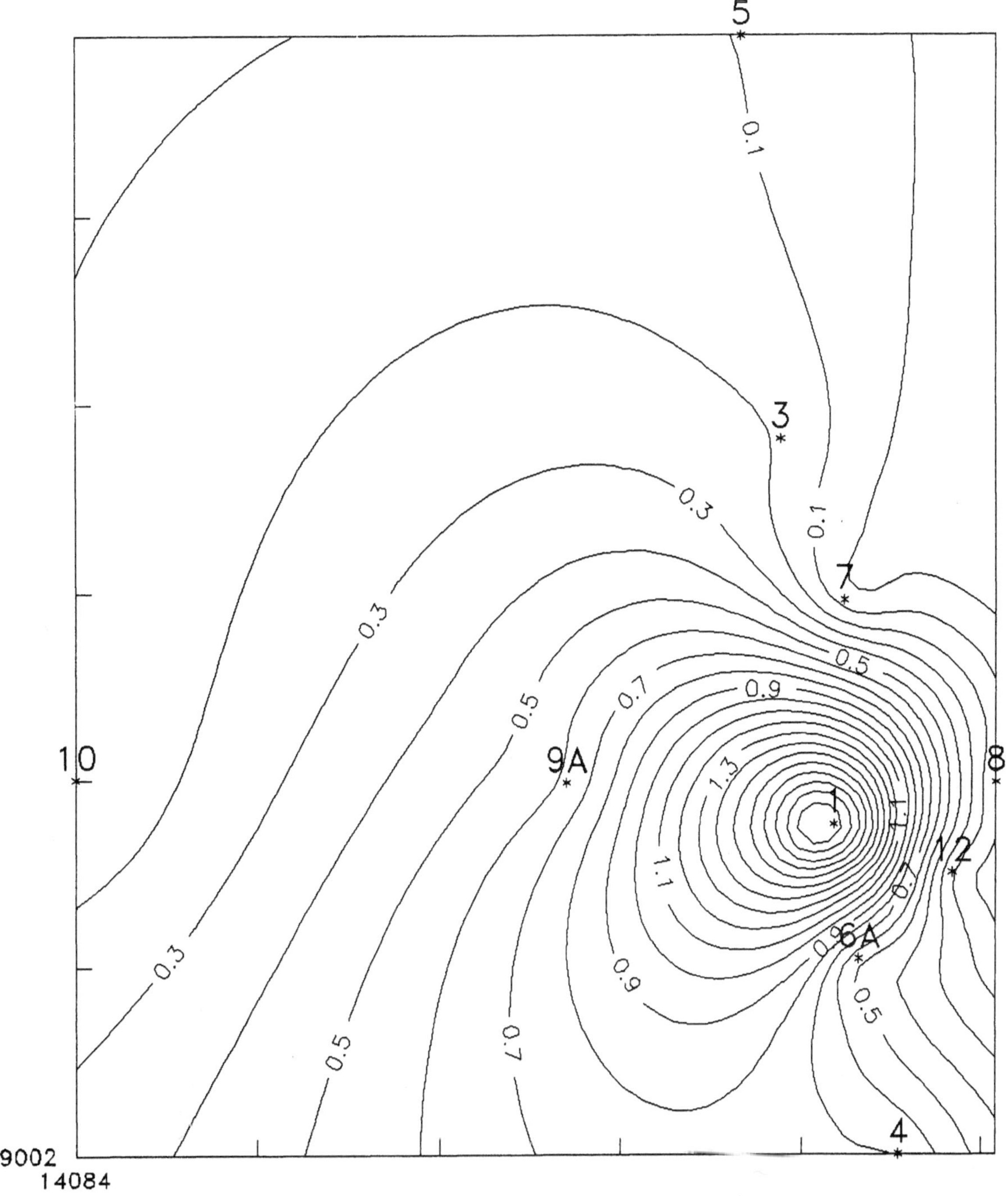

Figure 44. Areal distribution of particles of bone and charcoal in the fine-granule fraction of bulk basal samples for plotted cores. Contour interval: 0.1 particle/gram.

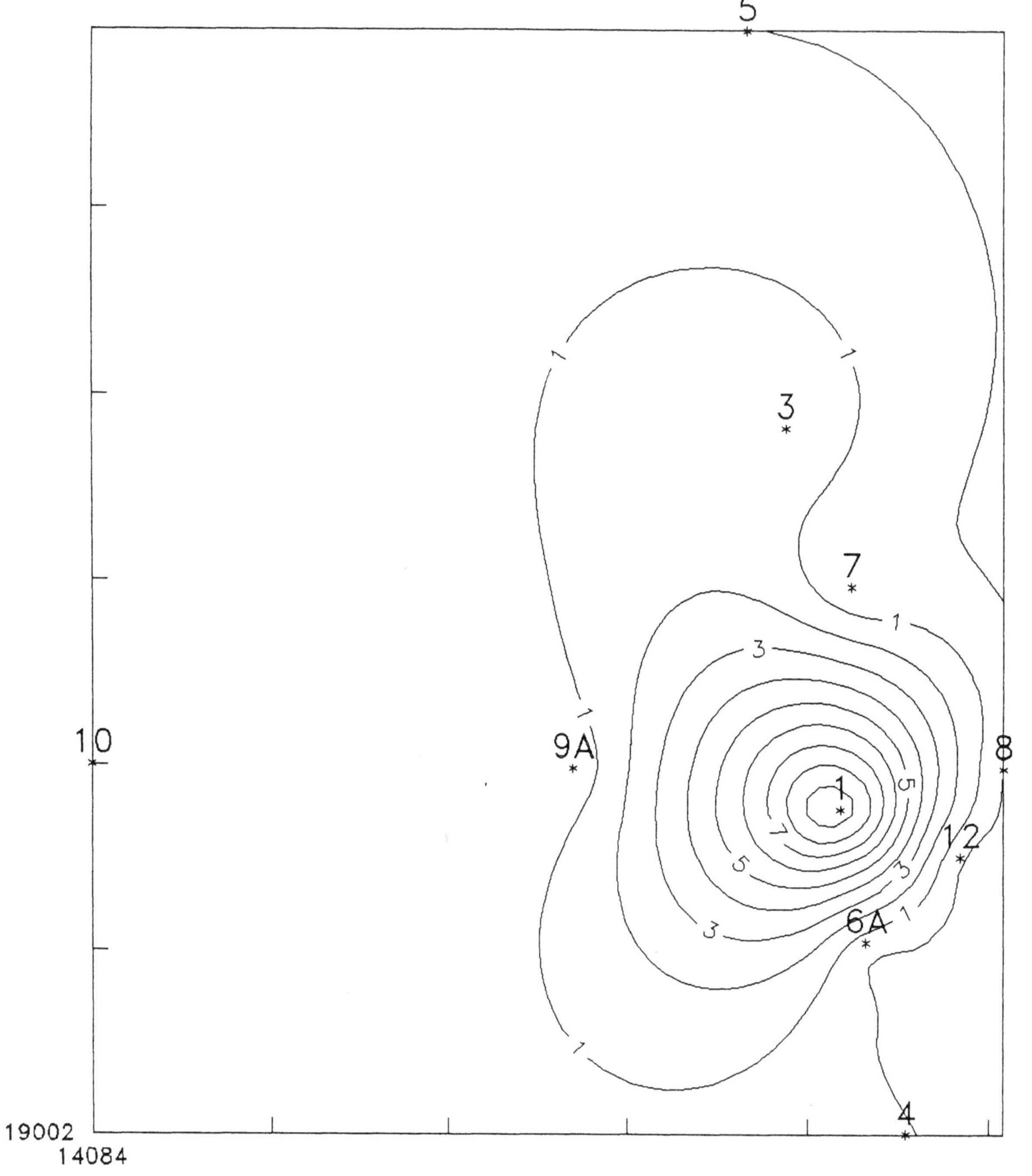

Figure 45. Areal distribution of particles of cultural material in the fine-granule fraction of bulk basal samples for plotted cores. Contour interval: 1 particle/gram.

After the abandonment of Paralia, including activity areas and possible structures on the terrace as far as 100 m west of the present shoreline, some colluviation and soil formation continued during the period 5000-4000 B.P. until the terrace began to be flooded by the rising sea level. Before this time, eastern portions of the site had been covered more or less with post-occupation deposits, by mechanisms described by Wilkinson and Duhon (see above).

The course of a marine transgression across any surface is a function of both the rate of vertical sea-level rise and the slope of the local ground surface: the flatter the surface, the more rapid the shoreline advance and, other factors being equal, the less disturbance and mixing of the terrestrial sediment cover will occur. In the vicinity of core OK85/1, with its relatively flat basal surface, the transgression is assumed to have moved rapidly. At the bottom of core OK85/1B the particle analysis of the 0-0.5 ϕ fraction (Figure 43) could be interpreted to show just slight mixing of a terrestrial sediment deposit with the earliest transgressive marine sediments. This mixture would constitute the bulk basal sediments from the core locations. Some of them contain greater amounts of relatively large ceramic sherds and stones than others, in an unpredictable distribution.

However, the cores around OK85/1 apparently bottomed in a partly artificial deposit containing residual coarse particles of limestone and exotic rocks of all sizes, the latter perhaps representing part of mud building material (sediment class D of Wilkinson and Duhon). Other particle types that were mixed but remained unremoved by the marine transgression are vertebrate bone fragments, plant and charcoal fragments, microdebitage, and ceramic sherds of all sizes up to several centimeters in maximum dimension. Preservation of all these types of material is good to excellent—significantly better than in the terrestrial deposits excavated nearby. Some edge rounding is evident on most of the sherds recovered, but they are significantly less worn than Neolithic sherds presently found in the swash zone at Paralia. There, small sherds occasionally weathering out of the 1973-76 excavation scarps have been abraded by a decade or so of wave activity. Almost all these sherds exhibit advanced edge rounding and complete loss of surface treatments (burnish, paint, incisions). If the sherds from the bottom of the 1981 and 1985 cores are comparable in mechanical strength to those presently on the Paralia beach, then the former were never subject to the degree of wave activity that characterizes this relatively high-energy environment. Contemporaneous basal sediment mixtures at locations to the north (OK85/3, 5, 7) and inshore (OK85/8, 12) perhaps represent somewhat thicker post-occupation colluvial deposits mixed with marine sediment, and thus contain fewer indicators of cultural activity.

The transgression, as it passed the vicinity of OK85/1 and continued eastward across the terrace, would have crossed a rising ground surface: the footslope of late Pleistocene stony red colluvium and its cover of later deposits associated with human activity, as well perhaps as stone structure foundations. These would have been already partially buried by post-occupation colluviation, but it is assumed here that some traces still protruded above the ground surface. As a modern analogue of the depositional environment during the marine transgression, one might consider the situation of the walls and other features partly submerged in shallow water at the Classical harbor site of Kenchreai near Corinth (Shaw 1972:Plates 8-13).

As the transgressing shoreline intersected the occupation deposits on the lower footslope, more mixing and redistribution of cultural material with marine sediments would occur than had taken place further down on the terrace. Stone wall foundations possibly provided hard substrates for increased populations of molluscs. In any event, the critical outcome of this mixing would be that nearshore areas downslope of the contemporary shoreline would receive homogenized deposits of reworked cultural material and shell in a marine sediment matrix.

The concentration peaks of charcoal, bone, and serpentinite fragments in the lower interval (320-380 cm) and central interval (160-220 cm) of OK85/1B (Figure 43) are taken to represent this hypothesized mixing that was occurring upslope of the core location, at the contemporaneous shoreline. The coarser size fractions, including cultural remains, were mixed and any primary context destroyed.

Based on the distribution curves of Figure 43, this proposed explanation requires that several relatively distinct areas of cultural deposits, and perhaps structures, were crossed by the advancing shoreline. By relating the depth of the particle maximum in Figure 43 to the local sea-level-rise curve of van Andel (1987:Figure 10), the earliest area, just described, might lie at depths of 8.5-7.9 m below present sea level. Later peaks of charcoal, bone, and serpentinite fragments, at 160-220 cm in Figure 43, would record another area of cultural deposits higher up the footslope, which was not reworked by the transgression until sea level was between six and seven meters below its present position.

Finally, only when the advancing shoreline rose to less than one meter of its present position (as recently as perhaps 800 years ago) did it reach upslope to the western edge of the excavated Paralia remains. Then more particles of cultural material were reworked into the bay bottom sediments, represented by the smaller peaks of bone, charcoal, and serpentinite fragments 20-30 cm below the top of core OK85/1B. Erosion of the occupation deposit at Paralia is continuing, as shown by the small active scarp backing the narrow cobble beach.

Conclusions

The second (1985) coring project produced little hard evidence to confirm or deny the theory that more Neolithic structures lie submerged off Paralia. Only in the area of core OK85/1 is there evidence of dense cultural material, and that is circumstantial.

The project has demonstrated the utility of diver-operated seabed coring to reach pre-transgressive land surfaces and their included cultural material, but it has also shown the limitations of the technique for recovering definitive contextual information. There may be little evidence of patterning in the cultural material, even in undisturbed samples of core size, and even if the core sample were to have intersected a deposit in primary context such as an occupation floor or midden. The sample size recovered from even a large-diameter core (10-15 cm) represents a volume within which not enough artifactual material may be found to detect any patterning. The ambiguity of the contextual nature of the deposit off Franchthi will remain until one or more test pits can be dug to the hard surface 9-10 m below sea level.

CHAPTER EIGHT

Holocene Environment of the Southern Argolid: A Pollen Core from Kiladha Bay[*]

Sytze Bottema

INTRODUCTION

During the past twenty-five years a network of pollen sites has been developed in Greece with the aim of reconstructing past vegetation and climate (Figure 46). This research has been almost invariably connected with investigations in the field of archaeology. The pollen record thus developed is mainly of Holocene origin, a period during which the influence of human habitation gradually exerted more and more pressure upon the natural environment. The distribution of pollen sites in connection with prehistoric settlements depends upon the presence of suitable sediments which are not always available. Although core locations are spread rather evenly over the Greek mainland, pollen diagrams prepared from the Peloponnesus are not of the quality met with in the north. This must be explained mainly by the different climatic conditions in the two areas. A core taken by John A. Gifford in Kiladha Bay fortunately forms an exception. The pollen diagram prepared for this material informs us about the development of the vegetation in that part of the Peloponnesus for the last seven millennia.

CORE LOCATION, GEOGRAPHY, CLIMATE, AND VEGETATION

The pollen diagram that will be discussed here has been prepared from a core taken from the bay (Figure 38) between Kiladha village on the mainland and the island of Koronis. Gifford registered a water depth of 10.2 m. The sediment core that was collected measured 4.5 m and was coded OK (Ormos Kiladha) 85/11. The lowest sample of 450 cm, a reddish sandy mud, was thought to represent a late Pleistocene soil whereas the remainder of the core was observed to be a homogeneous gray clay. Location OK 85/11 was chosen by Gifford because a drowned

*I am much indebted to Henk Woldring for his help in preparing the diagram, to Carell Lagerwerf for many discussions, to Dr. J.A. Gifford for critical reading of the manuscript, to Gertie Entjes-Nieborg for typing the manuscript, to Petri Maas for drawing the maps, and to Sheila van Gelder-Ottaway for improving my English usage.

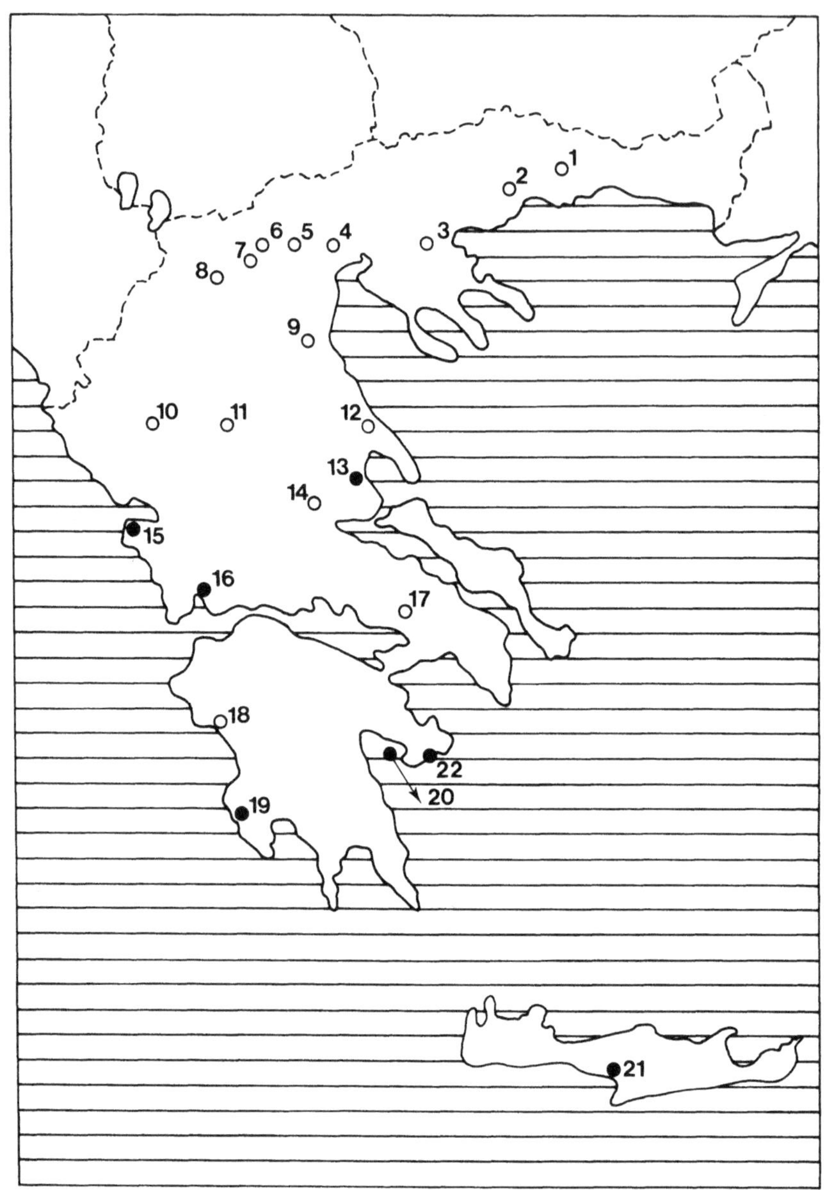

Figure 46. Pollen sites in Greece. Solid circles indicate sites discussed in text. 1. Gravouna (Turner and Greig 1975); 2. Tenagi Philippon (Wijmstra 1969); 3. Volvi; 4. Giannitsa; 5. Edessa; 6. Vegoritis; 7. Khimaditis; 8. Kastoria; 9. Litochoro (Athanasiadis 1975); 10. Ioannina; 11. Pertouli (Athansiadis 1975); 12. Viviis; 13. Halos; 14. Xinias; 15. Voulkaria (Wright 1972); 16. Trikhonis; 17. Kopais (Turner and Greig 1975); 18. Kaiafa (Wright 1972); 19. Osmanaga (Wright 1972); 20. Kiladha; 21. Aghia Galini; 22. Thermisia (Sheehan 1979). For locations numbered 3, 4, 5, 6, 7, 8, 10, 12, 13, 14, 16, 20, and 21, see Bottema 1974, 1979, 1980, 1982, 1988.

early Holocene stream channel was indicated there by van Andel et al. (1980). It could be expected that the time record would be longer there than in the other cores taken in shallow water. Running water courses are, however, generally not a reliable source for the development of a good pollen record. Sediment suitable for pollen analysis in such a location could have been formed only at a time when the sea level had risen sufficiently.

Gifford reports that the lowest sample of the core contained reddish sediment, which points to oxidation of calcareous matter, suggesting a late Pleistocene soil. The core very likely originates from the bank of the stream channel and not from the channel itself. The pollen archive developed from a time when the sea covered the stream channel.

The composition of the pollen assemblages in the clay sediment reflects past vegetation, but the record must also have been influenced by the distance from the land, which increased with time. The malacological information supplied by van Straaten informs us to some extent about this distance (see below).

The shape of Kiladha Bay for various time periods has been reconstructed by van Andel (van Andel et al. 1980; van Andel and Sutton 1987). The geography of the area is extensively treated by van Andel et al. (1980), Pope and van Andel (1984), van Andel and Lianos (1983), and van Andel and Sutton (1987), to which the reader is referred for relevant information.

The climate of the southern Argolid is discussed by van Andel (van Andel and Sutton 1987). Data obtained for Navplion give an average temperature for January and July of 10°C and 27°C, respectively. These data are thought to be valid for the area under discussion as well. Inferring from data observed for the Fourni valley and Navplion, annual precipitation must be about 500 mm. The pronounced Mediterranean type of climate in this part of Greece, especially defined by the seasonal distribution of precipitation, results in very dry conditions. The amount of precipitation in the Argolid is low because the area lies in the rain shadow, whereas part of the area of mountain ridges on the adjoining Peloponnesus receives up to 1200 mm.

The vegetation of the southern Argolid is discussed by Sheehan (1979) and van Andel (van Andel and Sutton 1987). As in many parts of the Mediterranean, long-lasting human activity has destroyed most, if not all, of the natural vegetation. Well-known degradation stages of Mediterranean vegetation, such as maquis and phrygana, are described. Vegetation which seems to be natural may be of a secondary character. The regeneration process proposed by Rackham (1983), following the sequence phrygana-maquis-kermes oak woodland, seems to be acceptable but is valid under the ruling climate regime only.

Information on the potential vegetation of the Peloponnesus can be obtained from the UNESCO/FAO (1968) map on the vegetation of the Mediterranean region by Bagnouls and Gaussen. The Argolid is situated in the Eu-Mediterranean belt mainly dominated by *Quercus coccifera*. In the northern part, stands of *Pinus halepensis* have been postulated as natural. Aleppo pine, however, is almost certainly the effect of anthropogenic activity, as is suggested by Vernet et al. (1987). At the higher elevations, deciduous oaks are postulated.

The main part of the Peloponnesus, especially the central mountains such as Taigetos (2407 m), Parnon (1935 m), Khelmos (2375 m), Erimanthos (2224 m), and Killini (2376 m), is covered by *Abies cephalonica* and *Pinus nigra*. In the north, on Erimanthos (2224 m), Bagnouls and Gaussen postulate beech forest although *Fagus sylvatica* is not found there today. Nor is beech listed in that area on the distribution maps prepared by Meusel et al. (1965). Studies on the vegetation history of mainland Greece (Bottema 1974, 1982) suggest that *Fagus* shifted to the north during the Holocene. Beech pollen percentages increase in northern Greece, especially after 4000 B.P., whereas they decrease in the southern part of the Pindus and Akarnania. It is not impossible that *Fagus* occurred in the Peloponnesus during the terminal Pleistocene, but conclusive information is lacking. The western humid submountain stage at about 800-1000 m is covered by forest of *Quercus sessiliflora*, *Q. cerris*, *Q. pedunculata*, and *Pinus nigra*.

Elevations below 800 m show a Eu-Mediterranean vegetation ascribed to the Olea-Ceratonion. This is more or less in conformity with Polunin's (1980) map on the vegetation of Greece. Polunin postulates a Mediterranean vegetation from about 0-800 m. At higher elevations (ca. 800-1200 m), an East-Central European transitional deciduous forest is postulated. Above 1200 m, Oro-Mediterranean coniferous forest should be present. In these forests, various other tree species play a subordinate role. Meusel et al. (1965) give the following species for the Peloponnesus: *Corylus avellana*, *Carpinus betulus*, *Ulmus glabra*, *Ulmus carpinifolia*, and *Juglans regia*, the latter only in the most northerly part. According to Rikli (1943-1948) *Castanea sativa*, *Platanus orientalis*, and *Juniperus foetidissima* are among the arboreal species found in the peninsula.

MALACOLOGY

The samples submitted for pollen analysis were also investigated for their malacological contents. No shell fragments were observed below a depth of 235 cm. From 235-195 cm scarce shell fragments were found, whereas the samples from 190-0 cm were very rich in marine molluscs. L.M.J.U. van Straaten (State University of Groningen) investigated these remains and kindly supplied the following information on the molluscan fauna.

The scarce shell fragments found at a depth of 235-195 cm are possibly from a lagoonal association. Above that level, an association is found which points to the presence of a shallow open sea at the time of deposition. The sea was at least 2 m deep with generally calm water. High percentages of *Bittium reticulatum* and other gastropods indicate a rich aquatic vegetation including *Poseidonia*. Such conditions are likely to have been present in the Kiladha area even after the water increased in depth to ca. 10 m at the location where the core was taken.

Van Straaten reports that the deposition of the sediment between 240 and 190 cm may have taken a relatively long time, or that hiatuses in sedimentation are hidden in the record. If the latter, it seems impossible that the sediment dried up and became exposed to the air in this part of the core since good preservation of the pollen proves permanent inundation. Van Straaten's statement on difference in sedimentation rate in the Kiladha core seems to be in accordance with the sea-level curve established by van Andel et al. (1980:Figure 3, f-curve).

DATING

In addition to palynological dating (see below), we have the results of radiocarbon dating. According to the curve of the sea-level rise published by van Andel et al. (1980), sediments present at a depth of 14.6 m below sea level should have been submerged ca. 6500 B.P. The lowest samples of nearby cores produced the following radiocarbon dates:

OK 85/1	6600 ± 250 B.P.	(Beta-15612)[7]
OK 85/1b	6860 ± 120 B.P.	(Beta-15613)
OK 85/1a	6720 ± 100 B.P.	(Beta-15614)

METHODS

From core OK 85/11, 68 samples for pollen analysis were taken at intervals of 5 cm. The samples were analyzed mainly at intervals of 10 cm. Whenever any conspicuous changes in the pollen composition were noticed, the samples were analyzed at intervals of 5 cm. Those parts of the diagram where the pollen spectra are separated by more than 10 cm were caused by incomplete core recovery by the Eykelkamp pulse-augering system (see Chapter 7). Missing parts are registered at 50-80 cm, 125-150 cm, 210-225 cm, 270-300 cm, 355-375 cm, and 430-440 cm. No pollen was found in the sediment below 425 cm. The samples were prepared by heavy-liquid separation (Bromoform-Alcohol mixture s.g. 2.0) followed by standard procedures as described by Faegri and Iversen (1973).

The pollen types identified for the Kiladha core OK 85/11 are shown in a diagram (Figure 47). The values calculated for each type in the respective spectra are drawn in a curve. These curves represent the relative values, expressed as percentages of a total pollen sum which includes all types that were counted except those of Chenopodiaceae and Liguliflorae. The large number of Chenopodiaceae found in the eight lowermost samples are thought to have been produced by a local vegetation. The reason why the pollen of the Liguliflorae have been excluded from the pollen sum will be explained in the next section.

DISCUSSION OF THE KILADHA POLLEN DIAGRAM

Construction of the Diagram

The order of the various pollen types shown in Figure 47 has been arranged rather pragmatically. The curves for the tree taxa are shown first, followed by the curve for the AP/NAP ratio, the main diagram. After the main diagram, the herb-type curves are represented. The anthropogenic indicators have been grouped together, more local water and marsh plants have been put at the end, and in between the only logical pattern is the grouping of the various genera of the same family. The pollen sum on which the percentages are based gives an indication of the statistical reliability.

Two pollen types appearing in large numbers have been excluded from the basic pollen sum, viz., Chenopodiaceae and Liguliflorae. In the eight lowermost spectra of the diagram, chenopod pollen is found in large quantities. This reflects the influence of the sea which gradually penetrated into the stream channel. Halophytic chenopods flourished along the edge of the water and deposited their pollen in the nearby sediment. After spectrum 8, sea level had risen sufficiently to force the chenopod vegetation far enough away to prevent a high pollen influx.

The reason for excluding the Liguliflorae from the pollen sum differs from that for excluding the Chenopodiaceae. Even if members of the Liguliflorae did grow close to the core location in large numbers, they would never have produced so much pollen. Liguliflorae are insect-pollinating, and they generally demonstrate low percentages in surface samples. High values for Liguliflorae can be found in pollen assemblages which have been severely corroded. In such cases Liguliflorae become strongly over-represented because they are very resistant to corrosion, oxidation, and mechanical or microbal attacks, and their shape is so distinctive (fenestrate) that they can be identified even in an advanced state of corrosion. Preservation was generally good in the Kiladha core, and the high Liguliflorae numbers were certainly not caused by corrosive action. Comparable behavior of Liguliflorae pollen has been found in other diagrams, e.g., from central Anatolia (Bottema and Woldring 1984(1986)). High values for Liguliflorae, *Centaurea solstitialis*-type, and other Tubuliflorae are found in cores from steppic areas. Cores from locations situated in areas that are heavily forested at the moment do not show high values for Liguliflorae, at least in those parts of the diagram which yield high arboreal percentages. It seems that Liguliflorae are especially connected with steppic conditions or at least with vegetations which are poor in trees.

Yet this does not explain why Liguliflorae may demonstrate high values in pollen diagrams while they are not found in pollen traps in modern vegetations. A possible explanation is given by Bottema and Woldring (1984(1986)), based on an observation in one of the small crater lakes of Zirelia (Reinders and Bottema 1983). The lakes of Zirelia are found in the plain of Almiros in southern Thessaly. During coring (11 m of soft clay that had been deposited in 1400 years, dated by radiocarbon) from a raft in the middle of the lakes, Bottema and Woldring observed that after about 1:00 P.M. a lot of dust settled on the water. The precipitation became even more clearly visible after a combine harvester started to work at some distance away. The cutting and threshing of wheat caused a steady precipitation of chaff and small pieces of straw and dust into the lake. At that time, the plain of Thessaly had maximum daily temperatures of between 40° and 45°C. The "culture steppe" (an area where the vast natural forest has been completely turned into farmland) must have been heated so much in the course of the day that rising air took dust and chaff into the sky. Over the cooler water of the lake a backflow took place, thus precipitating the dust that first had been taken into the air.

There was no discharge of streams into the crater lake. The rapid sedimentation was very likely caused by aeolian transport. The cored sediments contained high numbers of Liguliflorae pollen in relation to arboreal pollen. Tree pollen must have precipitated into the lake in normal quantities during the spring when air temperatures were much lower than in the summer, whereas pollen of Compositae growing in the open landscape, many of which flower in the summer, was collected by the upward air flow. The composite pollen production of a large area was concentrated and returned into the crater lake. Comparable effects can be seen in the modern pollen precipitation off the coast of West Africa (Hooghiemstra et al. 1986).

Because the pollen assemblages of Zone I of the Kiladha diagram strongly point to a very open vegetation, high Liguliflorae values may have been caused by the same mechanism as is assumed to have taken place in Zirelia and central Anatolia. For that reason the Liguliflorae have been left out of the basic pollen sum on which the percentages have been calculated. The reader may object to leaving this type out of the sum and wonder whether other types should also be excluded. However, the other herb types displayed values that did not deviate essentially from those found in 400 modern surface samples analyzed for Greece, Turkey, Lebanon, Syria, and Iran.

The order of presentation is only partly consistent. An attempt has been made to group the types according to their plant-sociological and ecological affinities. This approach is severely hindered by the low identification level of some of the pollen types. Only if all pollen types found can be identified up to species level can better grouping be realized.

Pollen Zones

To facilitate the discussion, the Kiladha diagram has been divided into zones and subzones.

Zone I (spectra 1-19). Low arboreal pollen values averaging ca. 30%. Low values for conifers and Mediterranean xerophytes. Large variety of herb types with relatively high values.

Zone II (spectra 20-31). High arboreal pollen values dominated by *Pinus*. Mediterranean xerophytic species show rather high values. This zone is divided into subzones. Subzone IIa (spectra 20-22) is characterized by increasing AP values. Cerealia-type pollen is still present with high values. Subzone IIb (spectra 23-31): AP values about 80% due to increasing *Pinus*, *Olea*, and *Quercus coccifera*-type.

Vegetation Reconstruction

The tree pollen in the Kiladha diagram, which partly represents species and partly genera, can be grouped in (Eu-)Mediterranean, montane, or riverine vegetations. Unfortunately, some pollen types represent several species which grow in very different habitats. *Pinus* illustrates the problem that may arise. Systematically and ecologically, the pine species vary greatly. The two pine species which can be expected in the Peloponnesus cannot be identified palynologically since they share the same type of pollen. This problem also occurs in many herb types.

The pollen assemblages of Zone I (Figure 47) are characterized by total tree pollen values of about 30%. The types contributing to these values are dominated by about 20% *Quercus cerris*-type, including deciduous and semi-deciduous oak species. *Quercus coccifera*-type, including *Quercus coccifera* and *Q. ilex*, amounts to only a small percentage.

Pistacia measures 1-3%. This taxon is always very much under-represented in the pollen rain. Studies of modern pollen precipitation in relation to the vegetation in Greece (Bottema 1974) and the eastern Mediterranean (Bottema and Barkoudah 1979) demonstrated that *Pistacia* values of a few percent point to a very common occurrence of this species in the vegetation.

Representatives of mesic forest characteristic of temperate Europe are present in low numbers: *Corylus*, *Tilia*, *Ulmus*, *Betula*, and *Alnus*. *Corylus* and *Tilia* will have occurred at higher elevations in the mountains. These two species are mentioned by Meusel et al. (1965) and occur at present. *Alnus* and *Betula* pollen must be ascribed to long-distance transport. Their presence (<1%) may be exaggerated by low local pollen production. Low production of local pollen is also indicated, for instance, by the high proportion of insect-pollinating taxa in the nonarboreal part of the diagram.

Coniferous pollen was scarce during the time of Zone I. *Abies* is present only in the upper part of the zone, and *Pinus* is present with low values (<5%). There are small amounts of fir pollen in spectra 11 to 15. It may be assumed that fir occurred somewhere in the Peloponnesus since even pure *Abies* forest seldom produces more than 10% *Abies* pollen in surface samples. Low pine pollen values as displayed here point to the absence of pine trees or to very low numbers of pine growing in the Peloponnesus. *Pinus* is a prolific pollen producer compared to *Abies*.

The dominating herb pollen shows a large diversity. The values for Gramineae are not only conspicuously low, but they are often lower than the values for the Cerealia-type. Either grasses were a minor constituent in the local and regional vegetation or grazing was so heavy that flowering was prevented. It seems more likely that not much grass cover was found in the area, because, even nowadays, over-grazed steppe produces a higher percentage of grass pollen than is shown in the diagram. In this connection, the Neolithic settlement on Paralia is of interest. Grain fields generally do not distribute pollen in large numbers. Outside a field of wheat or barley, pollen values are at most a few percent and sometimes even no Cerealia-type pollen is found at all. Much higher amounts of cereal pollen can be found where threshing takes place. Pollen of cereals often stays in the glumes and is subsequently released by threshing. It is also possible that pollen from the fields was washed by the rain into the stream channel. Whatever the explanation may be, cereal growing must have been very important during the period represented by Zone I and must have occurred very near the core location.

The high cereal-type pollen values are not the only anthropogenic indicators. The area must have been open, either because of dry conditions or because of farming activity or both, as can be concluded from relatively high *Asphodelus albus*-type values. This large Liliaceae species is typical in ploughed fields where the large bulbs easily survive if they are out of reach of the coulter. A Neolithic ard would have probably left the bulbs untouched.

Plantain (*Plantago lanceolata*) is fairly well represented. In temperate Europe ribwort plantain is thought to indicate grazing more than cultivation. Another type that strongly indicates grazing is *Poterium*. This type also includes *Sanguisorba minor*, but *Poterium spinosum* is more likely for the Mediterranean. This plant forms prickly cushions where forest or shrub vegetation has been degraded by grazing. *Mercurialis annua* pollen is common. It is a typical ruderal plant,

Figure 47 can be found at http://www.iupress.indiana.edu/em/email_images/franchthi/figure_47.jpg.

profiting from disturbance by man. *Cistus*, a pyrophile, scores high compared with other Greek diagrams, pointing to hot and dry conditions and possibly fires. Most of the taxa represented in this diagram are not unexpected. It is their relative importance in comparison with other Greek diagrams that draws our attention.

The Umbelliferae are worthy of mention. The *Eryngium*-type represents *Eryngium*, a species that favors dry habitats. Umbelliferae, which have not been specified beyond family level, demonstrate values of more than 10%. The combination of deciduous oak pollen and such high values of Umbelliferae very much resembles the pollen spectra produced by late Glacial and early Holocene vegetations in the Zagros Mountains in Iran (van Zeist and Bottema 1977). Early Holocene conditions in the Zagros seem to have favored a very open oak forest-steppe with a large variety of herbs.

It is no simple matter to reconstruct the natural vegetation in the Argolid or the Peloponnesus from the pollen record. The anthropogenic indicators and the observation that the sediment of Zone I contains a lot of small charcoal particles, which may have been produced by intentional fires, both point to strong human impact upon the environment during the time of Zone I. As no palynological information from the early Holocene is available, we are not informed about the time when human impact was negligible. The vegetation of the southern Argolid must have been of a very open character during Zone I. Trees, mainly deciduous oaks, formed at best a woodland at higher elevations. Other deciduous trees would have been rare, growing in limited numbers on favorable locations. As the landscape in the Peloponnesus is highly variable, more demanding species, such as *Corylus*, *Tilia*, and *Ulmus* may have been present on north slopes or in stream valleys at a higher elevation in the mountains. At lower elevations there was an open *Pistacia* vegetation with a lot of herb species, such as *Cistus*.

The effects of human activity are clearly visible in the pollen diagram. The high Cerealia-type values indicate that either grain fields had been laid out up to the edge of the Neolithic stream channel or that the inhabitants of the nearby Neolithic village did their threshing close to the coring site. If farming activity had occurred at some distance from the core location much lower Cerealia-pollen percentages would have been found.

Many of the herb pollen types present in Zone I may have been produced by plant species profiting from man-made habitats. If Neolithic people destroyed all or most of the forest at lower elevations, one might expect the spectra to be dominated by pollen from the trees growing on the mountain itself. Thus, modern pollen spectra from the cultivated coastal lowlands of northern Turkey, between Bafra and Samsun, are dominated by pine pollen. This is explained by relatively low local pollen production compared to transport from more distant areas where *Pinus nigra* is growing. On the other hand, the very low arboreal pollen values in Kiladha Zone I point to vegetations that were by nature of a very open character caused by almost steppic conditions, thus stimulating the growth of a variety of herbs.

The pollen assemblages in the upper part of the diagram, which is defined as Zone II, differ appreciably from those of Zone I. The total tree pollen percentages (AP) in Zone II increased from ca. 30% to ca. 80%, and the relative proportions of the respective types also changed drastically.

In the upper two meters of sediment, the charcoal content has very much decreased. Many marine molluscs are found there, indicating that the piedmont plain (van Andel 1987:Figure 21) had gradually drowned. The distance of pollen-producing vegetation from the catchment point, the core location, increased and quite soon the present situation was attained (van Andel 1987:Figure 12). It can be expected that especially the insect-pollinated types strongly decreased in proportion as no local vegetation occurred any more. That this cannot be the cause of the conspicuous change is indicated by surface-sample studies on the modern pollen precipitation in

Greece (Bottema 1974) and the Near East (Bottema and Barkoudah 1979), which show that the change in tree pollen values as in our Zone II cannot simply be explained by an increasing distance from the coring site to the mainland. A core taken in the Bay of Almiros near Volos close to the ancient city of Halos (Greece), in a rather similar situation, does not show an increase in pine pollen (Figure 50, below).

The strong increase in total tree pollen is caused by several species. *Olea* pollen, almost absent during Zone I, now reaches values of 10-15%. The same is found for the pollen of the evergreen oak-type. Deciduous oak pollen at first shows a decline, but it soon regains its former values. Other deciduous elements like hazel, lime, and elm are present in parts of the spectra, albeit in low numbers.

A conspicuous rise is displayed by the coniferous types *Abies* and *Pinus*. The share of *Abies* soon reaches ca. 4%. *Pinus* pollen reaches a maximum of ca. 35%. Pollen of *Platanus* (plane tree), almost absent from the previous zone, is now more often found.

Almost all herb types strongly decrease, as may be expected in view of the high arboreal values. The only type that now plays a relatively important role is that of the Ericaceae which had been almost completely absent during the previous phase. It is obvious that the appearance of Ericaceae is an important indication of changing conditions, connected with the change in tree pollen values. The appearance of Ericaceae pollen very likely points to an increase in precipitation or moister conditions.

The zoophilous as well as the anemophilous herb types show a decline. Not only do those types representing natural vegetations show a decrease, but the anthropogenic indicators also have much lower values than during the previous period. The vegetation found in the southern Argolid, and more generally in the Peloponnesus, seems to have become established in its present form at the time of spectrum 23. The period from spectrum 20 up to 23 (subzone IIa) shows the transition from the typical pollen assemblages of Zone I towards those of Zone II. During this transitional period, the most important tree was the Greek fir, *Abies cephalonica*. Fir must have been dominant in the mountainous parts of the Peloponnesus. As deciduous oak pollen values decrease, fir may have replaced the oaks.

Pinus also increased in numbers. The higher pollen percentages must partly be ascribed to *Pinus nigra* expanding into the mountain belt. However, one also has to consider the possibility of expanding *Pinus halepensis*. Vernet et al. (1987) were able to synchronize the appearance of the Aleppo pine with Neolithic or Bronze Age activity in southern France. If the Aleppo pine increased in the Peloponnesus, one may wonder why it did not appear earlier as there is ample evidence for early human activity in that part of Greece. At lower elevations, from sea level to a few hundred meters above, typical Eu-Mediterranean elements started to spread during the transitional period. Three representatives of xerophytic evergreen vegetation, viz., *Olea*, *Erica* cf. *verticillata*, and *Quercus coccifera* (type) demonstrate increasing values. Lentisk (*Pistacia lentiscus*) was present in a reasonably large amount already from the previous period. At the level of spectrum 23, modern conditions had arrived. Because of incomplete recovery, there is a hiatus between spectra 22 and 23. For that reason, it remains possible that modern conditions had arrived at a somewhat lower level. Increasing anthropogenic activity must be responsible for the expansion of juniper, which measures over 10% in the upper samples.

We are reasonably well informed about the present-day pollen precipitation in the Peloponnesus by the study of Sheehan (1979). The various vegetation zones produce pollen spectra that together will have contributed to the kind of assemblages found off the coast in the Kiladha core. At present, *Pinus* pollen occurs in moderate-to-high values all over the Peloponnesus, but especially in black pine forests. *Olea* pollen originates mainly from the maquis zone or deciduous forest. The natural vegetation to which *Olea* belongs is difficult to define. Phytogeographically, it is defined as an important constituent of the Olea-Ceratonion. A past vegetation in which *Olea* plays an important role is not a xerophytic evergreen vegetation of shrubby character, but a deciduous oak forest. In late Glacial and early Holocene times, olive was very common in thabor-oak forest (*Quercus ithaburensis*) in the northern Jordan valley in Israel. Evergreen-oak pollen is mainly present in lower or higher maquis. Deciduous-oak pollen in the Kiladha core has dropped to about 5% in the upper spectra. Sheehan did not find *Quercus* of the deciduous type exceeding 2%, pointing to the fact that this taxon had recently become very rare. The values of the Ericaceae are about the same for the modern pollen rain as those of Zone II. They are mostly derived from maquis or deciduous forest. There is a striking difference between the subfossil record of *Pistacia* in Kiladha and Thermisia and the modern pollen precipitation. *Pistacia* is very well represented in the pollen diagrams, but in the surface samples this type is met with in higher numbers only in the Franchthi Cave area. The representation of *Abies* comes up to expectations (Bottema 1974). The almost complete absence of *Juniperus* in Sheehan's surface samples is puzzling, as this type has a share of 10% at most in the subrecent part of the Kiladha core. However, this may be a matter of preservation in the surface samples. All vegetation types studied by Sheehan are characterized by dominant AP values. This agrees completely with the Zone II evidence in Kiladha.

The fact that forest vegetation rapidly conquered the Peloponnesus during Zone II does not imply that anthropogenic influence was absent. The high *Olea* values indicate that extensive olive culture had developed, and cereal farming was still practiced in the Argolid. Weeds, such as *Mercurialis annua* and *Plantago lanceolata*, were still found. Compared to the previous period (Zone I) the total area of arable land would have been smaller, but a large part of the lower Mediterranean belt was used for olive orchards.

The pollen assemblages of Zone II reflect a vegetation that differs appreciably from that of Zone I. Consequently, climatic conditions responsible for the development of this kind of vegetation must have differed from those present during Zone I.

On the basis of the vegetation reconstructed for the time of Zone I, it can be postulated that the climate was much drier than at present. If the global temperature of the Holocene is considered, there seems to be no reason to attribute the very open character of the vegetation in the southern Argolid to a much higher temperature, dry conditions being a more likely cause. The oak woodland points to a climate with an average precipitation of about 300-350 mm for the lower elevations. It is evident that the mountainous part of the Peloponnesus at that time also received considerably less rainfall, as is suggested by the very low representation of tree pollen of montane origin. It seems that the southern Argolid was in the rain shadow during the time of Zone I. The rapid expansion of AP values at the beginning of Zone II points to an increase in precipitation, soon attaining the level of today.

It is questionable whether it is permissible to translate the pollen record into terms of climate, as is done here. In fact, the pollen diagram clearly demonstrates the role of man. The anthropogenic indicators may be translated inadvertently into a climatic effect. It is, however, very unlikely that Neolithic or Bronze Age people who were subsequently present in the southern Argolid and other parts of the Peloponnesus destroyed the natural forest—not only in the lower plains and valleys, but also in the mountain belt—to such an extent. Nowhere in Greece have indications been found for important influence on the forest vegetation by Neolithic habitation. During Zone I, trees were rather scarce in the southern Argolid, but their numbers remained stable for several millennia, as is concluded from the rather constant tree-pollen values. In their study on the late Quaternary alluviation and soil formation of the southern Argolid, Pope and van Andel (1984) also see minimal influence of Neolithic man on the landscape.

Human occupation of the southern Argolid in general and the Franchthi Cave area in particular is extensively treated by van Andel et al. (1980, 1987). Information is supplied on settlement pattern and density, eventually connected with erosion. Van Andel measured the sediment supply and its variation in time for Kiladha Bay. The lowest sedimentation was found in the earlier Neolithic (8000-6000 B.P.). The amount almost doubled from about 6000 B.P. to 3500 B.P. The later Neolithic and much of the Bronze Age (Helladic) are thought to be represented by pollen Zone I in the Kiladha diagram (Figure 48).

Van Andel et al. (1980:Figure 13) reconstructed a marked increase in sedimentation in the Kiladha Bay area from ca. 3500 B.P. to about 1500 B.P. They proposed that, after that time, the sediment supply dropped by about 25%. The amount of sediment deposited during the time represented by the Kiladha pollen core is not in accordance with this reconstruction. During Kiladha Zone I (ca. 6700–ca. 3200 B.P.), 245 cm of sediment were deposited. For the last 3200 years, 175 cm of sediment are measured. The date of 3200 B.P. is based upon extensive palynological information discussed in the final section (below). Thus, during the later Neolithic and the Bronze Age, ca. 0.7 mm/yr was deposited, whereas for the last 3200 years (largely the time of the Greek "Iron Age") sedimentation decreased to ca. 0.5 mm/yr. The sedimentation rate for the upper part may be somewhat higher if a stillstand during the beginning of Zone II is taken into account. The upper part of the sediment differs considerably from the lower part as is indicated by the presence of marine molluscs and the absence of charcoal. This may point to a different mode of sedimentation.

For the southern Argolid, van Andel and Sutton (1987) describe two kinds of events having taken place during the last 4000 years. A debris flow is dated around 4500–4000 B.P., whereas stream-flood deposits occurred about 300 B.C.–50 B.C. (as dated by pottery). Debris flows can be caused either by the climate becoming drier or by land clearance. Stream-flood deposits occur when climate becomes wetter or, in this case, existing terracing is neglected (van Andel and Sutton 1987:Figure 6). The latter possibility was proposed because there was no evidence for an increase in precipitation. The evidence from the Kiladha pollen record strongly points to an increase in precipitation for the Argolid during Zone II, viz., after the Helladic period. Increased rainfall and neglect of terracing may have jointly contributed to the occurrence of stream-flood deposits.

COMPARISON OF THE KILADHA DIAGRAM WITH OTHER PALAEOBOTANICAL INFORMATION FROM GREECE

In this section, the palaeobotanical evidence obtained for lowland sites in the south of Greece and the island of Crete will be compared with that of the Kiladha core.

Peloponnesus

Information on the postglacial vegetation history of the Peloponnesus is given by Sheehan (1979) and Wright (1972). Sheehan investigated deposits from coastal lagoons in the southern Argolid, the oldest sediments of which date back to about 4400 B.P. in Limni Thermisia. Compared to deposits from deeper water, lagoonal sediments often suffer from oxidation, resulting in the absence of pollen. Pollen is sometimes present but in a state of corrosion, or the record shows hiatuses. Even if pollen is recovered, counts may be very low and statistically less reliable. As is the case in many clay deposits, organic remains are either scarce or absent. Sheehan tried to solve these problems by combining 30-cm-long samples of two correlated cores to obtain a radiocarbon date. It is evident that no precise dates could be expected, only an order of magnitude.

Notwithstanding such problems, Sheehan collected quite substantial evidence on the younger Holocene vegetation development of the southern Argolid. His conclusions are generally in

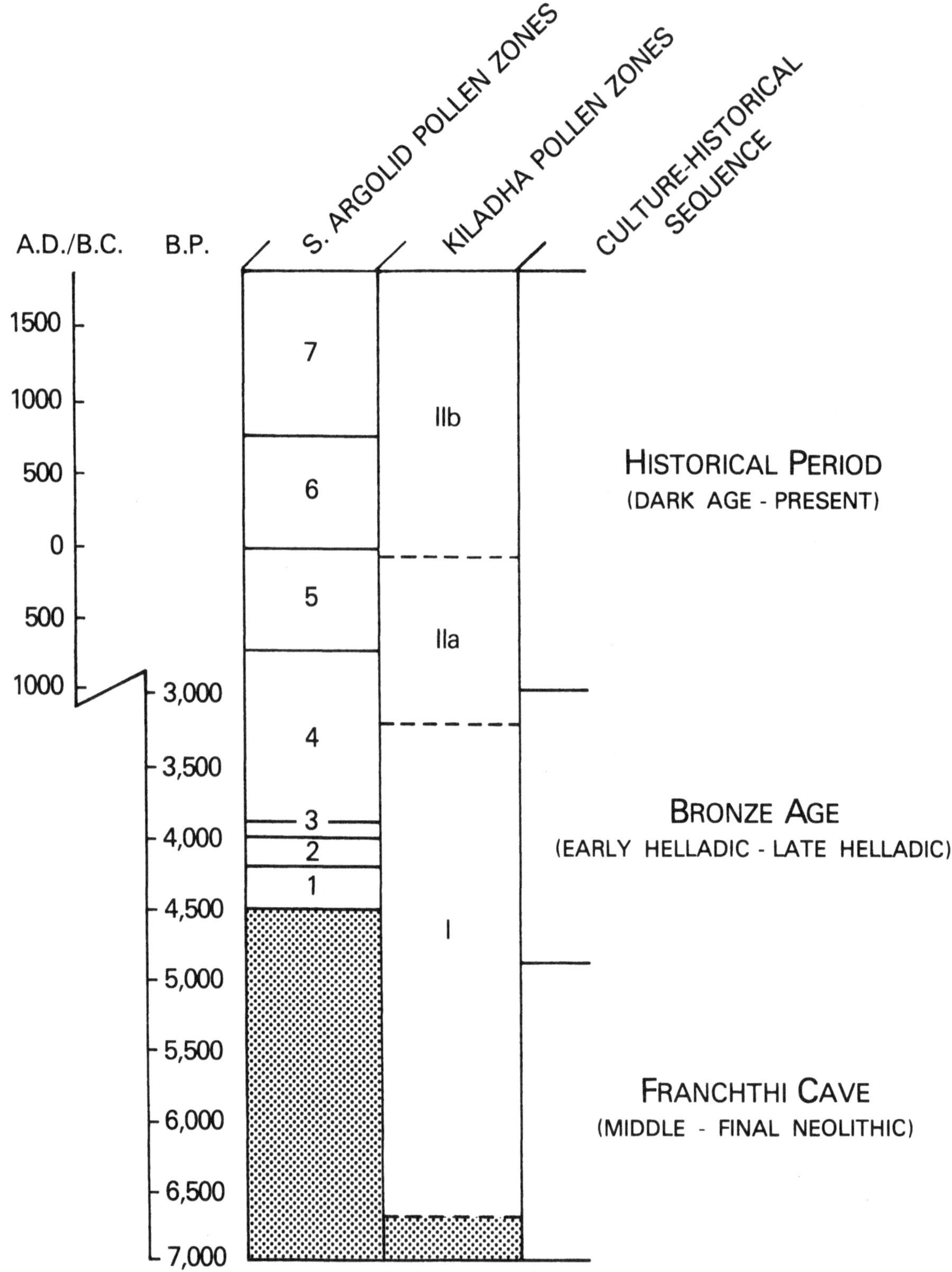

Figure 48. Pollen zones and culture sequence in the southern Argolid from Middle Neolithic to the present (after Sheehan 1979 and Jacobsen 1976).

agreement with those of the present author. Sheehan states that during the fifth millennium B.P. a more mesic type of forest must have been present in the southern Argolid, whereas the present author is inclined to speak of dry conditions. Sheehan's statement is based upon the discovery of *Ilex* and *Aesculus* grains. Both tree species are insect-pollinated and are only rarely found. In the Kiladha samples *Ilex* and *Aesculus* were not found, but there was a single pollen grain of *Carya* in each of two spectra. *Carya* occurred in this area during the Tertiary. Its pollen is redeposited and, although in low numbers, was regularly met with in Greek deposits. Although impossible to prove, the *Ilex* and *Aesculus* grains may have been produced by trees present in some very favorable location in the mountains. This in itself does not prove general mesic conditions, but the grains could also be of secondary origin. If the fifth millennium witnessed mesic conditions in the area east of Kiladha, in the Thermisia region, one would have expected more pollen from deciduous trees.

Sheehan's conclusion that "in place of forest, much of the land may have been given to field crops" (Sheehan 1979:46) is in agreement with the Kiladha record and holds at least for the piedmont plain as it is reconstructed by van Andel (van Andel and Sutton 1987). Crops would have been grown on the piedmont plain or on valley floors. On the steeper sides of mountains or river valleys, forest would still have been present if the climatic conditions permitted tree growth.

In the lower part of the diagram of Limni Thermisia, *Pinus* percentages are often much higher than in the comparable part of Kiladha Zone I. It is very conspicuous, however, that such high *Pinus* values are found in spectra in which a very low number of pollen grains could be counted, often only about 10% of the pollen sums in the Kiladha diagram.

Sheehan dates by interpolation the beginning of olive cultivation in Thermisia at about 2700 B.P. Two radiocarbon measurements are available. This date is of the same order as, although somewhat younger than, those from other radiocarbon-dated diagrams in Greece where the beginning of olive cultivation is dated.

Wright (1972) already concluded from the Osmanaga cores that olive growing had not yet developed in the Bronze Age and that it became important from about 3000 B.P. onward. The development of true maquis vegetation took place very late, ca. 2000 B.P. according to Sheehan. It seems likely, as is concluded from other diagrams in the eastern Mediterranean, that typical Mediterranean maquis developed after ca. 3000 B.P. This is mainly supported by the appearance of important numbers of *Quercus coccifera*-type pollen. Most constituents of the maquis are hardly or not represented in the pollen precipitation. It has been shown (Bottema 1974; Bottema and Barkoudah 1979) that evergreen oak represents Eu-Mediterranean maquis very well in the modern pollen record.

Limni Trikhonis

From the west coast of mainland Greece, in Akarnania, a diagram prepared from a core taken in Limni Trikhonis (Figure 49) is now available (Creer et al. 1981; Bottema 1982). The lake of Trikhonis is located 38°36′N, 12°30′E at an elevation of about 20 m above sea level. The average January temperature in that part of Greece is 10°C and ca. 25°C for July. Annual precipitation measures about 750-1000 mm. The lake lies in a transitional zone of Mediterranean xerophytic and deciduous oak forest (Polunin 1980). The sediment represents about the last 6000 years. Zone II includes a layer of volcanic ash, palynologically dated about 3200 B.P. Dating by radiocarbon, paleomagnetism, and by pollen is not in agreement (discussion in Creer et al. 1981). The magnetic age of zone II is too young compared to the radiocarbon and palynological age. In favor of an age of ca. 3200 B.P. for the ash layer is the very good palynological correlation

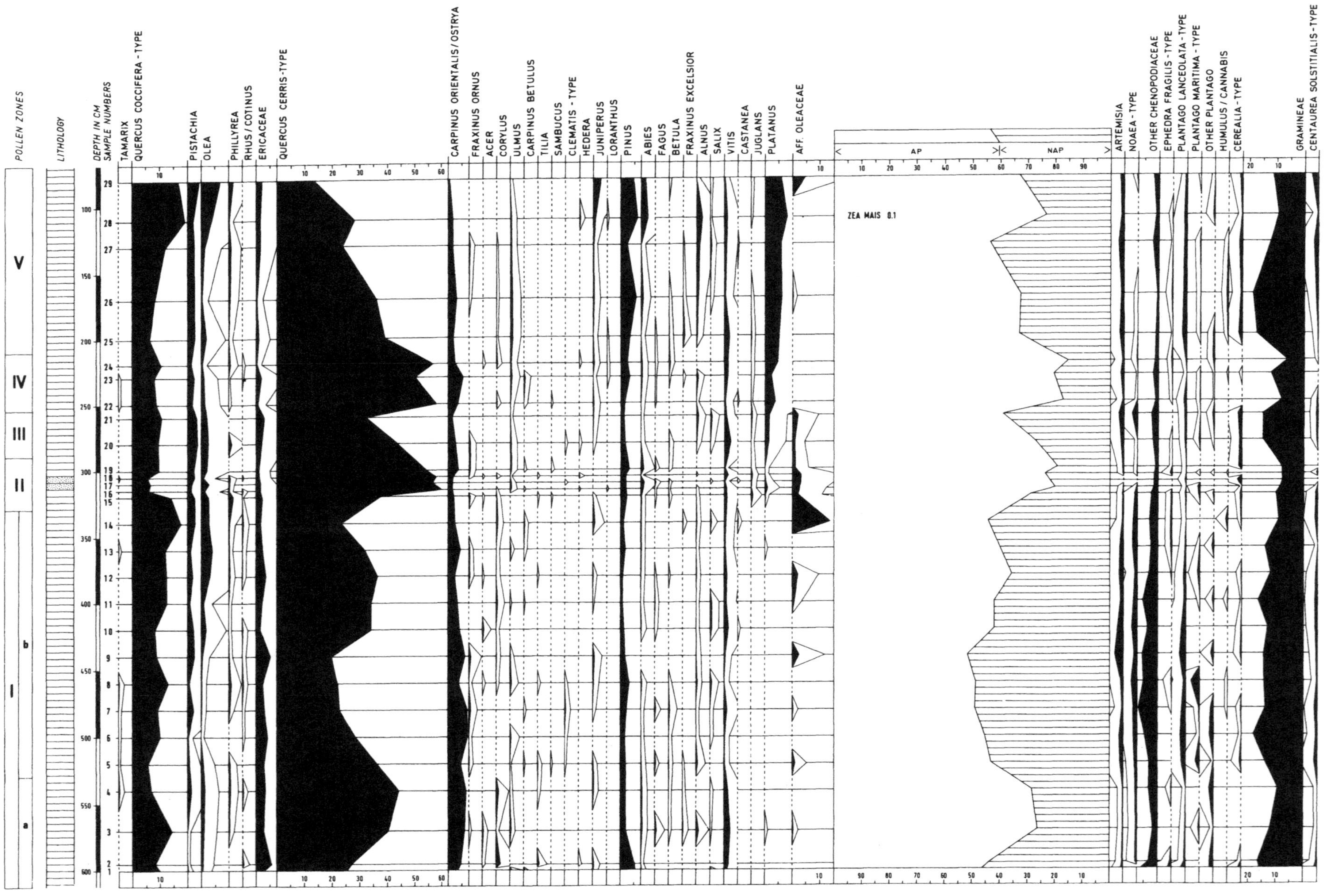

Figure 49. Main part of Trikhonis pollen diagram.

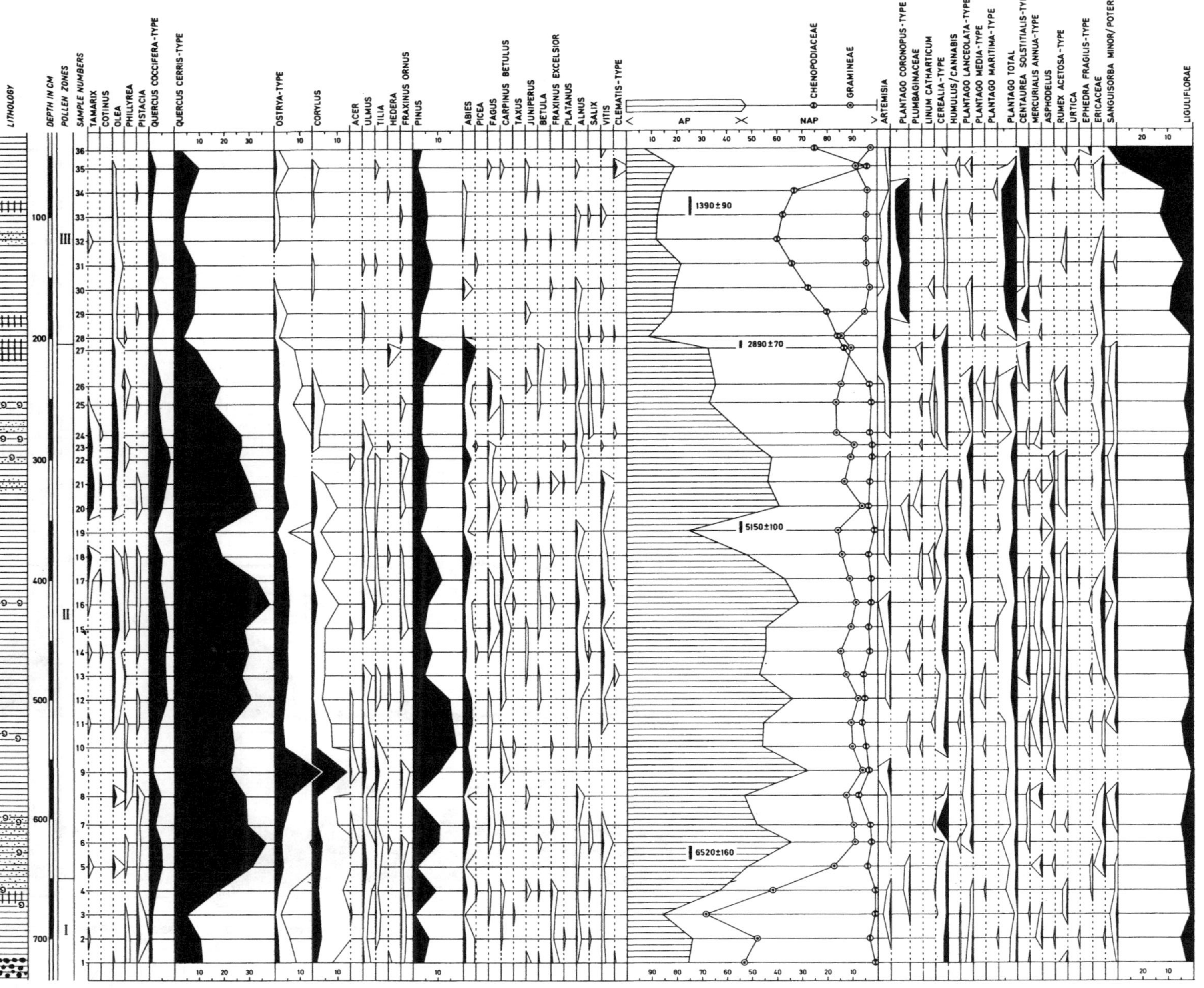

Figure 50. Main part of Halos pollen diagram.

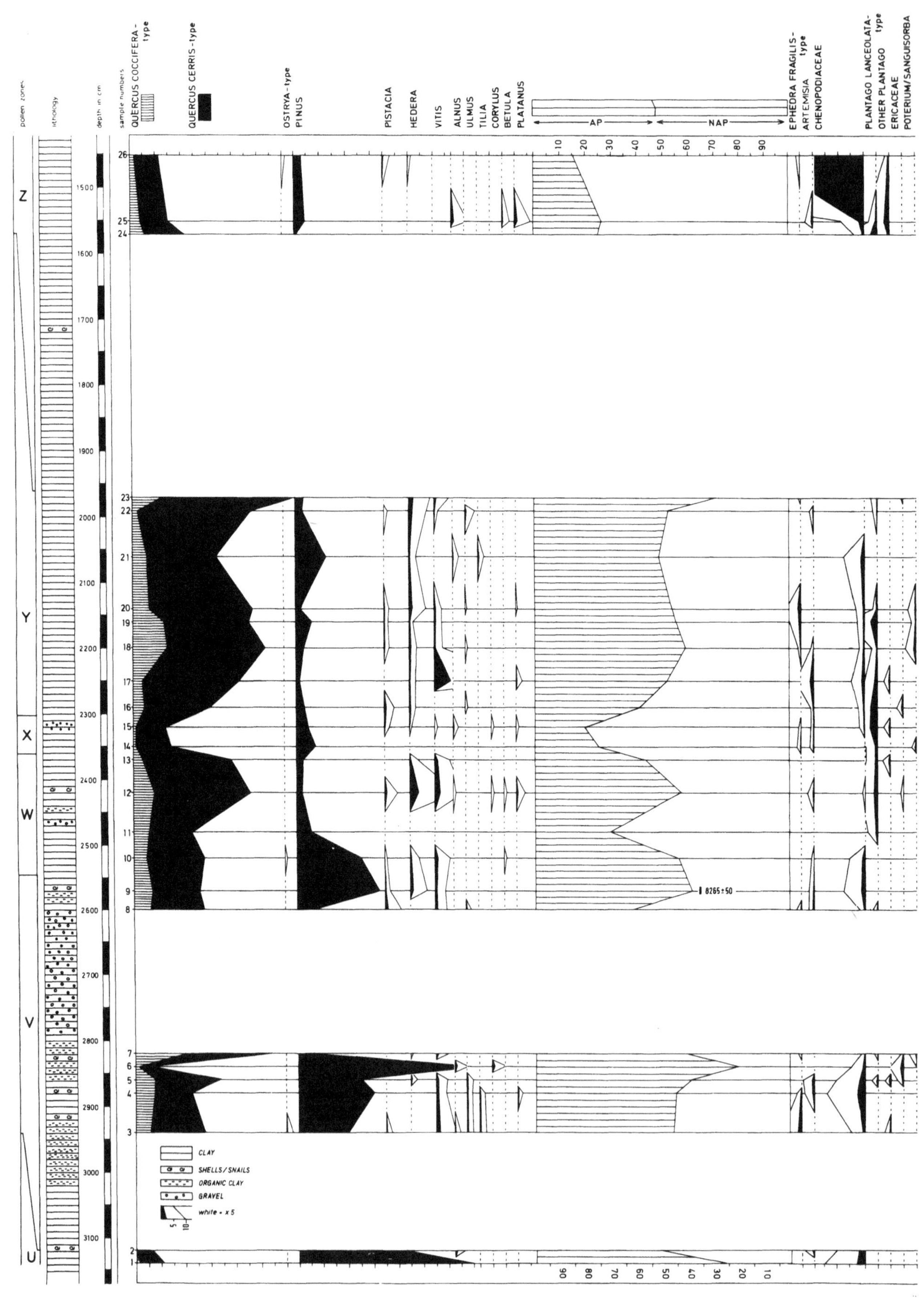

Figure 51. Main part of Aghia Galini pollen diagram.

with C-14-dated diagrams from Greece and Southwest Turkey of which the nearest evidence comes from Voulkaria (Wright 1972), where the increase in olive pollen has been dated after 3040 ± 120 B.P. (I-2866).

Zone I of the Trikhonis diagram demonstrated lower AP values than the following zones II, III and IV, suggesting that conditions for tree growth improved after 3200 B.P. Compared to the Kiladha diagram, this is, however, expressed rather weakly.

Halos

A sediment core from the Eu-Mediterranean vegetation zone in Thessaly has been taken at sea level near the archaeological site of Halos (Bottema in Reinders 1988) (Figure 50). At present, very little natural vegetation is left in the coastal zone or in the adjacent plain of Almiros. According to Voliotis (1973) the coast would be in the zone of the Oleo-Ceratonion. Further inland, still under the influence of the sea, a narrow zone of *Quercus ilex* would have been present. The plains still further inland were once occupied by Ostryo-Carpinion. Rainfall for the area is restricted almost completely to the winter months, autumn, and spring, and hardly reaches 500 mm. The average January temperature for Volos is about 7°C. Summers are very hot.

The Halos sediment, as was also the case in the Kiladha core, started to form on a red Pleistocene soil that was flooded by the rise of sea level. Sandbars were formed in front of the developing bay. Between the coast and the sandbars, sediment was deposited by two small streams. The Halos core has been radiocarbon-dated at four levels (Figure 50), and sedimentation seems to have started at about 7000 B.P. Part of the herb-pollen types at the bottom of the sediment reflect local marsh vegetation. Their numbers depress the upland tree values.

From ca. 6500 B.P. onward, a constant decrease of the tree pollen values is witnessed. The deciduous zone of oak and hopbeam, found in the Almiros plain and in the foothills further inland, suffered from destruction by man. This effect is somewhat exaggerated by abnormally high values of Chenopodiaceae and Liguliflorae in the upper zone III from about 2500 B.P. onward. The chenopods indicate the gradual filling of the basin accompanied by salinization. The influence of man upon the environment seems to have been the main factor that changed the vegetation. In the Halos record no signs of a change in climate can be detected, either around 3200 B.P. or at any other time.

Aghia Galini

A 31-m-long core originating from the Eu-Mediterranean vegetation zone at sea level near Aghia Galini, on the south coast of Crete, contained pollen in the lower half only (Bottema 1980). Even there, several hiatuses occur (Figure 51). At present, temperatures for this part of Crete are 11.8°C for January and 27.4°C for July (Gortynos, Mesara plain). The annual precipitation at Timbaki, about 8 km southeast of Aghia Galini, recorded from 1951-1960, averages 410 mm.

From sea level to 300 m, a vegetation zone is present that includes *Pistacia lentiscus*, *Ceratonio siliqua*, and *Olea europaea*. From 300-1000 m the following constituents are mentioned: *Quercus coccifera*, *Q. ilex*, *Arbutus unedo*, *Pistacia terebinthus*, *Spartium junceum*, *Erica*, *Pteridium*, *Quercus pubescens*, and *Pinus brutia*. A selection of pollen types from the Aghia Galini diagram is shown in Figure 51. From a depth of 27.80 m, a radiocarbon date of 8265 ± 50 B.P. (GrN-6672) was obtained. If a constant sedimentation rate is assumed, the upper 5000 years are not represented by the pollen record.

Up to about 8000 B.P., typical xerophytic evergreen Eu-Mediterranean vegetation does not play a role in the Aghia Galini area. Forest vegetation was mainly formed by deciduous or semi-deciduous oaks and pine, possibly *Pinus brutia*. After 8000 B.P., the pines disappeared and most of the forest consisted of deciduous oaks and, to a lesser extent, evergreen oaks. Herb pollen values point to the presence of, for instance, Umbelliferae.

The open oak forest that developed after ca. 8000 B.P. points to dry conditions not favorable for the growth of pine. Very conspicuous is the absence of *Olea* in the pollen record for at least the older half of the Holocene, whereas olive accounts for 8% to 12% of the modern pollen precipitation in this part of Crete. It may be rather premature to postulate the absence of *Olea* as a natural constituent of the vegetation of Crete on the basis of only one pollen diagram. It should be stressed, however, that the olive has very good pollen production and dispersal. The pollen evidence from the Aghia Galini area demonstrates a tendency towards drier conditions after about 8000 B.P.

A comparison of the pollen sites discussed above with the pollen record of the southern Argolid demonstrates a larger contrast between middle and upper Holocene vegetation in the latter than in other parts of Greece. This may be true for climatic conditions as well.

Comparison of the Pollen Evidence of the Kiladha Core with the Seed Record of Franchthi Cave

The charred plant remains retrieved during the excavations of Franchthi Cave have been treated by Hansen (1978; forthcoming a-b). This record dates back to the Palaeolithic, and the upper limit extends to the Final Neolithic. Hansen's Zone VI, the Middle, Late and Final Neolithic, is covered by the Kiladha pollen diagram, but the upper part of the pollen record is not present in the seed record.

The origin of the charred seeds and plant remains in accumulation layers of open-air sites or in caves is still a matter for discussion, but the presence of a variety of species such as presented by Hansen has undoubtedly an important indicative value. Some of the taxa identified by Hansen (forthcoming a) are also represented in the pollen diagram. It should be stressed that, in the analysis of (charred) seeds, the identification level is generally much higher than in pollen analysis. Seeds of Cruciferae and various Leguminosae are frequently found in the Franchthi record, and these taxa are also fairly well represented in the pollen diagram. Of the tree species, the nuts of *Pistacia* are present in the macrofossil record. *Pistacia* must have been an important constituent of the vegetation of the southern Argolid during the Neolithic, as indicated by the pollen values, and the nuts seem to have been readily available to the inhabitants of Franchthi. Seeds of einkorn wheat (*Triticum monococcum*), emmer wheat (*T. dicoccum*), and two-row barley (*Hordeum distichum*), as well as spikelet forks and glume bases of these species, were common. This is in agreement with the pollen record, which displays important values for Cerealia-type pollen.

ENVIRONMENTAL CHANGES AND HUMAN HABITATION IN THE SOUTHERN ARGOLID AT THE END OF THE FOURTH MILLENNIUM B.P.

For northwestern Europe a pollen zone has been established that starts at about 2500 B.P. and lasts up to the present. This zone was called the Subatlantic and, compared with the preceding phase, it was assumed that the climate became more oceanic. It is not clear whether an identical phase is present in the eastern Mediterranean. Synchronization still forms a major problem, as the climatic phase in the eastern Mediterranean described in this report definitely started earlier (by perhaps 700-1000 years) than the Subatlantic period of temperate Europe.

The change from a dry climate to one that was relatively moist cannot be dated precisely in the Kiladha record. The transition from Zone I to Zone II took place ca. 2700 B.P., if a constant rate of sedimentation is assumed, inferring from the assumed date of 6700 B.P. at 425 cm obtained by correlation with nearby radiocarbon-dated cores OK85/1, lA and lB.

The Zone I/II transition in Kiladha can also be compared and crossdated with identical events found in other pollen diagrams from Greece and Turkey that have been dated by radiocarbon (Bottema 1974; 1982; Bottema and Woldring 1984(1986)). Such correlation dates the Zone I/II transition at about 3500-3200 B.P. It must be stressed, however, that the changes in the pollen record at that time may differ appreciably from one location or area to another. This is easily explained by the fact that conditions in the eastern Mediterranean and the Near East vary widely as regards topography and climate. Nevertheless, a common feature of many sites is that some new pollen types appear at about 3200 B.P. (Bottema 1982). Apart from more general anthropogenic indicators, the appearance of pollen of *Juglans* (walnut), *Platanus* (plane tree), and *Castanea* (sweet chestnut) has drawn attention. In the Kiladha diagram, these types do not play a role, and walnut and sweet chestnut do not grow that far south according to Meusel et al. (1965). The most important type in Kiladha to correlate with dated diagrams from Greece and Turkey is *Olea*.

The characteristics of the pollen assemblages for Greece and southwestern Turkey dated around 3000 B.P. mainly point to the appearance of an advanced horticulture and agriculture. However, the spectra also demonstrate traits pointing to an increase in humidity or to much cooler summers. The arguments for lower temperatures during the summer after ca. 3200 B.P. have been given in Bottema and Woldring (1984(1986)).

The mechanism behind the dramatic change in vegetation, climate, and human activity is not yet understood. One could assume that a more humid climate developed around 3200 B.P. and that prehistoric farmers in the eastern Mediterranean profited from it. But that does not explain the cause of the change in climate. An event that may be connected with the environmental changes discussed above is the rather catastrophic volcanic eruption of Santorini, which has been the subject of much discussion. Baillie and Munro (1988) date the eruption at 1628-1626 B.C. by retarded growth in oak tree rings. The dating of the Santorini eruption is critically reviewed by Pyle (1989) who points to the large scatter of radiocarbon dates and the ambiguity of indirect dating methods. A layer of volcanic ash has been described for a sediment core from the lake of Trikhonis (see above). In the Trikhonis core (Figure 49), the ash layer coincides with a short period of regeneration of the natural vegetation. Indicators of farming decrease or disappear, and deciduous oak in particular strongly expands. The coincidence suggests that the area was abandoned for some time, permitting the regeneration of forest.

A volcanic deposit was discovered by D.G. Sullivan in a core taken from Köycegiz Gölü on the southwest coast of Turkey. The sediment at 414-423 cm was described as clayey sand by van Zeist et al. (1975). Organic sediment on top of the tephra at 389-401 cm was dated 3070 ± 55 BP (GrN-6451). According to Sullivan, the chemical and physical properties of the deposits point to tephra of the Santorini (Thera) eruption. Sullivan (1988) traced Santorini Minoan tephra in western Turkey in the small lake Gölcük, 90 km east of Izmir. A pollen diagram of the Gölcük sediment is in preparation. It is still not clear how far the effect (supposing that there was an effect) of the Santorini eruption extended and what the impact upon the environment was. To what extent was mainland Greece affected by this event? What was the effect upon the plant cover, and at what time of the year did the ash rain occur? To what extent can a volcanic eruption change the climate? All kinds of answers have been given to these questions (Halstead 1982).

We know from past eruptions that the global temperature may decrease about 1-2°C if a large amount of ash is released in the air. However, after one to a few years, temperatures regain their previous levels. In this respect, the correlation of planetary movement and climate proposed by Fairbridge (1987) is of interest. Fairbridge suggests that the position of the sun and the planets

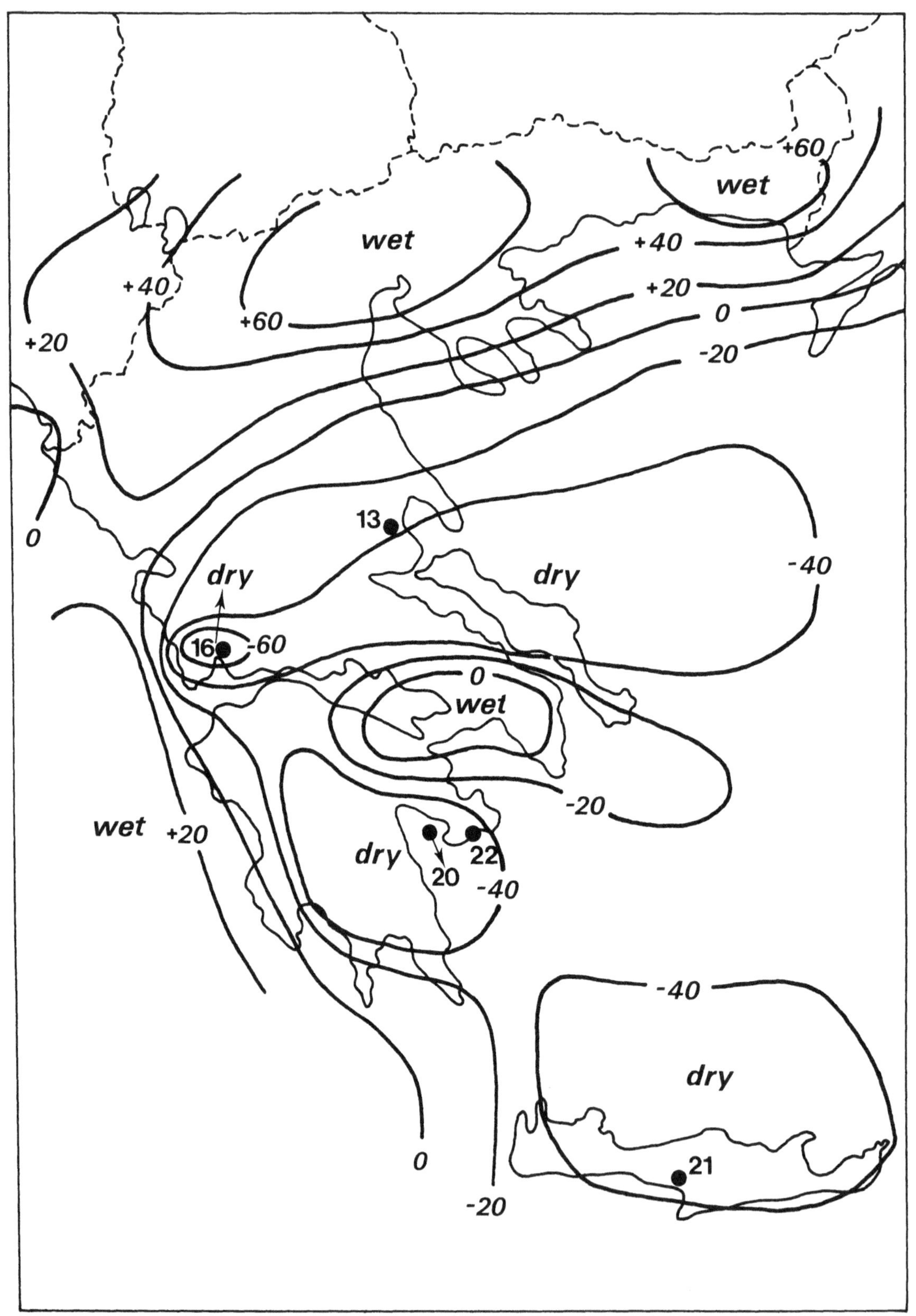

Figure 52. Abnormally dry and wet areas in Greece in January 1955 (after Bryson et al. 1974). Pollen sites discussed in text are indicated by solid circles (cf. Figure 46).

in certain configurations strongly influences climate as well as volcanic activity. The volcanic activity would increase because of changes in gravitation. Thus, changes in climate and volcanic activity would have a common cause, and mutual influence, if present, would not last very long.

Whatever the effect of volcanic activity may have been, it certainly cannot explain all the changes that took place towards the end of the fourth millennium B.P. While the fall of the Minoan culture on the island of Crete has been explained by the Santorini eruption, radiocarbon-dated to ca. 3300 B.P., some authors suggest another catastrophe to have caused the downfall of the Myceneans about 300 years later. Invading barbarians from the north (Childe 1958:157), raids by the "Sea Peoples" who destroyed Mycenean trade (Stibbe 1964), and variations on such themes have been brought forward to explain the sudden disappearance of the Myceneans from the Argolid.

Another suggestion was made by Carpenter (1966), who thinks that the Mycenean decline was caused by a prolonged drought that disrupted agriculture. Carpenter suggested that a period of severe drought occurred around 1200 B.C. (1966:46) in the Argolid, but not in northern Greece or other parts of southern Greece, including Attica. This idea was strongly criticized by Wright (1968), although not much evidence against the drought theory could be provided. Carpenter's theory is supported by Bryson et al. (1974), who stated that "if a year can be found that has the appropriate pattern to fit the field evidence from some past century, there is no meteorological reason why that pattern could not exist as the dominant pattern for a century or more." In fact, such a pattern occurred in 1954-1955 (Figure 52).

The cause of the extreme drought may be looked for in volcanic activity. Baillie and Munro (1988) draw attention to the event of 1159 B.C. (measured from tree-ring growth in calendar years) that is almost certainly linked with the eruption of Hekla. According to them, it took 19 years for the trees they investigated to return to a normal pattern of tree-ring growth. It is not impossible that the age of the conspicuous changes in pollen diagrams from Greece and western Turkey, around 3200 B.P., is connected with this event. Baillie and Munro (1988:346) note Kelly and Sears's study of the climatic impact of explosive eruptions causing pressure changes resulting in quite different weather patterns.

If we scan the Kiladha diagram, there are no clear signs of a pronounced drought effect around the Zone I/II boundary that can be deduced from the pollen assemblages. One may wonder whether short and extreme fluctuations in the climate are expressed in the pollen rain and can be read from pollen diagrams. Fluctuations in the weather are very normal, but such fluctuations are inconspicuous in the pollen record because of the way the samples are taken. In general, the thickness of a sample is 1 cm of sediment. In the Kiladha diagram, the number of samples is 31, representing 7.4% of the sediment that covers ca. 6700 years. One sample represents about 16 years on average. If we assume that ten to twenty years of extreme drought change the composition of the pollen rain, the chances of tracing that in the pollen spectra are slight because the space between the spectra varied from 5 to 20 cm and the dry period could be present between the spectra. A dry period that can ruin a farming economy affects annual plants, such as cereals, much more than perennial herbs or deep-rooted trees. The continuous curve of the Cerealia-type does not support an extremely dry period. It is only during Zone II that this pollen type strongly reacts at the time that the forest expands. The lack of palaeobotanical evidence in favor of a dry period in the Argolid weakens the statement by Bryson et al. (1974:50) "that the evidence is sufficient to justify Carpenter's drought hypothesis as the only one presently available that is consistent with extant evidence."

Developing Carpenter's theme, however, the January 1955 map of Bryson et al. (1974) that shows the departure from normal in percentages has one very attractive aspect. Instead of applying this to an assumed drought period connected with the disappearance of the Myceneans, it could be applied to the whole of Kiladha Zone I. The dry conditions that ruled the Peloponnesus at least from the beginning of the seventh millennium to the end of the fourth millennium occurred at the same time that conditions in other parts of Greece witnessed an increase in moisture.

The pollen record of Greece, the eastern Mediterranean, and the Near East invariably points to the end of the fourth millennium B.P. as a conspicuous transition in terms of vegetation and climate, but especially crucial in the prehistory of man. The author is of the opinion that the events on Crete and the Peloponnesus are not isolated, but that they are in some way connected with more widespread phenomena, natural and/or man-induced.

APPENDIXES

The Onshore Investigations: Supporting Data

APPENDIX A

The Stratigraphic Contexts of the Paralia Walls

The prime objective of this volume has been to describe the archaeological sediments with a view toward understanding their mode and sequence of deposition. During this work, however, it has been possible to place the built structures in a preliminary stratigraphic order. This is presented here in a provisional manner with full awareness that the final site phasing may in fact rearrange the order somewhat. (See plan, Figure 25, and balloon photograph, Plate 1.)

Wall A[8]	Q5. In the northern section of Q5N, strata III, IV, V, and possibly VI have been cut by a foundation trench filled by stratum VII. Wall A is therefore contemporary with VII and is apparently postdated by strata XXIII and XXIV. Wall A is below Wall B and above Wall H (see Jacobsen and Farrand 1987:Plates 55 and 56).
Wall B[8]	Q5. Wall B is a late wall built on or just within Q5 XXIX (Jacobsen and Farrand 1987:Plate 55). It is within or postdated by Q5 XXXII. It is above Wall A. [Wall B was removed before the photograph in Plate 1 was taken.—EDITOR]
Wall C[8]	Q5. Wall C rests partly on Q5 III, which had accumulated behind a boulder. Wall C was apparently built to incorporate that boulder. In the southern section of Q5N, strata IV and V have accumulated behind Wall C, which in turn acted as a barrier across the slope. This is the type sequence for the class B and C sediments (Chapter 4). Wall C is stratigraphically earlier than Wall A.
Wall D	Q5. Stratum XIV appears to have accumulated immediately behind Wall D and therefore must immediately postdate that wall (Jacobsen and Farrand 1987:Plate 54).
Wall E	QR5 (and very southern edge of Q5). Wall E appears to be an early wall behind which Q5 XVI accumulated. Q5 XVII was built against Wall E (Jacobsen and Farrand 1987:Plate 50). QR5 IV postdates the wall. Wall E was refaced by Wall J at a relatively early date. Wall F appears to have been built against E, probably after Wall E had suffered some collapse.
Wall F	Q6, just penetrates into Q5. Wall F appears to have been built against Wall G. The artificial surface of Q5 XXVII was built against Wall F. This "floor" is also built against Wall H, and therefore Wall F, stratum XXVII, and Wall H are roughly contemporary. Wall F is postdated by Q5 XXVIII.

Wall G	Q5. Wall G is built upon 15-20 cm of reddish talus, which in turn rests upon stony red colluvium. It may have been bonded to Wall C, but at a relatively late phase of that wall's use. The C/G relationship remains uncertain, however. Wall G was probably in use at the same time as Walls F and H and Floor Q5 XXVII.
Wall H	Q5. Wall H is contemporary with Q5 XXVII (therefore with Wall F and possibly Wall G). It just penetrates into square Q6N where it is built upon Q6 stratum IV or is immediately postdated by Q6 stratum VIIa (Jacobsen and Farrand 1987:Plate 55). Wall H is below Wall A. N.B. Wall A in Q5 north section is built upon or is contemporary with Q5 XXI and XXII. These in turn are equivalent to the top units of Q6N VII.
Wall J	Wall J is a late refacing of Wall E.
Wall K	P5. Strata P5 III and IV accumulated behind Wall K (Jacobsen and Farrand 1987:Plate 48). It is postdated by strata XV and XI, which also postdate Wall L. Wall K may have been contemporary with Walls A and Q, but it was not possible to prove this in the field. Wall K may have acted as a barrier to prevent talus inundating structure LMN. The equation LMN = K = A does not contradict the overall stratigraphy.
Wall L	P5. Wall L is postdated by strata XI and XV. Strata P5 XIV and XII are probably part of the same construction phase as Wall L: pisé superstructure and floor, respectively. Wall L is contemporary with Walls M and N.
Walls M and N	P5. See Wall L (*supra*).
Walls P and R	P5. Walls P and R are possibly contemporary with Wall Q, but this is uncertain.
Wall Q	P5. Wall Q was constructed approximately on top of stratum P5 XVII (Jacobsen and Farrand 1987:Plate 55). It is postdated by P5 XVIII. Its relationship to P5 XVII makes it postdate Q6N VII and puts it at a similar stratigraphic level to Wall A. P5 XIII was built against it, and it therefore is part of the same construction phase as structure LMN.
Wall S	P5. The stratigraphic context here is unclear. If Wall S can be related to Wall Q, it can then be placed in its stratigraphic context.
Wall T	Q4. It was not possible to relate Wall T to the main stratigraphic sequence, but it is probably immediately postdated by the units east of it: Q4:109-129.
Wall U	O5. This is uncertain, but O5 strata II-IV appear to have accumulated behind Wall U.
Wall V	O5. Wall V is postdated by at least O5 strata XVI and XVII. It is at the same stratigraphic level as Wall L in P5.
Wall W	L5. Wall W was first exposed during the excavation of Units 18 and 19 (stratum V). It was completely exposed by Unit 26 (IV/V). During the excavation of Unit 31 (IV), soil was removed from between stones of the wall. Units 18-26 presumably postdate Wall W, which must therefore predate stratum V. Wall W is within stratum IV sediments (Figure 35). As its base is within stratum IV, it was probably built at that time.

Wall X — L5. Wall X was first exposed during the excavation of Unit 62 (strata VI and IX). Units 70-76 lay against the wall and postdate it; Unit 76 was situated near its base. Except for Unit 70, which belongs to stratum VI, all belong to stratum X. Wall X must predate stratum VI, probably also stratum X. It was most likely built between strata X and XII, but the stratigraphic control is weak. (Cf. Jacobsen and Farrand 1987:Plates 57 and 58.)

Wall Y — Q6. Wall Y was built upon stratum Q6 VI. It was postdated by Q6 VII (Jacobsen and Farrand 1987:Plate 52). Therefore, it is probably contemporary with Walls F, G, and H.

Wall Z — QR5. Wall Z is a small curved structure below QR5 stratum V.

Wall AA — L5. Wall AA was removed during the excavation of Unit 15. Contexts to the east of wall: Units 4, 9, and 11 (all of stratum L5 V). Contexts to the west of wall: Units 6 and 12 (stratum V?). Units 4, 6, 9, 11, and 12 accumulated against the wall and probably postdate its use. Unit 15 will also include some material that postdates the wall's use. Wall AA should postdate Unit 17 (stratum V), which lies beneath it.

Structure BB — L5. Structure BB is not a built wall but an area of disturbance represented by stratum VII, either a pit or a wall-robbing trench. If the latter, the stones were robbed during or after the deposition of stratum VI.

Wall CC — L5. The relationship of Wall CC to Wall AA is uncertain, but they are probably approximately contemporary. Wall CC has sediments of stratum VI accumulated against its northern face (Figure 35). It then appears to have collapsed onto that stratum.

APPENDIX B

Catalogue of Strata

This appendix presents descriptions of major stratigraphic units for most grid squares or grid-square sections in the Paralia excavations. Following each heading, references are given to master and secondary section drawings, which illustrate the strata being discussed. These references are to plates appearing in Jacobsen and Farrand 1987, unless otherwise noted. In the "Description" portion of the discussion of each stratum, "S.D." refers to the horizon references of Susan Duhon (see Chapter 2).

The following is a directory of the grid squares or sections discussed in this appendix:

Grid Square/Section	*Page*
L5	145
O5N	149
P5	153
Q5N	158
Q5S	162
Q5 East	165
Q5S West	167
QR5	168
Q6N North	170
Q6N East	171
Q6N South	173

L5 MAJOR STRATIGRAPHIC UNITS

Master section drawings: Figure 35, this volume; Plate 44
Secondary section drawings: Plates 43, 57-63

I

Position:	At base of succession as elsewhere on Paralia. Gradual interface with II (boundary type 5).[9]
Geometry:	Random stones. Top of layer dips roughly downslope.
Description:	Yellowish red (5YR 5/6 moist) clay loam. Locally sandy, abundant stones, all sizes to boulders. High Fe_2O_3; low organic carbon. S.D. L9 (V B 22b). Sedimentary class A.
Context quality:	In situ, undisturbed.
Cultural material:	Absent.
Units:	L5:54.
Interpretation:	Late Pleistocene and early Holocene subsoil and ground surface (see sedimentary class A).

II

Position:	Above I. Upper boundary distinct (type 4).
Geometry:	Weakly developed strata dip to west.
Description:	Yellowish red (5YR 4/6 moist) loam, abundant talus stones mainly less than 5 cm, long axis. Localized fall-sorting indicative of active talus; voids common. High Fe_2O_3, low organic carbon. S.D. L8 (V B 21b).
Context quality:	Not disturbed, but note that human skull fragments in Unit 48 may be intrusive. In addition, localized movement on active talus slope gives continuous re-sorting.
Cultural material:	Present throughout.
Units:	L5:44-52, 43 at interface with III, 53 at II/I interface. L5NE:59, 60, 62, 63, 64, 65, 66, 67, 68; 58, 61 mixed.
Interpretation:	Active talus accumulation, occupation in vicinity, but probably not actually at this point.

III

Position:	Above II. Boundary with IV above, clear (type 3) where thin reddish layer appears in section.
Geometry:	Subhorizontal, some stones and sherds set horizontally. Five to six large fish vertebrae, two of which were articulated, noted in L5:39.
Description:	Dark brown (10YR 3/3 moist), brown when dry; silt loam, single-grained. Occasional stones but less stony than II; localized charcoal. Low clay, high organic carbon, low Fe_2O_3. S.D. L7 (IV C 4). Sedimentary class B.
Context quality:	In situ; minimal disturbance, gradual accretion of sediments.
Cultural material:	Present throughout. Thin reddish layer at top of III L5:37; L5NE:50 appears to be floor, possibly related to robbed-out "wall" of stratum VII.
Units:	L5:39-41; Units 38 and 42 probably mixed with IV. L5NE:54-57, 59-61; 52, 54, 58, and 62 probably mixed.
Interpretation:	Steady accretion of sediment on subhorizontal surfaces with in-situ occupation at top, possibly throughout layer.

IV

Position:	Above III. Gradual boundary with V (type 5). Cut by VII to west in north scarp.
Geometry:	Subhorizontal as for III. Articulated fish vertebrae removed in Unit 50 indicate minimal disturbance.
Description:	Dark brown (7.5 YR 3/2 moist), pale brown when dry; silt loam, few stones in section. Moderately high Fe_2O_3. S.D. L6 (IV C 3) and S.D. L5 (IV C 2). Sedimentary class C.
Context quality:	Minimal disturbance; gradual accretion of sediments.
Cultural material:	Present throughout. Thin red layer in vicinity of Unit 30 (L5) may be second floor.
Units:	On possible "floor" L5:37; L5NE:50, 52. L5:27-30, 32-36. Units 25, 26 probably mixed. L5NE:45, 48, 49, 52. Units 34, 35, 42, 43, and 46 probably mixed.
Interpretation:	Steady accretion of sediments on subhorizontal surfaces, possibly with in-situ occupation.

Note on III and IV: These form a virtually continuous sequence of aggradation on subhorizontal surfaces. Flat-lying stones and sherds are common, and two incidences of articulated fish vertebrae in subhorizontal positions reinforce the impression of minimal disturbance. The possible floors indicate in-situ occupation. The deposits appear not to have been disturbed by cultivation. A possible east-west wall (W) exposed in Units 21-30 (L5) appears to have been in use during stratigraphic unit IV. The disturbed area VII which cuts IV (including the possible floor of Unit 50) and upper III may represent a robbed-out northwest-southeast wall. The accumulation upon subhorizontal surfaces implies some terracing downslope in order to trap the soil.

V

Position: Above IV. Although only gradual interface with IV below, the sedimentary difference between IV and V is considerable. IV/V boundary interpreted as stratigraphic discontinuity (type 2). Cut by VII to south (type 1 boundary). In north scarp, distinct boundaries above and below.

Geometry: Unclear, but has partly accumulated behind boulder in south scarp and behind Wall AA later.

Description: Dark reddish brown (5YR 3/4 moist) clay loam; abundant angular talus stones but subrounded non-limestone gravel also present; occasional voids. High clay, high Fe_2O_3, low organic carbon.
S.D. L4 (III C 1).
Stratum V is much more stony in L5 than in L5NE. The stones decrease rapidly in the vicinity of a possible collapsed wall (Wall CC) visible in east scarp. To north of this wall, V is replaced by VI and a less stony variant of V continues beneath this possible wall into the north scarp.

Context quality: Uncertain. No gross disturbance obvious, possibly continuously re-sorted as in talus.

Cultural material: Present throughout. Possible wall (CC) visible in east scarp may relate to north-south wall (AA) exposed between Units 2 and 15 in L5 and removed in Unit 15.

Units: L5:4, 5, 8, 9, 10, 11, 17, 18, 20. Units 23 and 24 on interface. Contexts of uncertain reliability in trench center: 6, 7, 12, 16, 19, 21. Unit 3 transitional to VII above.
L5NE: Owing to possible cross-cutting of stratum VII, all sediments of V in L5NE *may* be mixed. Cross-cut or mixed: 26, 29, 30, 32, 33, 35, 36, 38, 40, 43. Mixed at interface: 25. Unmixed: 28.

Interpretation: A complex layer of uncertain genesis. High talus content, high Fe_2O_3, high clay matrix resembles basal colluvium; cultural material suggests presence of occupation in vicinity. The two possible walls, AA and CC, partly contain stratum V material, but this also runs beneath Wall W. Slumping from upslope may account for the stony southern part of V.

VI

Position: Above V. Interface with V diffuse but smooth. Clear difference between sediments of V and VI suggest stratigraphic discontinuity of at least Type 3. This *may* represent a hiatus.

Geometry: Restricted to L5NE and L5NW where the sediment body dips gently to west. Filled pits 1 and 2 in northwest.

Description: Very pale brown (10YR 7/4 dry) to pink (7.5 YR 7/4 dry or 10YR 7/2). Silt loam, few stones, very calcareous with common $CaCO_3$ nodules. High silt, low organic carbon, and smectite dominant clay mineral.
S.D. 3 (II B 22). Sedimentary class H.

Context quality: Not disturbed except where cut by VII (see section).

Cultural material: Present throughout and includes possible industrial use of silt.

Units: L5:13, 14, 22 (from pit).
L5NE:13, 17, 18, 19, 23, 24, 29, 32. Unit 1 possibly mixed.
Pit 1: 63-67. Pit 2: 95-98.
L5NE, possibly VI but not in trench scarp: 4, 5, 6, 8, 9, 10, 12, 14, 16, 20, 25, 34, 40.
L5NW, relatively unmixed: 58-61, 70. Mixed: 56, 57, 62, 68, 86-88.
Judging from soil descriptions, 96-98 may be slightly mixed.

Interpretation: Very distinctive deposit which may have been used for industrial purposes. The abundance of $CaCO_3$ nodules suggests that it may have been calcified originally.

VII

Position: Cuts III, IV, V and VI (type 1).

Geometry: Forms pit or trough in section. Excavator noted it as soft area limited to northwestern corner of L5NE. Sketch plans and unit notes suggest, however, that an elongate northwest-southeast feature extended across entire square (see L5NE:11). This entire feature is tentatively included within VII.

Description: Brown (10YR 4/3) loam, abundant stones, very mixed, stones at random. Locally very soft. Sedimentary class J.

Context quality: Intrudes as disturbance through four stratigraphic units. Although noted and well defined in some excavation units, elsewhere, notably in whole trench passes, material from VII is probably mixed with that of IV and V.

Cultural material: Present throughout.

Units: All L5NE:7, 11, 15, 37, 39, 41, 44, 47, 49, 51, 53. Possibly of VII or mixed interface: 2, 3, 16, 20, 21, 27, 30, 33, 35, 36, 38, 43.

Interpretation: Either a pit cut from the top of stratum VI or disturbance resulting from stone-robbing. If the latter, it might have been a stratum IV wall (i.e., Wall BB) robbed during or a little after stratum VI.

VIII

Position: Above V, below IX.
Geometry: North-south lens in east scarp, otherwise uncertain.
Description: Brown (7.5 YR 4/4) stony loam. Sedimentary class F.
Context quality: Poorly defined, probably mixed with V below and IX above.
Cultural material: Present throughout.
Units: L5:2, 3.
Interpretation: High talus component possibly contemporary with VI to north.

IX

Topsoil: For full description with analytical data, see Chapter 2.

Strata X-XIII are all situated in L5NW.

X

Position: Below VI; against and above wall in southwest of L5NW.
Geometry: Uncertain.
Description: Brown (10YR 4/3) loam, relatively stone free.[10]
Context quality: Of variable quality, stratigraphic control weak.
Cultural material: Present throughout.
Units: 69, 78, 81, 82. Slightly mixed: 71-78.
Interpretation: Uncertain, but Wall X must predate this stratum.

XI

Position: Below VI, in center of trench.
Geometry: Uncertain.
Description: Brown (10YR 5/3) stony.
Context quality: Of uncertain reliability, probably mixed with VI and XIII.
Cultural material: Present throughout.
Units: 79, 80, 88, 89, all relatively mixed. Units 91-93 mixed with XIII.
Interpretation: Uncertain.

XII

Position: Below X in southwest of trench.
Geometry: Stratum occurs at various elevations.
Description: Strong brown (7.5 YR 5/6).
Cultural material: Present throughout.
Units: 83, 84.
Interpretation: Although this resembles the basal red colluvium (stratum I), the presence of abundant artifacts indicates that this is a cultural deposit which possibly includes some colluvium.

XIII

Position: Below XI in center of trench.
Geometry: —
Description: Strong brown (7.5YR 5/6). Locally stony.
Context quality: Mixed with XI.
Cultural material: Throughout.
Units: 90, 91-94, 99.
Interpretation: As for XII.

O5N MAJOR STRATIGRAPHIC UNITS[11]

Master section drawings: Plates 45-47, 54
Secondary section drawings: Plates 64, 65

Strata II-III in north scarp only.

I

Red colluvium, as elsewhere on Paralia. Sedimentary class A.

II

Position: Above I, moderately distinct interfaces above and below (type 4).
Geometry: Gently dipping layer, continues up to boulder in section.
Description: Very pale brown (10YR 7/4 dry) loam, common medium gravel.
Context quality: Good.
Units: 83-86. Unit 81 possibly cross-cut.
Interpretation: See below.

III

Position: Above II, below IV. Diffuse boundary above and below (type 4).
Geometry: Subhorizontal layer, again accumulated behind boulder to west.
Description: Reddish yellow (7.5YR 7/6 dry) loam. Common medium gravel; soft.

Context quality: Probably cross-cut during excavation.
Units: 80. Units 81 and 83 probably cross-cut with II.
Interpretation: See below.

Strata IV, V, VI, VII, and IX are visible in north and east scarps, and stratum IX in south scarp as well.

IV

Position: Above III, below V. Distinct upper interface emphasized in north scarp by thin layer of reddish clay loam (included within IV).
Geometry: Thick, roughly horizontal accumulation.
Description: Complex layer comprising: reddish yellow (7.5YR 7/6 dry) and light yellowish brown (10YR 6/4 dry), soft and loose silt loam and loam. Abundant gravel. Reddish yellow (5YR 5/6 dry) layer: hard with occasional stones; forms upper interface in north scarp.
Context quality: Appears well defined. See below.
Units: 46, 60, 61, 63, 65, 66, 67, 73, 74, 77. Near IV/V interface: 60. Near III/IV interface: 78.
Interpretation: Sedimentary evidence equivocal. Strata II-IV could be talus accumulation behind barrier situated immediately downslope. Alternatively, the reddish layer, III, appears to be a redistributed red colluvium (class A, not class D). In addition, pottery from Unit 65 joined that from O5NE:32 and 35 (in stratum VI) and a complete vessel was recovered from IV (Plate 46). The pottery joins and whole pot argue for contemporaneity or near contemporaneity of IV-VI. In 1974, stratum III was interpreted as "backfill." These layers might have accumulated in a pit, but the paleoslope beneath at 31° is only a little steeper than the midslope above. See also Interpretation of V-VII.

V

Position: Above IV, merges up into VI, diffuse interface (type 5).
Geometry: Rough horizontal layer. Stops to west in north scarp at red-hued lens, possibly related to red layer IX. In east scarp, layer is of variable thickness.
Description: Light yellowish brown (10YR 6/4 dry) silt loam, occasional stones.
Context quality: Although distinct in section, quality uncertain.
Units: 59. Possibly 49NE and 46NE. See stratum VI.
Interpretation: See stratum VII.

VI

Position: Above V, below VII, merging interfaces above and below.
Geometry: Roughly horizontal layer, rather poorly defined in spite of distinctive "dark gray" color. In north scarp, pinched out to west by VII.
Description: Grayish brown (10YR 5/2 dry) silt loam, occasional stones. Gray color may derive from high proportion of charcoal dust, but no data available. A heat-blackened sherd was recorded in 05NE:32.
Context quality: Well defined, but appears cross-cut locally on section drawings.
Units: All O5NE:30-33, 35, 36, 38. N.B. Mixing of excavation unit tags prior to final drawing resulted in loss of information for V, VI, VII, and IX.
Interpretation: See stratum VII.

VII

Position: Above VI. Diffuse boundary with IX above (type 4).

Geometry: Roughly horizontal, but of varying thickness. In east scarp, pinches out to south. In north scarp, extends beyond VI and merges with V below. Eight subhorizontal sherds noted.

Description: Very pale brown (10YR 7/4 dry) silt loam, rare-to-occasional stones.

Context quality: Well defined in section. No evidence of cross-cutting on section drawing.

Units: Only 23NE and 27NE. See stratum VI.

Interpretation: V-VII. All appear to belong to single complex, but frequent horizontal sherds indicate accretion on horizontal surfaces. Apparent link of V with VII in north scarp and associated pinching out of VI possibly suggest a rapid rate of deposition. Abovementioned interunit joins also suggest rapid rate of deposition from IV-VII. If VI originally contained much charcoal, this might suggest an ash dump. Following accumulation of IV, surface appears to have aggraded steadily in horizontal increments. The rate of deposition cannot be stated here but, judging from the stones/sherd orientation, the accumulation of V-VII was not instantaneous. It might be the result of steady but quite rapid aggradation of a series of ash dumps. Following their deposition, V-VII were overlaid by a zone of stratum IX deposits. There was possibly a phase of erosion between the accumulation of VII and IX.

VIII

Position: Below IX, diffuse interface in east scarp becomes distinct (type 4) in south.

Geometry: Small layer with gently dipping upper interface.

Description: Brown (10YR 5/3 dry) silt loam. Rare medium-to-fine gravel. In section indicated by symbols for gray loam, silt loam, and brown loam.

Context quality: Small context, possibly some mixing with IX above.

Units: 50, 51, 56, 57, 58, 88, 89, 90.

Interpretation: Occupies similar stratigraphic position to V-VII but not joined, therefore marked separately. Appears to represent aggradation on controlled slope.

IX

Position: Above V, VI, VII, and VIII. Upper interface generally diffuse but quite clear in east scarp.

Geometry: Occupies most of eastern half of O5. In east scarp drops down to south to progressively overlie VII, VI, V, and VIII.

Description: Reddish yellow (7.5YR 6/6 dry) sandy clay loam. Rare medium-to-fine stones, common small serpentinite pebbles. Layer most obvious in south scarp. In north scarp, where it attains highest elevation, IX contains abundant medium-to-large stones. Sedimentary class D.

Context quality: Although locally clear in section, this layer was cross-cut in many places.

Units: Of uncertain reliability: 12, 13; for 12-19NE, see note for stratum VI.

Interpretation: Color and presence of numerous serpentinite pebbles suggest that this sediment was introduced to site. Stones in northeast of grid square contained within IX may derive from collapsed wall. Stratum IX might have come from its collapsed superstructure.

X

Position: Above IX. Well defined in east scarp, poorly defined with diffuse interfaces elsewhere.

Geometry: In east scarp: broad zone of talus stones with boulders infilling trough.

Description: Light yellowish brown (10YR 6/4 dry) loam, soft and loose. Abundant medium-to-coarse gravel, unoriented. Sherds also at random, some vertical or at steep angles. Sedimentary class G.

Context quality: Active talus, therefore will include much material rolled from upslope.

Units:	4, 6, 7, 8, 12, 17, 19, 20, 22, 34.
Interpretation:	Active talus, possibly accumulated behind wall or boulders, but only clear evidence shows on south scarp. Merges up into topsoil (XX) in north scarp. In places appears to have soil B horizon developed in upper 20-30 cm.

XI

Position:	Small patch of silt, very clearly situated between boulders in southeastern corner.
Geometry:	Uncertain, but defined by two boulders.
Description:	Light gray (10YR 7/2 dry) fine, well-sorted silt loam. Contains common, small, white chalk-like inclusions vaguely similar to burnt limestone. Sedimentary class H.
Context quality:	Well defined and clear, probably good context but stratigraphically very late.
Units:	Indeterminate.
Interpretation:	Very similar to L5 VI and in similar stratigraphic position. See L5 VI and text.

XII onwards south scarp only.

XII

Position:	Above I, relatively clear with type 4 interface above and below.
Geometry:	Dips parallel to paleoslope of underlying red colluvium.
Description:	Two components. Above: reddish yellow (7.5YR 7/6 dry) silty clay loam, stones absent. Below: light yellowish brown (10YR 6/4 dry) loam, few stones.
Context quality:	Uncertain but appears well defined.
Units:	94, 95, 98, 99, 100-103. Possibly also 104-105.
Interpretation:	Uncertain. Red-hued material may be introduced sediment, gray appears to have accumulated on a controlled slope. This is location of attenuated sequence in P5NE, and the red may be equivalent to P5 II.

XIII

Position:	Above XII, below XIV. Diffuse interface defined by stone content.
Geometry:	Triangular accumulation behind boulder of Wall K.
Description:	Light yellowish brown (10YR 6/4 dry) loam, soft, loose. Abundant medium-to-coarse gravel. Sedimentary class G.
Context quality:	Incorporates material from upslope.
Units:	43, 87, 92, 93.
Interpretation:	Accumulated behind Wall K. Equivalent to P5 III or IV.

XIV

Position:	Above XIII, merges up into topsoil (XX).
Geometry:	Small stone-free lens downslope of large boulder.
Description:	Brown (10YR 5/3 dry) silt loam, occasional stones.
Context quality:	Uncertain.
Units:	30-34, 38-40.
Interpretation:	Probably accumulated in lee of boulder. Correlated with P5 V.

XV

Position:	At base of excavated sequence, below Wall V, merges up into XVI.
Geometry:	Thick accumulation between Wall V and stones in scarp which might represent extension of Wall L from P5. Many horizontal sherds.
Description:	Mainly pale brown (10YR 6/3 dry) loam. Occasional stones of all sizes. Soft and loose.

Context quality: Although deep and poorly defined, appears to be relatively good context with little obvious disturbance. Possibly includes material rolled from upslope.

Units: 124, 125, 130-138.

Interpretation: Aggradation of horizontal increments possibly within or adjacent to built structure. The soft matrix and numerous stones suggest input of talus-type material, but not active talus slope. Correlated with P5 XI.

XVI and XVII As for XV, very unclear interface between XVI and XV and between XVI and XVII. Interpretation as for XV. Units: 112, 113, 118, 127, 128, 129.

XVIII

Position: Above XVII, overlies Wall V; associated deposit (shown "gray" on Plate 47) overlies Wall K. Merging interfaces above and below.

Geometry: Gently dipping layer or horizon, parallel to modern ground surface.

Description: Light brown (7.5YR 6/4 dry) clay loam with fine gravel.

Context quality: Probably incorporates much material from upslope. Of uncertain reliability.

Units: 24, 25, 26, 31, 32, 33, 34, 112.

Interpretation: Possibly accumulated downslope of wall (not lettered), which then collapsed on top of it (see XIX). May also include soil B horizon. Correlated with P5 XV.

XIX

Position: Above XVIII, merges up into topsoil.

Geometry: Similar to topsoil but includes dipping layer of large stones which appear to represent collapsed wall of late stratigraphic date.

Description: Yellowish brown (10YR 5/4 dry) loam with abundant stones which enclose many voids. Sedimentary class F.

Context quality: Very late and includes material from upslope.

Units: 5, 6, 9, 15, 16, 20, 21.

Interpretation: Collapsed wall which has progressively collapsed downslope.

XX Topsoil; see descriptions from elsewhere on Paralia. Sedimentary class K.

P5 MAJOR STRATIGRAPHIC UNITS

Master section drawings: Plates 48, 49, 54, 55
Secondary section drawing: Plate 66

I

Position: At base of sequence as basal red colluvium elsewhere. In P5, this is mixed or merges with II above, which might be a later deposit introduced by man.

Geometry: As elsewhere, but note that very steep upper interface in Unit 158 may result from the excavation of "wallslot" for Wall K.

Description: Yellowish red (5YR 5/8 moist) sandy clay loam, hard. Fine gravel-boulders. Occasional $CaCO_3$ coatings on stones and as nodules. Sedimentary class A.

Context quality and cultural material: Rather dubious, mixed with artifacts from overlying strata.

Units: 118, 155, 158; mixed with II. 118 also mixed with III.

Interpretation: As elsewhere.

II

Position:	At interface between base of cultural deposits and top of I. Interface with III variable, between clear in southeast to diffuse in northeast.
Geometry:	Variable. Usually thin layer over I. Generally follows slope, but in east scarp forms thin capping over stone in section.
Description:	Reddish yellow (7.5YR 7/6 dry) sandy clay loam, rare stones. Sedimentary class A or D.
Context quality:	Uncertain, but readily confused with I beneath. Possibly forms intrusive later deposit along base of Wall K to east. In this case, the small reddish patch and others like it may provide the contamination noted during the excavation of Units 155 and 158.
Cultural material:	Present throughout.
Units:	118, 155, 158 mixed with I. Unit 194 possibly mixed with XI.
Interpretation:	Difficult to distinguish from I. Possibly a paleosol B horizon, but locally appears to represent an introduced sediment for building purposes. Introduced artifacts might be expected.

III

Position:	Above I and/or II, merges up into IV in north scarp. Distinct upper interface in east scarp *appears* to continue to south as roughly horizontal surface. Stratum IIIa occupies the northern 2 m of P5 (eastern half), and IIIb, the southern 2 m.
Geometry:	North scarp: wedge-shaped with lower interface parallel to paleoslope and upper interface of slightly more gentle gradient. East scarp: very thin to north (IIIa) becoming much thicker to south, where it subdivides into upper relatively stone-free units and lower stony units.
Description:	Dark yellowish brown (10YR 4/4 dry) loam to silt loam. Stone content varies from virtual talus gravel in north scarp to stone-free silt loam in east scarp.
Context quality and cultural material:[12]	Very poorly defined in north scarp where III merges into IV. In east scarp, where stone content is generally less, it appears well differentiated. Stratum IIIb, being thicker, should be less contaminated, but the possibility of contamination exists alongside Wall K, which appears to have been placed in a wall slot.
Units:	Contained within stratum on section drawing: 113, 117, 119, 136, 137, 140, 143. Near III/IV interface: 114, 115; III/VI interface: 107, 112.
Interpretation:	Strata IIIa and IIIb, although similar sediments at similar levels, may be of different dates. Stratum IIIb occupies southern half of trench and stops at a large boulder in center of east scarp. To north of this, IIIa continues but appears to be much thinner; in northern face, it contains much talus and has accumulated behind Wall K, which it appears to postdate. Stratum IIIa appears to represent an attenuated sequence, and probably for a long period talus material moved freely downslope and out of the area of P5. In IIIb, note possibility of contamination where a small patch of red-hued sediments existed alongside Wall K. This might be equivalent to VII in Q5.

IV

Position:	Above III in northeastern quadrant of trench. Upper interface with V distinct (type 4).
Geometry:	Almost rectangular sediment body; upper and lower interfaces roughly parallel to modern ground surface. Weakly bedded, single beds have relatively gentle dips: e.g., 105, ca. 5° to west.
Description:	Light yellowish brown (10YR 6/4 dry) loam. Abundant medium-to-coarse angular-to-subangular gravel. Two well-rounded beach-type pebbles, soft and loose. Sedimentary class G.

Units: Within stratum: 89, 91, 93, 95(?), 97; near III/IV interface: 114, 115. Near IV/V interface: 47, 49, 81, 89.
Interpretation: Talus deposit incorporating abundant cultural material. Accumulated behind Wall K and postdates it.

V

Position: Above IV, merges into X (type 5).
Geometry: Stone-free lens of similar attitude to IV. Sherds vary from subhorizontal to roughly parallel to slope of modern ground surface.
Description: Brown (10YR 5/3 dry) loam, occasional stones. Sedimentary class C.
Units: 38, 58. Near V/X interface: 32.
Interpretation: Stone-free lens, possibly merely a localized development, as a result of the two boulders to east in north scarp having filtered out the coarse talus gravels.

VI

Position: South of IV and possibly lateral variant of it. Above III. Merged into both IX and X, interfaces unclear.
Geometry: Lens, attitude uncertain.
Description: Brown (7.5YR 4/4) loam, occasional stones.
Units: 102; near III/IV interface: 107, 112.
Interpretation: Occupies trough between two talus lobes. As with V, possibly results from localized interception of stones by boulders or bushes.

VII

Position: Above III, below VIII and IX. In south scarp also above a stone-free sediment of 5YR-7.5YR hue. Clear interface (type 4) above and below.
Geometry: Gently dipping lens which pinches out to west in south scarp.
Description: Pale brown (10YR 6/3 dry) loam. Medium-to-coarse angular gravel. Sedimentary class G.
Units: 103, 106. PQ5:45, 47.
Interpretation: Talus lens accumulated behind Wall K.

VIII

Position: Between VI and VII, physically above both. Interfaces relatively distinct, type 4.
Geometry: Lens in transverse section only.
Description: Gray brown silt loam, few stones.
Units: 50, 51; 105 on interface of VI, VII, VIII.
Interpretation: Probably localized trough between two talus lobes or developed in sheltered position in lee side of obstruction as in V.

IX

Position: Above VI, VII, and VIII, merges up into X (type 5).
Geometry: Poorly defined, amorphous stratum, dips gently to north.
Description: Very pale brown (10YR 7/3 dry) silt loam. Common medium-to-coarse gravel, frequently subhorizontal. Note that section is transverse to slope. Sedimentary class F.
Units: From P5:27; from PQ5:37, 38.
Interpretation: Slope accretion with some talus input.

X

Position: Merges down into V, VI, IX, and XI; merges up into topsoil, XIX.

Geometry: Extensive horizon, 10-25 cm deep, parallel to modern ground surface.

Description: Light-yellowish-brown-to-light-brown (10YR-7.5YR 6/4 dry) clay loam. Occasional-to-common stones of all sizes. Relatively high Fe_2O_3, low organic carbon. S.D. Q3 (B21). Sedimentary class F.

Units: 10, 11, 14, 15, 18 and 25. PQ5:36.

Interpretation: Not a sedimentary or archaeological layer, but soil B21 horizon developed on a relatively stable slope.

XI

Position: Above II, below XV. Merging interface above and below.

Geometry: An inverted triangle in section. Some sherds have steep dips to west.

Description: Dark yellowish brown (10YR 4/4 dry) loam. Occasional-to-common stones. Very soft and loose towards base, although becomes harder towards Wall K.[13]

Context quality: Although poorly defined in section, layer appears to have been bounded to east by Wall K and to west and south by Walls M and L; also clearly overlaid by XV. Possibly localized mixing.

Cultural material: Throughout.

Units: 182, 183, 188. Near interface with XV: 132, 181.

Interpretation: Uncertain. Appears to be variable "fill" between Walls K, L, and M. Sherd orientation suggests it *might* have resulted from spillage over Wall K.

XII

Position and Geometry: Unit 191: between Walls Q and L, clear interface above (type 3). Units 74 and 76: against stones of Wall Q in west scarp.

Description: Dark brown (7.5YR 4/4 dry) locally 5YR hue, clay loam, rare stones. Sedimentary class D.

Context quality and cultural material: Well defined during excavation but possibly includes some introduced material.

Units: 74, 76, 191.

Interpretation: Walls M, L, and Q were associated with reddish-hued sediments, probably introduced to the site as wall or floor construction materials. Unit 191 may be an in-situ floor or floor foundation, whereas Units 74 and 76 were more likely used in wall construction.

XIII

Position: Thin layer against Wall L in north and Wall N in south. Above XII in north, northwest and west scarps. Rather diffuse layer, merges up into XIV or XV.

Geometry: Wedge of sediments between Wall N in southwest (thickest) and Wall L in northeast (thinnest).

Description: Dark brown (10YR 3/3 slightly moist). Loam with some gravel.

Context quality: Appears to be contained between walls of structure, therefore possibly well defined. Unit numbers, however, undetermined.

Cultural material: Present throughout, associated with in-situ occupation(?).

Units: Few units can be clearly related to this deposit: 191 might belong; 79 and 90 more correctly belong to XV, which overlies Walls L and N.

Interpretation: As this is closely related to a possible floor (XII), it might be either a floor or the rubbish thereon. Alternatively, it might represent a phase of debris accumulation following abandonment.

XIV

Position and Geometry:	On top of Wall L. In section, forms a thin wedge of sediment to west of wall, diffuse boundaries above and below in section. Within trench, however, some was clearly plastered onto top of wall.
Description:	As for XII. Water sieving showed numerous small serpentinite pebbles in >2 mm fraction. Sedimentary class D.
Context quality and cultural material:	Probably includes introduced material.
Units:	186. Near XIV/XV interface: 180.
Interpretation:	Sediment introduced, possibly for wall construction, later collapsed and disintegrated.

XV

Position and Geometry:	In north scarp, below XVI and above XIV and XI. Forms gently dipping layer in northwest of trench where it overlies Walls N and L. Built up against Wall Q. Merging boundaries, type 5, above and below.
Description:	Dark brown (7.5YR 4/2 slightly moist) loam to silt loam. Relatively stone-free in north scarp, more stones in west scarp.
Context quality and cultural material:	Probably incorporates material from upslope.
Units:	Good contexts: 66, 67. XII/XIII/XV interface: 79, 90. XIV/XV interface: 128.
Interpretation:	Late deposit which appears to have overwhelmed and infilled the structure(s) formed by Walls L, M, N, and Q. Also postdates lower portions of Wall K, probably upper wall stones as well.

XVI

Position:	Above XV and below topsoil (XIX), diffuse interfaces (type 5) above and below. In small northwest scarp, forms horizon immediately below large boulder.
Geometry:	In north scarp, forms a gently dipping horizon, apparently a continuation of X.
Description:	Brown stony loam, possibly with "B" horizon developed. Sedimentary class F.
Context quality and cultural material:	Includes material from upslope.
Units:	22, 27 and 29.
Interpretation:	As for X but incorporating some semi-active talus.

XVII

Position:	Base of excavated sequence in southwest of P5, merges up into XVIII.
Geometry:	Subhorizontal layer overlying a reddish-hued "surface" in PQ5 (22 and below), approximately equivalent to Units 77 and 97 or a little lower in Q5N.
Description:	Dark gray-brown (19YR 4/2, slightly moist) clay loam. Stones occasional to common. Sedimentary class E.
Context quality:	Uncertain, see interpretation of XVIII.
Cultural material:	Possibly some introduced material.
Units:	PQ5:28, 29.
Interpretation:	See XVIII.

XVIII

Position:	Above XVII, merges up into topsoil.

Geometry: Thick accumulation, geometry undetermined.

Description: Dark-brown-to-dark-gray-brown (10YR 3/3-4/2 slightly moist) clay loam, occasional stones. The <2.8-mm residue of Units 46, 57, and 68 contained numerous subrounded-to-well-rounded stones which included common serpentinites and green stones. Sedimentary class E.

Context quality and cultural material: See Interpretation.

Units: PQ5:14, 16, 18, 19, 20, 21, 27. P5: 37, 43, 45, 46, 57, 68, 69, 71. Units near XVIII/XIX interface: 3, 4, 8, 12, and 19.

Interpretation of XVII and XVIII: XVII is similar to the upper parts of Q6N (stratum VIIc). In PQ5 and Q5N, XVII or its equivalent overlies a reddish deposit (a "surface" in excavation notebook) which was probably introduced for building purposes. It lies near the bottom of Walls A and K and may either represent a floor/floor foundation or may be a collapsed superstructure. A possible surface exists above XVII (P5) in vicinity of Units 69 and 71. Collapsed building debris (daub and plaster, according to excavators) was found in XVIII and, along with a group of large stones, may have collapsed from Wall Q onto this surface. XVIII postdates Wall Q; XVII would appear to be roughly contemporary with its use.

XIX Topsoil. A horizon of modern soil, it includes much talus and in certain areas has aggraded slightly as a result of incorporation of archaeological spoil. Sedimentary class K.

Q5N MAJOR STRATIGRAPHIC UNITS

Master section drawing: Plate 56

I

Position: At base of succession as elsewhere on Paralia. Gradual boundary with II above.

Geometry: Random stones, upper interface dips downslope. For paleoslope surface, see Figure 20.

Description: Yellowish red (5YR 4/6 moist) clay loam. Hard with many boulders.
S.D. Q10 (IV B 22b). Sedimentary class A.

Context quality: In situ, undisturbed.

Cultural material: Pottery absent but occasional bones recorded. Shells and charcoal also present but not necessarily of cultural origin.

Units: Good contexts: 81, 84, 88, 90-96. Mixed interface with II: 78.

II

Position: Above I, below III. In north scarp, clearly differentiated from III above, but the distinction was less clear in south scarp. Rather mixed interface between II and III possible.

Geometry: Coarsely bedded, dips to west in accordance with slope of top of colluvium.

Description: Yellowish red (5YR 4/6 moist) silty clay loam forms relatively sparse matrix. Abundant stones of variable size which grade into angular talus gravel (1-4 cm, long axis) above.
S.D. Q9 (IV B 21b).

Units: Good contexts: 31, 67, 68, 70, 72, 74, 76. Mixed interface: 27-30, 64-66; with I below: 78.

Context quality: Unmixed, but in south scarp stratum II was not differentiated from III; therefore, possibly becomes mixed with III towards south.

Cultural material: Considerable decrease in cultural material within units of II/III interface (27-30, 64-66). The unmixed II units have little cultural material.

Interpretation: Active talus slope. The lack of cultural debris argues for a pre-occupation date (i.e., with respect to Paralia only). Probably a late Pleistocene/early Holocene slope deposit.

III

Position: Above II. Gradual boundary to IV above.

Geometry: Wedge of sediment thickens to west. Upper interface has lower dip than the lower. No apparent bedding.

Description: Brown (7.5YR 5/4 dry) loam, soft. Many angular stones at random. S.D. Q8 (III C 3). Sedimentary class B.

Context quality: Good. Part of continuously aggrading sequence with IV above. No mixing or disturbance, although excavation notebook suggests possibility of slight cross-cutting of layers.

Cultural material: Present throughout.

Units: Unmixed contexts: 58, 60-63. Mixed interface with IV: 25, 26, 56, 57. With II: 27-30, 64-66.

Interpretation: Stony slope deposit containing abundant cultural material. Unlike II, not an active talus. During accumulation of III, ground surface slope appears to have lessened in conjunction with aggradation of deposit.

IV

Position: Above III. Merges into V above, from which it can be distinguished by a change in stone content.

Geometry: Trapezoidal sediment body with slight downslope dip.

Description: Light brownish gray (10YR 6/2 dry) silt loam. Common angular stones. Low Fe_2O_3, high organic carbon. S.D. Q7 (III C 2). Sedimentary class B.

Context quality: Good. Part of continuous, aggrading sequence with III below and V above. No mixing or disturbance although as with III possibility of slight cross-cutting because stratum thins to east.

Cultural material: Present throughout.

Units: Eastern sequence, not indicated on section drawings; good contexts: 23, 24; mixed interface with V: 20-22; mixed interface with III: 25, 26. Main sequence, indicated on section drawing; good contexts: 51, 53, 54, 55; mixed interface with V: 50; with III: 56, 57.

Interpretation: Slope deposits dominated by silt-loam matrix. This together with gentle dip of sediment body implies some slope control and aggradation of fine sediment, probably behind wall.

V

Position: Above IV. Abrupt interface with VI above (type 2 or 3). Cut to west by VII.

Geometry: Sedimentary body rectangular in section, dips gently downslope. Many subhorizontal sherds.

Description: Light brownish gray (10YR 6/2 dry) loam, massive. Rare angular stones. Low Fe_2O_3, moderately high organic carbon. S.D. Q6 (III C 1). Sedimentary class C.

Context quality: Good. Although cut by VII to west, this was recognized and separated during excavation.

Cultural material: Present throughout.

Units: Eastern sequence, good contexts: 13-16, 18.
Eastern sequence, mixed with VI: 12; with IV: 20-22.
Main sequence, good contexts: 44, 45, 47, 48.
Main sequence, mixed with VI: 43; with IV: 50.

Interpretation: Stones excluded by decrease in slope gradient, an upslope barrier or some other impediment. Note, however, that fine sediments have continued to aggrade, therefore first suggestion quite likely. Probably accumulated behind Wall C or structure of similar age. Later cut during construction of Wall A.

VI

Position: Above V. Upper interface, wavy, distinct but becomes diffuse upslope (type 4). Cut to west by VII.

Geometry: Wedge-shaped, thins upslope. Slight dip to west.

Description: Light brown (7.5YR 6/4 dry) loam. Contains some rounded serpentinite pebbles. More clay than V, high $Fe_2 0_3$, low organic carbon.
S.D. Q5 (II B 23). Sedimentary class D.

Context quality: Relatively clear and unmixed except to east, where introduced from elsewhere.

Units: Eastern sequence, both probably mixed: 11, 12 (with V).
Main sequence, good contexts: 39, 40.
Main sequence, mixed with VII: 36, 37, 41; with V: 43.

Interpretation: Perceived reddish yellow deposit. Out of sequence and contains stones foreign to site. Sediment probably introduced to site from formerly dry valley floor for building purposes. Either floor or collapsed from wall. If latter, not from Wall A, which it appears to predate.

VII

Position: Feature cut through VI and V and parallel to Wall A on east side. Discernable in both plan and section. Clearly *cut* boundary to east, merges into VIII or IX above.

Geometry: See Position.

Description: Variable. Above: light yellowish brown (10YR 6/4 dry) loam, merges down into light brown (7.5YR 6/4 dry) loam. Fill surrounds many fist-sized stones which lie immediately behind Wall A. Sedimentary class J.

Context quality: Although a cut along the west side of wall was originally recognized during excavation, this interpretation was later discarded. On the eastern side of the wall, VII was apparently clearly distinguished and the finds separated accordingly.

Cultural material: Present throughout.

Units: Present in main sequence only. Good contexts: 38, 42, 46, 52. Possibly mixed contexts: 35 (with VIII), 36, 37, 41 (with VI), 49 (with V).

Interpretation: Cut through V and VI. Then filled with stones and soil to accomodate Wall A. The two different fills may be re-sorted from the original deposits V and VI.

XXX

Position: Above VI, VII and XXIV, below XXXII. Generally unclear boundaries above and below.

Geometry: Long, thin, poorly defined layer transitional to IX above.

Description: Light yellowish brown (10YR 6/4 dry) clay loam; common angular cobbles. Moderately high $Fe_2 0_3$ and organic carbon.
S.D. Q4 (B 22). Sedimentary class F.

Context quality: Poorly defined and likely to have been mixed during excavation. Possibly subject to continuous re-sorting.

Cultural material: Present throughout.

Units: Uncertain (excavation unit tags had remained in section when first drawn in 1973). All probably mixed: 9, 10, 32, 33, 34A, 35.

Interpretation: Soil B horizon developed in upper solum. Distinguished on basis of strong color and structure (S.D. Q4). Not prehistoric.

XXXII (Topsoil)

Position: Below ground surface. Merges down into XXX in north scarp.

Geometry: Parallels ground surface 40-60 cm deep.

Description: Brown (10YR 4/3 to 7.5YR 4/3, dry) clay loam, common angular stones, granular structure. High organic carbon.
S.D. Q1, 2. (A 1, A 3). Sedimentary class K.

Context quality: Mixed by movement of material from upslope, faunal mixing, etc.

Cultural material: Throughout but mixed.

Units: 1-8, probably 17.

Interpretation: Soil A horizon. During excavation probably also included material from soil B horizon (S.D. Q3).

XXI[14]

Position: Wedge-shaped deposit to west of and against foot of Wall A. Merges up into XXII.

Geometry: As above.

Description: "Reddish" clay loam; no other data available. Sedimentary class D.

Context quality: Poorly defined.

Cultural material: Uncertain.

Units: Possibly 105.

Interpretation: Little data available. Possibly a sediment introduced from elsewhere to act as "floor." Alternatively, collapsed from wall but appears to predate Wall A.

XXII

Position: Above XXI. Merges up into XXIII and XXIV.

Geometry: Thin layer, dips gently to south, thickens to west. Extends to base of Wall A in east.

Description: "Brown-red brown," clay loam, many small pebbles. Sedimentary class E.

Context quality: Poorly defined during final study, therefore of uncertain quality; excavator, however, considered it to be good context. Strip along western side of Wall A separated out as Unit 105.

Cultural material: Present throughout.

Units: Unmixed contexts: 97-104, 106. Possibly mixed: 80 (with XXIII and XXIV); 86, 87 (with XXIV); 105 (uncertain but probably with XXII).

Interpretation: Considered by excavators to be possible floor.

XXIII

Position: Above XXII, below XXIV. Accumulated against Wall A.

Geometry: Poorly defined, but appears to have been triangular wedge extending west of Wall A.

Description: Brown (10YR 4/3, 5/3 dry) clay loam. Described as containing "red inclusions" on original section drawing. Sedimentary class E.

Context quality: Not present during final redrawing, but notebooks and original section drawings suggest undisturbed context.

Cultural material: Present throughout. The "red inclusions" *may* be material which has fallen from wall superstructure.

Units: Possibly mixed with XXII and XXIV: 77, 80.

Interpretation:	Debris accumulated against wall, possibly includes material fallen from wall.

XXIV

Position:	Above XXII and XXIII, below XXX. Upper and lower interfaces uncertain.
Geometry:	Thick deposit, thickens to west.
Description:	Brown (10YR 5/3 dry) clay loam. Common large angular stones.
Context quality:	Apparently good.
Cultural material:	Present throughout.
Units:	Good contexts: 71, 75, 85. Possibly mixed: 32, 33, 34A, 69 (with XXX); 77 (with XXIII); 80 (with XXII, XXIII); 86, 87 (with XXII).
Interpretation:	Postdates use of wall. Forms part of extensive sediment body which extended into top of Q6N.

Q5S MAJOR STRATIGRAPHIC UNITS[15]

Master section drawings: Plates 50, 54, 55

I

Position:	Base of sequence. Clear interface with XVI above (type 4) in southwest trench. Stratum XV above possibly cuts I. In southeastern sounding gradual interface with Ib above.
Geometry:	Forms dipping paleoslope at base of sequence.
Description:	Reddish yellow (5YR 6/6 dry) sandy clay loam. Abundant angular stones up to boulder size. Sedimentary class A.
Context quality:	No contamination, although some material possibly incorporated from overlying deposits by faunal activity, etc.
Cultural material:	In southwest, a little pottery in all contexts except 209. In southeast, pottery present in lowest excavated unit from within I.
Units:	Southeast: 194. Southwest, good contexts: 206, 208, 209. Mixed interface: 205.
Interpretation:	Basal red colluvium of late Pleistocene/early Holocene land surface.

XVI

Position:	Above I. Merges laterally into XV, which, if it is a real feature and fill, is postdated by XVI. Clear upper interface with XXVII (type 3).
Geometry:	Small exposure, appears to dip gently downslope at a lesser gradient than I/XVI interface.
Description:	Yellowish brown (10YR 5/4 dry) silt loam. Occasional large stones above, increasing to common below. Sedimentary class B.
Context quality:	Good, well-defined, and sealed context. Only possible disturbance is XV, the units of which were separated out during excavation.
Cultural material:	Present throughout.
Units:	200-202.
Interpretation:	Sediment accumulated behind Walls C and E resulted in a gradual decrease in the surface slope and the creation of a terrace.

XV

Position:	Adjacent to Wall E. Fill of possible feature cut into I. Fill merges laterally into XVI.
Geometry:	Narrow slot alongside Wall E.
Description:	Fill: yellowish-red (5YR 5/6 moist) with occasional large stones.
Context quality:	Appears to have been cut into I only, *not* through fill XVI.

Cultural material:	Pottery sparse.
Units:	204, 203.
Interpretation:	Not certain, but possibly a shallow trench excavated to accommodate the substantial Wall E.

XVII

Position:	Above XVI; distinct interface, type 2/3 with IX above.
Geometry:	Virtually horizontal layer.
Description:	Yellowish red (5YR 5/6 moist) sandy clay loam. Rare-to-occasional small stones. Sedimentary class D.
Context quality:	Good, well defined.
Cultural material:	Present throughout.
Units:	197-199.
Interpretation:	Sediment appears to have been introduced from elsewhere and laid as surface (floor?) up to and against Walls E and C. It is possible that some of the included finds were introduced from elsewhere.

IX

Position:	Above XVII. Merges up into XVIII; IX was distinguished from XVIII on basis of a clean surface encountered during excavation. No sedimentary break evident in section. To west, diffuse interface to XIX above.
Geometry:	Thick amorphous layer, dips to west.
Description:	Light yellowish brown (10YR 6/4 dry) loam. Common medium gravel, occasional coarse.
Context quality:	Large stratum, poorly defined, especially above, therefore some likelihood of mixing.
Cultural material:	Present throughout.
Units:	Good contexts: 187, 195, 196; probably mixed with XIX and XVIII: 185, 186.
Interpretation:	Uncertain. Sediment accumulated on top of possible floor XVII and against Wall E. Also included a possible surface at IX/XVIII interface. Stratum IX possibly resulted from the gradual accretion of slope sediments.

XVIII

Position:	Above IX, merges into topsoil XXXII and laterally into XIX.
Geometry:	Poorly defined layer dipping to west, roughly parallel to modern ground surface.
Description:	As for IX.
Context quality:	Poor. Likelihood of cross-cutting, interface mixing, and, towards the top, continuous re-sorting as a result of localized talus movement. Material from near IX/XVIII interface probably from good context.
Cultural material:	Unit 186, excavated from vicinity of interface with IX, yielded abundant cultural material.
Units:	All possibly mixed: 161, 184-186.
Interpretation:	Uncertain. Probably accumulation of slope debris on former occupation levels. Strong possibility of some cultural debris having come from upslope, but this layer is not a fully developed talus.

XIX

Position:	Above IX and XVIII very diffuse interface to XX and XXXII above.
Geometry:	Lens, dips to west, roughly parallel to modern ground surface.
Description:	Light yellowish brown (10YR 6/4) clay loam. Common to abundant gravel. Sedimentary class F.

Context quality: Very poor to poorly defined, even in section. Probably includes much material rolled from upslope.
Cultural material: Present, but of dubious value in terms of succession. Probably abundant residual material.
Units: 68, 69, 158.
Interpretation: Possibly post-occupation reactivation of talus.

XX

Position: Above Wall E. Merges into topsoil XXXII. Above XIX.
Geometry: Very poorly defined layer dipping to west.
Description: Similar to XIX but fewer stones. Sedimentary class F.
Context quality: As XIX.
Cultural material: As XIX.
Units: 6, 23, 24, 25.
Interpretation: Few stones compared with XIX, probably due to local factors such as boulders which have acted as sediment traps for coarse material.

XXXII Topsoil as for Q5 North.

Strata Ib and following are situated at eastern end of Q5S south section.

Ib

Position: Above Ia below VIII. Merging boundary above and below.
Geometry: A thin layer above Ia; approximately follows top of red colluvium.
Description: Dark brown (7.5 YR 4/4 moist) loam. Abundant medium-to-coarse subangular gravel in soft matrix.
Context quality: Good, although because derived from talus-type deposit, may include material rolled from upslope.
Cultural material: Present throughout.
Units: Good: 193; possibly mixed with VIII: 192.
Interpretation: Talus developed on top of red colluvium; probably simultaneous with occupation in vicinity but not in situ.

VIII

Position: Above Ib, merges up into X and IX above.
Geometry: Gently dipping layer with upper interface roughly parallel to modern ground surface. Many subhorizontal stones.
Description: Light brownish gray (10YR 6/2 dry) silt loam. Abundant medium gravel to 8 cm, long axis. Soft matrix. Sedimentary class B.
Context quality: Good. Gradual accretion of sediments; possibly some re-sorting resulting from talus movement.
Cultural material: Present throughout.
Units: 188-191; 192 on Ib/VIII interface.
Interpretation: Talus, less active above. Subhorizontal stones suggest accretion of sediments on subhorizontal surface, possibly behind a wall or boulder.

X

Position: Above VIII, diffuse boundary with XI. To west, steep, reversed, oblique boundary to IX.
Geometry: Wedge-shaped, thickens downslope to IX/X interface; no bedding.
Description: Pale brown, 10YR 6/3 (d) silt loam. Common stones but less than VIII. Matrix dominates.

Context quality: Cross-cut by units 185 and 186. A rather unclear stratum. Finds are liable to be mixed.
Cultural material: Present throughout.
Units: 185, 186, both mixed with IX.
Interpretation: The stratigraphy is unclear above IX and VIII, and this stratum is no exception. The geometry and stone content suggests that it accumulated during a phase of slope control either up- or downslope of a wall. The reversed oblique boundary with IX may indicate the former presence of a wall or that a wall remains within the balk. Similar to XVI to west but not necessarily same age.

XI

Position: Above X, merges into XXXII above and IX/XVIII to west.
Geometry: Poorly defined triangular deposit, thins downslope.
Description: Pale brown (10YR 6/3 dry) silt loam. Common stones to 10 cm, long axis. Many subhorizontal stones and sherds, others with slight dip to west.
Context quality: Units limited to this stratum during excavation, therefore appears to be relatively unmixed.
Cultural material: Present throughout.
Units: 183, 184, possibly mixed interface.
Interpretation: Still some talus accumulation, but matrix dominates, which implies some slope control. On plan in excavation notebook, it appears to have accumulated behind Wall D which, however, does not clearly appear in section.

XIII

Position: Top of XI, gradual interface all round.
Geometry: Subhorizontal lens.
Description: "Reddish brown" loam lens. Sedimentary class D.
Context quality: Poorly defined.
Cultural material: Uncertain.
Units: Uncertain.
Interpretation: Probably introduced sediment. It extends up to what might have been a collapsed wall which had once existed above Unit 148, but which subsequently collapsed downslope.

Q5 EAST MAJOR STRATIGRAPHIC UNITS[16]

Master section drawing: Plate 54

Ia Stony colluvium as elsewhere on Paralia. Sedimentary class A. More details in stratum I, Q5N and Q5S.

Ib

Position: Gradual interface to Ia beneath. Boulder above.
Geometry: Very thin bed beneath boulder.
Description: Strong brown (7.5 YR 5/6 dry) appears gray brown in section. Few stones.
Context quality: Very small, possibly also mixed.
Cultural material: Present.
Units: Probably 191, 192.
Interpretation: See VIII, Q5 south section.

XII

Position: Above boulder, above Ib. Gradual interface with XIII above, (type 4); gradual interface with XIb above (type 5).

Geometry:	Roughly horizontal body of sediment; some subhorizontal stones.
Description:	Pale brown (10YR 6/3 dry) silt loam. Common coarse, angular gravel and cobbles.
Context quality:	Good, well-defined context up to Wall D to west.
Cultural material:	Present throughout.
Units:	182-184.
Interpretation:	Frequent stones imply some talus movement but probably not fully active; matrix dominates. Continues in south scarp as less stony deposit XIa. Clearly variable, both across and downslope.

XIII

Position:	Lens between XII below and XIb above. Gradual, type 4 interface.
Geometry:	See above.
Description:	Brown (7.5YR 5/4 dry) loam with occasional stones. Sedimentary class D.
Context quality:	Rather poorly defined.
Cultural material:	Sediment and contained artifacts may have been introduced from elsewhere.
Units:	Parts of 181, 182, but probably mixed.
Interpretation:	Appears to have been associated with Wall D, but exact relationship not proven. Similar to XIII in south scarp, which might also be related to collapsed wall at same stratigraphic position as D (same wall?).

XIb

Position:	Gradual interface (type 5) to XIV above. Above XIII.
Geometry:	Subhorizontal layer; occasional subhorizontal stones.
Description:	Pale brown (10YR 6/3 dry) silt loam, occasional medium-to-coarse stones.
Context quality:	Because of general diffuse interface, a rather poorly defined layer.
Cultural material:	Present throughout.
Units:	Includes 181-182, but both mixed with XIII.
Interpretation:	Probably accumulated when some slope control screened out many stones but allowed accumulation of fine sediments.

XIV

Position:	Above XIb, below XXXI. XIV/XXXI interface, stratigraphic discontinuity of type 2.
Geometry:	Roughly horizontal.
Description:	Light yellowish brown (10YR 6/4) loam. Occasional stones.
Context quality:	Quite well defined by Wall D to west. Excavators appear to have distinguished this from stony layer above (stratum XXXI).
Cultural material:	Throughout.
Units:	121, 125, 128, and 130.
Interpretation:	Finds dominated deposit that accumulated on controlled slope. Appears to have accumulated behind Wall D.

XXXI

Position:	Above XIV, merges into topsoil (XXXII) above.
Geometry:	Horizontal bed lying on slightly concave-up surface.
Description:	Yellowish brown (10YR 5/4) loam. Abundant angular gravel with occasional stones to 30 cm. Sedimentary class G.
Context quality:	Although well defined, likely to incorporate material rolled from upslope. Apparently, well defined by excavators.
Cultural material:	Probably much residual material from upslope.
Units:	121, 125, 128, 130.

Interpretation:	Episode of talus accumulation behind Wall D.
XXXII	Topsoil: 40-50 cm thick. See Q5N XXXII.

Q5 SOUTH, WEST SECTION, MAJOR STRATIGRAPHIC UNITS[17]

Master section drawing: Plate 55

I

Position:	At base of sequence. Merges into XXV (type 5).
Geometry:	Small exposure, geometry undetermined.
Description:	Yellowish red (5YR 5/6-4/6) clay loam. Occasional angular stones. Sedimentary class A.
Context quality:	One undisturbed unit.
Cultural material:	Absent.
Units:	Unmixed: 226. At I/XXV interface: 225, 227.
Interpretation:	Top of colluvium only.

XXV

Position:	Above I. Upper interface with XXVI, gradual, type 4.
Geometry:	Thick, horizontal layer.
Description:	Brown (7.5YR 4/4) to yellowish red (5YR 4/6 moist) loam, occasional stones.
Context quality:	Appears relatively uncontaminated, but see XXVI below.
Cultural material:	Present throughout.
Units:	Good contexts: 221, 223, 224. Possibly mixed with XXVI: 222; possibly mixed with I: 225, 227.
Interpretation:	Although reddened, this is not an undisturbed basal colluvium, but it may have been mixed during the early phase of occupation.

XXVI

Position:	Above XXV. Clear upper boundary with XXVII (type 3).
Geometry:	Thick horizontal layer, stones appear horizontal.
Description:	Yellowish brown (10YR 5/4 dry) loam, occasional angular stones. Softer to south. A group of fist-sized stones occurs at southern end of scarp below Wall F. These stones fill a possible foundation cut made to accommodate the wall. The sediment in this cut resembles stratum XXVI, which may therefore intrude in XXV at this point.
Context quality:	Appears uncontaminated, sealed by XXVII above.
Cultural material:	Throughout.
Units:	Good: 218, 219, 220. XXV/XXVI: 222. XXVI/XXVII: 217.
Interpretation:	No clear origin, but apparently an accretion of fine but rather poorly sorted sediments; some slope control and input of talus material.

XXVII

Position:	Above XXVI, very clear upper and lower interfaces (type 3).
Geometry:	Horizontal; runs from Wall F to Wall H.
Description:	Reddish yellow (5YR 6/6 dry) silty clay loam; hard, many calcium carbonate nodules, rounded and angular gravels including serpentinites. Low organic carbon, moderately high Fe_2O_3. S.D. sample A (see Appendix E). Sedimentary class D.
Context quality:	In section, appears uncontaminated. The presence of human bones, however, suggests disturbance. See Interpretation.

Cultural material: Present throughout, but see Interpretation.
Units: Good: 214-216. XXVI/XXVII: 217.
Interpretation: Sediment runs up to both Walls F and H and contains material (e.g., serpentinite pebbles) foreign to site. It was probably introduced to the site from elsewhere and may therefore contain artifacts and human bones also from elsewhere. Interpreted as floor built up against Walls F and H.

XXVIII

Position: Above XXVII, merges up into XXIX (type 5).
Geometry: Roughly horizontal.
Description: Pink (7.5YR 5/4 dry) silt loam, common angular stones, many of them large.
Context quality: Appears good in section.
Cultural material: Present throughout.
Units: Good: 213. Possibly mixed XXVIII/XXIX: 212.
Interpretation: Uncertain. Although this could be talus, this cannot be clearly demonstrated from the transverse section.

XXIX

Position: Above XXVIII, below topsoil (XXXII).
Geometry: Thick subhorizontal layer in transverse section.
Description: Reddish brown loam, occasional stones below, becoming very stony above.
Context quality: Probably poor, also subject to contamination from material rolling from upslope.
Cultural material: Present throughout.
Units: 63, 64, 66, 100, 102 and 210.
Interpretation: In the north, where it joins with Q6 VIIb, layer appears to have been on top of Wall H, where it may have been the wall superstructure. Wall A was possibly cut into XXIX. The upper stony part of XXIX may result from a reactivation of talus movement following the abandonment of the site.

XXXII Topsoil, dark yellowish brown, 10 cm in south, 30 cm in north, probably mixed.

QR5 MAJOR STRATIGRAPHIC UNITS[18]

Master section drawings: Plates 51, 55
Secondary section drawing: Plate 70

I

Position: Not in section but below II.
Geometry: Not determined.
Description: Light brown (7.5 YR 6/4 dry) loam, occasional stones.
Context quality: Good, sealed by II.
Units: 37, 38.
Interpretation: Gradual aggradation behind Wall E.

II

Position: Above I, upper interface with V clear (type 3).
Geometry: Variable. Although appears in section as inverted triangle, this is in fact same deposit as XVII in Q5S, i.e., a horizontal layer.
Description: Reddish yellow (7.5 YR 6/6 dry) loam. Rare gravel, common small serpentinite pebbles. Sedimentary class D.
Context quality: Good, well defined.

Units: 32-36.
Interpretation: Introduced from elsewhere for building purposes. Possibly a floor or material collapsed from wall. Possibly contains artifacts introduced from elsewhere.

III

Position: Below V, interface with V, gradual.
Geometry: Small area in southeast of trench, possibly fill of Structure Z.
Description: Brown (7.5 YR 5/4 dry) loam, common angular gravel.
Context quality: Uncertain.
Interpretation: Possibly part of structure associated with Wall Z.

IV

Position: Base of sequence, west of Wall E and against it. Merges up into V.
Geometry: Thick deposit but section exposed too small to describe shape.
Description: Pale brown (10YR 6/3 dry) silt loam-loam. In general, stones rare but these increase in number towards top, e.g., in Units 13 and 14; also in 16/17 near IV/V interface where a gravelly deposit was present downslope of gap in Wall E.
Context quality: Good, especially in lower levels. In upper units, likely to incorporate material from upslope.
Units: Good contexts: 16, 17, 22, 24, 31, 39, 40, 41. Units near interface with V: 13, 14, 15 and 18.
Interpretation: Steady accumulation of fine sediments downslope of Wall E, south of Wall F. More talus input towards top where spillage over Wall E.

V

Position: Above II and III, merges up into VI above (type 5).
Geometry: Thick; upper interface roughly parallel to modern slope.
Description: Light brown (7.5 YR 6/4 dry) loam. Complex of sediments containing abundant angular stones with isolated lenses of talus gravel. Sedimentary class F.
Context quality: Because this forms a complex of minor sedimentary variations, this may include several episodes of deposition. No great disturbance, however.
Units: Good: 9-12, 30, 31. Near interface with VI: 5-8, 25-27. Near interface with IV: 13-15, 18.
Interpretation: Gradual accretion of slope deposit which includes episodes of talus accumulation above and locally behind Wall E. Actually filters through gap in wall in one place, and a small talus patch is developed in upper IV.

VI

Position: Above V. Gradual interface (type 5) above and below.
Geometry: Thin layer, upper and lower interface roughly parallel to modern slope.
Description: Dark brown (7.5 YR 4/4 dry) loam; common to abundant gravel, locally, fully developed talus. Sedimentary class F.
Context quality: Incorporates some material from upslope, also possibly mixed during excavation as a result of merging interfaces.
Units: Good: 4. Near interface with VII: 3. Near interface with V: 5, 6, 7, 8, 25, 26, 27.
Interpretation: Although no fully developed talus blanket was noted in section, layer does incorporate localized reactivation of talus. Also, weakly developed soil B horizon.

VII Topsoil. Approximately 20 cm thick but thinner in west scarp. Sedimentary class K.

Q6N NORTH SECTION, MAJOR STRATIGRAPHIC UNITS

Master section drawing: Plate 56

I

Position:	Base of sequence as elsewhere; merges into III.
Geometry:	Unknown depth; upper interface irregular with gentle dip to west.
Description:	Brown (7.5 YR 5/4 dry) to yellowish red (5 YR 5/6 dry) clay loam. Hard, many subangular stones and boulders. High Fe_2O_3, low organic carbon. S.D. R7 (II B 22b), S7 (II B 2b). Sedimentary class A.
Context quality:	Probably mixed with material from III.
Cultural material:	Present in small quantities in all units except 71.
Units:	Good: 71. Possibly mixed with III: 70, 72. (These data are from the excavation notebook.)
Interpretation:	Basal colluvium, locally disturbed.

III

Position:	Above I. Distinct but possibly interrupted boundary with IV and V above.
Geometry:	Gently dipping towards west.
Description:	Brown (7.5 YR 5/4 dry) clay loam. Occasional-to-common stones of varying size. Charcoal present locally. High organic carbon in S6. S.D. R6 (II B 21b), S6 (II A 1).
Context quality:	Presence of II A1 horizon in S6 suggests a full buried soil remains in S. In R this horizon has probably been truncated and removed. Stratum V above appears to be a cut feature, and it is possible that this might account for local truncation of the buried soil A horizon.
Cultural material:	Present throughout.
Units:	Good: 60, 61, 63, 64, some localized mixing possible.
Interpretation:	Buried soil A and B horizons, locally mixed or truncated.

IV

Position:	Above III. Distinct interface, type 3 to VI above. Possibly cut interface (type 1) with V to east, but not very clear.
Geometry:	Wedge-shaped; thickens to west. Upper interface subhorizontal.
Description:	Light brownish gray (10YR 6/2 dry) loam, common stones. Low Fe_2O_3, high organic carbon. S.D. S5 (C 2).
Context quality:	Good, possibly locally disturbed or crosscut with IV.
Cultural material:	Throughout.
Units:	Good: 38, 40, 51, 53, 54. Possibly of IV: 50. Near III/IV interface: 55, 56, 58.
Interpretation:	Gradual accretion of sediments with much cultural material. Presence of $CaCO_3$ nodules, although possibly related to soil development on site or precipitation from springs, could equally have been introduced to site with soil brought in from elsewhere.

V

Position:	Above III, cuts IV. Distinct interface (type 3) with VI above.
Geometry:	Possible feature and fill. Shape unclear.
Description:	Brown (10YR 5/3 dry) silt loam. Common stones, becomes gravelly beneath. High organic carbon. S.D. R5 (C 2). Sedimentary class J.

Context quality: Appears to be a coherent feature excavated as 36, 37.
Cultural material: Present throughout.
Units: 36, 37.
Interpretation: Possible feature and fill cut in IV, sealed by VI.

VI

Position: Above IV and V. Distinct upper and lower interfaces (type 3).
Geometry: Thin subhorizontal layer. Slight jog in center of section which corresponds to western end of V.
Description: Best distinguished in profile S. Light brown (7.5 YR 6/4 dry) loam, many stones. Greater than 2 mm fraction yielded frequent well-rounded fine gravel and single specimen of marine gastropod *Bittium reticulatum*.
S.D. S4: C 1. Sedimentary class D.
Context quality: Well defined.
Cultural material: Present throughout, but sediment possibly introduced from elsewhere.
Units: Good: 35. VI/VII interface: 33.
Interpretation: Sediment of reddish hue, probably introduced. May have been laid as floor.

VII

Position: Above VI.
Geometry: Very thick complex layer. No consistent internal divisions could be made. For example: a single lens, VIIb, apparently dipped from Units 20, 21, and 22 in center of trench down to 27 in west of trench. Upper units, at least above Unit 23, possibly entire deposit VII, characterized by sherds dipping gently to west 25° or less.
Description: Mainly grayish brown (10YR 5/2 dry) to light brownish gray (10YR 6/2 dry) loam (distinguished as clay loam on section drawings because of relatively high clay content; see text). Common stones, locally abundant and of all sizes. Also common large potsherds with fresh breaks associated with most stony areas. Contains VIIb: lenses of yellowish red (5YR 5/6 dry) clay loam. Very common *Cerastoderma glaucum* (cockle). High organic carbon.
S.D. R1, 2, 3 (B 21, B 22, C 1). S1, 2, 3. (B 21, B 22, B 23). VIIa and VIIc = sedimentary class E; VIIb = sedimentary class D.
Context quality: Very complex. Contains lenses of angular stones and reddish-hued sediments, the latter of which were probably introduced from elsewhere. During excavation sediment color and texture were seen to vary laterally from north to south (soil profile T illustrates this point).
Cultural material: Present throughout. Units 20-22, 27 possibly introduced.
Units: Good: 7-15, 17-19, 23-26, 28, 29, 31, 32. Mixed: 1-6. VI/VII interface: 33; uncertain: 16; VIIb: 20-22, 27.
Interpretation: Thick accumulation which could not be resolved into coherent stratigraphy. Contains lenses of introduced material. Although abundant angular rubble in places, the associated sherds were not abraded as is normal for those associated with talus. The many dipping sherds imply continuous accretion on slopes less than 25°, but not instantaneous dumping.

VIII As for VII. Above VII, below IX.

Q6N EAST SECTION, MAJOR STRATIGRAPHIC UNITS[19]

Master section drawing: Plate 53

I

Position: At base of sequence. Merges up into III (type 5).
Geometry: As for I, north scarp.

Description:	Yellowish red (5YR 5/6 dry) clay loam. Hard, many stones of varying size. Some charcoal. High $Fe_2 0_3$, low organic carbon. S.D. T5 (II B 22b). Sedimentary class A.
Context quality:	Presence of charcoal where sampled suggests not sterile at this point.
Cultural material:	As above.
Units:	Only 69 in scarp.
Interpretation:	Basal colluvium as elsewhere.

III

Position:	Above I. Gradual interface to V above in north. Distinct (type 2) to VI above in south.
Geometry:	Roughly horizontal upper interface.
Description:	Brown (7.5 YR 5/4 dry) clay loam. Many stones and deposit becomes talus gravel to south. Relatively high $Fe_2 0_3$, low organic carbon. S.D. T4 (II B 21b).
Context quality:	Uncertain
Cultural material:	Present throughout.
Units:	Uncertain.
Interpretation:	As for Q6N, north section, III. Probably same layer, but note well-developed talus gravel to south. This has a brown upper horizon that *might* be a buried soil A horizon. This, however, could not be verified in the field .

V

Position:	Above III, merges with VI to south and with VII above. Cannot, in fact, be distinguished from latter.
Geometry:	Small patch only.
Description:	As for VI, Q6N, north section.
Context quality:	As for VI, Q6N, north section.
Cultural material:	As for VI, Q6N, north section.
Units:	36, 37.

VI

Position:	Above III; runs up to V and the two deposits have a diffuse mutual interface (type 5). Diffuse interface (type 5) to VII above.
Geometry:	Roughly horizontal layer.
Description:	Light brown (7.5 YR 6/4) silty clay loam. Frequent stones of all sizes. S.D. T3 (B 23).
Context quality:	Uncertain in east section.
Cultural material:	Uncertain in east section.
Units:	Probably as for Q6N, north VI.
Interpretation:	Roughly horizontal layer, possibly deliberately laid. See Q6N, north VI.

VIIa

Position:	Above V/VI.
Geometry:	Very poorly defined deposit with very diffuse interfaces which interdigitate with VIIb.
Description:	Light brown (7.5 YR 6/4 dry) loam. Many stones of various sizes to 16 cm, long axis. N.B. = S.D. T2 (B 22) which also includes lenses of VIIb. Sedimentary class E.
Context quality:	See Q6N, north VIIa.

Cultural material: See Q6N, north VIIa.
Units: Only 28 for certain.

VIIb

Position: Lens which interfingers with VIIa and also runs to south where it immediately overlies Wall H. Relatively clear boundary, above and below (type 3). Although apparently below VIIc, this is part of a complex which includes VIIa, b, and c.
Description: Yellowish red (5 YR 4/6 moist) loam. Numerous shells of *Cerastoderma glaucum* (cockle). Sedimentary class D.
Context quality: Probably includes introduced material.
Units: 20-22, 27.
Interpretation: Mud superstructure for either Wall A or Wall H, or a sedimentary cover over Wall H. If related to Wall H, possibly cut by Wall A.

VIIc

Position: Above VIIb.
Geometry: Thin layer, thickens to north but see comment below.
Description: Pink (7.5 YR 7/4 dry) silt loam. Many angular stones. S.D. T1 (B 21). Sedimentary class E.
Context quality: As for Q6N, north VIIc.
Cultural material: As for Q6N, north VIIc.

The difference between profiles R and T was evident during excavation, but it proved impossible to resolve these differences into discrete stratigraphic units. The diffuse boundaries and dipping lenses appeared to unite VIIa, b and c (Q6N, east section) into one complex equivalent to these strata in the north section.

IX Topsoil, only thin layer of which remained unexcavated. Sedimentary class K.

Q6N SOUTH SECTION

Master section drawing: Plate 52

Sedimentary strata as for north section.

II

Position: Below III.
Description: Strong brown-to-yellowish-red clay loam. Includes parts of Units 60, 61, 63, and 64. No other information is available.

APPENDIX C

Field and Laboratory Methods

The strongly calcareous nature of the sediments on Paralia complicated laboratory procedures and the interpretation of analytical data. Primary carbonates in the form of limestone sand and fragments of shell are abundant in the samples, as are secondary carbonates which occur both as discrete nodules and as finely dispersed in the matrix. In order to deal with this problem, pretreatments of samples prior to analysis were used as indicated below.

The pretreatments tended to remove secondary carbonates, but they leave primary carbonates relatively intact. Finely comminuted particles of limestone and shell, however, may have been removed by the pretreatments, especially by prolonged treatment with hydrochloric acid. In retrospect, uniform treatment of the samples with sodium acetate buffer would have been preferable.

Particle-size data present particular problems of interpretation. Inspection under the microscope reveals that the major part of the sand- and silt-sized fractions consists of aggregates of finer particles cemented by carbonates, limestone sand, and fragments of shell. The weight percent of sand, especially, varies according to no discernible pattern whether or not the sample was pretreated. For this reason, particle size is also reported recalculated on a sand-free basis.

Since the pretreatments did not remove the carbonates entirely, it cannot be assumed that the more vulnerable analyses, particularly cation exchange capacity and extractable cations, were unaffected by the high carbonate content of the samples. Therefore, these data must be interpreted cautiously.

Cation-exchange capacity represents the ability of a soil to hold certain cations which it may exchange with other cations from a liquid or other solid phase. This reversible process depends primarily on the quantity and type of clay minerals and on the quantity and kind of organic matter present. The extractable cations are the principal cations held on the exchange sites in the soil. Calcium-carbonate equivalent may include other carbonate species soluble in cold hydrochloric acid. The method of measurement does not allow the separation of primary and secondary carbonates.

Organic phosphate measurement was considered as a procedure which might have aided in the separation of deposits of human compared to geological origin. The procedure was not employed for lack of proper control sections away from the site, and because extensive use of the site by herds of goats today combined with the shallowness of the deposits would have led to inconclusive results. The considerable time and expense involved was therefore not considered merited.

FIELD METHODS

The profiles were described in the field in 1976, employing the system of the United States

Department of Agriculture *Soil Survey Manual* (USDA 1951, 1962). Samples from each described horizon were bagged and shipped to the United States.

LABORATORY METHODS

In accordance with USDA regulations concerning imported soil samples, approximately half of each sample was sterilized by steam heat in an autoclave in order to facilitate safe handling in the laboratory. Unsterilized samples were treated with special care. Most procedures were carried out using sterilized samples. Clay mineralogy and other x-ray work used unsterilized samples.

All samples were sieved for 2 mm and 80 mesh (sterilized) and 100 mesh (unsterilized) and stored in cardboard containers (sterilized) and glass jars with screwtops (unsterilized).

Particle Size

Samples were pretreated to remove carbonates for particle-size analysis by adding 1N HCl and digesting on a steamplate until sample pH was between 3.5 and 4.0 (Jackson 1979:36). Particle size was also run on all samples without pretreatment. After removal of organic matter with H_2O_2 and dispersion, the pipet method (SCS 1972:Procedure 3A) was used to separate the clay (<2 μm) and fine silt (2–16 μm) fractions. Sand (63 μm-2 mm) was found by sieving and coarse silt (16–62 μm) by subtraction.

pH

Soil pH was determined in a 1:1 soil-water suspension (Black 1965:922).

$CaCO_3$

Calcium-carbonate equivalent was measured gravimetrically by weighing a flask containing 10 ml of 3N HCl, adding 1 g of soil, and reweighing after the reaction was completed. The amount of $CaCO_3$ equivalent was calculated from the weight loss (Black 1965:1388-1389).

Organic Carbon

Organic carbon was determined by acid-dichromate digestion followed by titration with ferrous sulfate (SCS 1972:Procedure 6A1). This method does not detect elemental carbon or charcoal.

The following procedures were run after pretreatment for carbonates with a sodium-acetate buffer of pH 5 without heating (modified from Jackson 1979:34).

Extractable Iron and Manganese

The sodium-dithionite extraction procedure was used (SCS 1972:Procedure 6C1). Concentrations of iron and manganese in the extract were determined with a Varian-Techtron model 1000 atomic absorption unit according to the following specifications:

Iron

wavelength	248.3 nm
flame	air-acetylene, oxidizing
slit	0.2 nm
lamp current	5 mA

Manganese

wavelength	279.5 nm
flame	air-acetylene, oxidizing
slit	0.2 nm
lamp current	5 mA

Extractable Bases

Extractable bases were determined by soaking the soil sample overnight in NH_4OAc, pH 7.0, followed by leaching with an additional 200 mls of NH_4OAc (SCS 1972:Procedure 5A1). Concentrations of bases in the extract were determined by atomic absorption using a Varian-Techtron model 1000 AA unit according to the following specifications:

Sodium

wavelength	589.6 nm
flame	air-acetylene, oxidizing
slit	0.2 nm
lamp current	5 mA

Potassium

wavelength	766.5 nm
flame	air-acetylene, oxidizing
slit	0.5 nm
lamp current	5 mA

Calcium

wavelength	422.7 nm
flame	nitrous oxide-acetylene, reducing
slit	0.2 nm
lamp current	15 mA

Magnesium

wavelength	285.2 nm
flame	air-acetylene, oxidizing
slit	0.5 nm
lamp current	5 mA

Lanthanum chloride was added to samples and standards of Mg and Ca to reduce interferences.

Cation-Exchange Capacity

The leachate from the above procedure was rinsed with ethyl alcohol and distilled. The distillate was titrated with HCl (SCS 1972:Procedure 5A1) to determine CEC.

Base Saturation

Base saturation was calculated by dividing the sum of the NH_4OAc-extracted bases by the CEC (SCS 1972:Procedure 5C1).

Mineralogy

Bulk mineralogy was determined qualitatively by preparing a slide from the 100-mesh unsterilized sample and x-raying. A Phillips-Norelco XRG-2500 x-ray generator and diffractometer with a copper target was used. The slide was scanned at a rate of 2°2Θ/minute from 2° to 60°2Θ. Samples were also examined under low magnification with a binocular microscope.

Clay mineralogy was determined by preparing oriented slides with the $< 2\mu m$ fraction. Duplicate slides were x-rayed before and after heating to 450°C and 600°C and after glycolation by saturating with ethylene glycol for 48 hours. The slides were scanned at a rate of 2°2Θ/minute from 2° to 35°2Θ with a Phillips-Norelco XRG-2500 x-ray generator and diffractometer using a copper target.

Further information on the clay minerals is included in Appendix D.

APPENDIX D

Clay Mineralogy

The clay minerals are defined for this study as follows. Kaolinite has a 7.2Å basal spacing and does not expand with glycolation. Illite has a 10Å basal spacing and does not expand with glycolation. Palygorskite has a 10.5Å basal spacing and does not expand with glycolation nor collapse with heating to 450°C. Chlorite has a 14Å basal spacing and does not expand with glycolation nor collapse with heating to 450°C. Smectite has a 17Å basal spacing after glycolation. Other expandables have basal spacings between 10.5Å and 17Å before heating, and expand to greater than 17Å with glycolation; they collapse to 10Å after heating.

A very rough semi-quantitative estimate of relative proportions of the clay minerals was obtained by measuring x-ray diffraction pattern peak areas according to the following scheme:

kaolinite	7.2Å peak, glycolated
illite	10Å peak, glycolated
palygorskite	10.5Å peak, glycolated
chlorite	14Å peak, heated to 600°C
smectite	17Å peak, glycolated
expandables	area under the curve between 10.5Å and 17Å; unheated—14Å peak area; heated to 600°C—17Å peak area, glycolated.

Expandables exclude smectite, but possibly include vermiculite, random-mixed layer minerals, and expanding chlorites. Palygorskite may include hydrated illite.

All of these are common soil-clay minerals except for palygorskite. Palygorskite (here considered synonymous with attapulgite) is a soil-clay mineral of somewhat restricted occurrence, but it is nevertheless widely reported in the literature on soil clays in arid and semi-arid regions (for example: Vanden Heuvel 1966; Millot et al. 1969; Paquet et al. 1969; McLean et al. 1972; Glass et al. 1973; Hassouba and Shaw 1980).

Soils in these regions are most likely to provide the necessary alkaline environment for palygorskite. Other requirements include low alumina and high silica and magnesium concentrations (Zelazney and Calhoun 1977). A close association between palygorskite and high levels of carbonate was observed by some authors (for example: Vanden Heuvel 1966; McLean et al. 1972; Millot et al. 1969; Frye et al. 1974).

Morphologically, palygorskite is distinct from the other clay minerals discussed, since instead of being platy, it forms elongate laths. This characteristic morphology was used to advantage in order to check that the 10.5Å peak was due to palygorskite and not to hydrated illite or some other species. Accordingly, two samples were selected (R7 and Q4) and mounts made for use with the transmission electron microscope. Photomicrographs of these samples show the presence of elongate laths. This information, in conjunction with the x-ray diffraction peak of 10.5Å, is considered adequate evidence for the presence of palygorskite. There is a difficulty, however, since this 10.5Å peak is observed on all patterns including those obtained after heating to 600°C. According to Caillère and Hénin (1961), this peak should no longer be present after this treatment. No explanation for the retention of this peak is offered here.

APPENDIX E

Miscellaneous Samples

Several isolated samples, labeled A, B, C, and D, not part of a described profile, were also analyzed. Samples A and C are from discontinuous bodies of reddish, clayey materials from different locations on the site and were analyzed because of particular questions raised by the excavators. Sample B is closely associated with a Neolithic wall and is possibly part of a mud superstructure. Sample D is from an outcrop of the paleosol north of the site, along the sea-cut escarpment.

The samples are described below:

A Reddish yellow (5YR 6/6) silty clay loam, yellowish red (5YR 4/6) moist; massive; hard; many carbonate nodules; rounded and angular gravels; serpentinite gravels. Sample collected from material laminated on the surface of the west scarp of Q5S.

B Light brown (7.5YR 6/4) clay loam, reddish brown (5YR 4/4) moist; massive; cemented with carbonate; rare cobbles and shells. Removed from stones of Wall M in P5.

C Light brown (7.5YR 6/4) clay loam, yellowish red to strong brown (5YR - 7.5YR 4/6) moist; massive; hard; rare angular gravels; serpentinite gravels. From QR, Unit 33.

D Pink (5YR 8/4) loam, yellowish red (5YR 5/8) moist; moderate medium granular; hard; cobbly; roots; bee nest burrows. From an outcrop of paleosol along the shore approximately 80 meters north of the Paralia excavations.

These samples are clay loams relatively high in iron oxide and low in organic carbon. CEC is also low. Sample D is also unusually high in calcium carbonate, extractable sodium, and base saturation. The mineralogy is dominated by calcite and quartz in the <2-mm fraction and by kaolinite and illite in the clay-mineral fraction. Samples A and B come from deposits of Middle Neolithic age. The age of the deposit from which sample C is taken has not yet been determined (Wilkinson and Vitelli 1979). These three samples are similar to the sediments of horizons IIB23 in soil profile Q and IIIC1 in profile L and probably of similar origin. Sample D, although taken in order to study the paleosol away from the site, is overlain by unexcavated Neolithic deposits. It does not, therefore, furnish an independent sample for comparison.

APPENDIX F

Tables of Laboratory Data

PROFILE Q: PARTICLE-SIZE ANALYSIS (%)

		TOTAL <2-MM FRACTION								SAND-FREE			
		Without Carbonates Removed				*Carbonates Removed*				*Without Carbonates Removed*		*Carbonates Removed*	
Sample	*Depth (cm)*	*<2µm*	*2-16µm*	*16-62µm*	*>62µm*	*<2µm*	*2-16µm*	*16-62µm*	*>62µm*	<2µm	2-62µm	<2µm	2-62µm
Q1	0-20	32.2	23.1	15.3	29.4	35.4	15.8	10.5	38.3	46	54	57	43
2	20-38	31.8	21.5	13.6	33.1	40.5	18.2	12.1	29.2	47	53	57	43
3	38-53	32.8	24.5	14.8	27.9	38.0	17.8	11.9	32.3	46	54	56	44
4	68-83	34.1	24.2	18.6	23.1	34.1	14.9	6.6	44.4	44	56	61	39
5	83-108	24.0	21.7	13.6	40.7	32.3	25.0	14.3	28.4	40	60	45	55
6	108-123	17.1	28.2	19.0	35.6	21.4	35.0	19.9	23.7	27	73	28	72
7	123-158	15.0	36.9	21.3	26.8	15.0	25.9	14.1	45.0	21	79	27	73
8	158-181	22.4	26.7	14.6	36.3	24.3	28.9	14.4	32.3	35	65	36	64
9	181-228	36.8	30.0	15.1	18.1	43.9	31.9	12.8	11.4	45	55	50	50
10	228-253	35.0	20.3	11.7	33.0	42.1	23.5	17.6	16.8	52	48	51	49

PROFILE Q: CHEMISTRY

		Extractable Bases									
Sample	*pH (1:1)*	*Ca*	*Mg*	*Na*	*K*	*CEC*	*Base Sat. NH_4OAC*	*Fe_2O_3*	*MnO_2*	*Organic C*	*$CaCO_3$*
		(me/100g)					*(%)*				
Q1	7.0	20.1	5.2	8.1	1.4	47.6	73	1.59	0.03	3.06	35.7
2	7.1	24.4	3.9	8.1	1.3	51.6	73	1.73	0.04	1.84	39.8
3	7.2	24.1	4.0	6.8	1.3	50.5	72	1.73	0.04	1.20	41.4
4	7.2	23.8	4.6	7.2	1.4	43.8	84	1.89	0.05	1.36	42.3
5	7.3	16.6	3.8	8.5	1.2	38.0	79	1.95	0.04	0.79	43.9
6	7.1	17.1	3.2	9.9	1.1	48.7	64	1.00	0.03	1.08	45.2
7	7.4	20.0	4.7	12.8	1.2	48.7	80	1.03	0.04	1.40	41.9
8	7.4	12.3	4.8	8.8	1.3	42.8	63	1.77	0.05	0.78	38.7
9	7.4	12.0	3.0	11.9	1.6	37.4	76	2.28	0.07	0.28	43.6
10	8.2	14.6	2.9	12.6	1.6	37.8	84	2.65	0.07	0.29	38.9

PROFILE R: PARTICLE-SIZE ANALYSIS (%)

		TOTAL <2-MM FRACTION								SAND-FREE			
		Without Carbonates Removed				*Carbonates Removed*				*Without Carbonates Removed*		*Carbonates Removed*	
Sample	*Depth (cm)*	<2µm	2-16µm	16-62µm	>62µm	<2µm	2-16µm	16-62µm	>62µm	<2µm	2-62µm	<2µm	2-62µm
R1	0-30	25.5	24.8	12.5	37.2	32.3	21.3	14.8	31.5	41	59	47	53
2	30-52	24.0	29.2	20.1	26.6	29.1	24.9	16.8	29.2	33	67	41	59
3	52-80	21.2	26.7	17.4	34.7	25.1	23.1	16.3	35.4	33	67	39	61
4	80-103	20.8	30.8	20.1	28.3	26.1	26.7	19.8	27.4	29	71	36	64
5	103-130	20.8	33.0	20.0	26.3	24.4	26.5	21.9	27.2	28	72	34	66
6	130-135	28.6	29.1	20.6	21.7	28.0	26.1	15.3	30.6	37	63	40	60
7	135-155	32.4	27.3	16.5	23.8	31.4	21.1	9.9	37.6	42	58	50	50

PROFILE R: CHEMISTRY

Sample	pH (1:1)	Extractable Bases Ca	Mg	Na (me/100g)	K	CEC	Base Sat. NH$_4$OAC	Fe$_2$O$_3$	MnO$_2$ (%)	Organic C	CaCO$_3$
R1	7.3	22.3	4.2	11.4	1.6	52.8	75	1.32	0.03	1.58	47.3
2	7.7	21.8	4.5	10.4	1.6	47.8	80	0.53	0.02	1.26	48.1
3	8.3	22.1	5.0	10.0	1.3	45.2	85	1.16	0.04	1.28	44.3
4	8.6	23.7	4.0	9.3	1.2	48.7	78	1.09	0.05	1.39	46.2
5	8.6	18.0	4.7	10.9	1.3	49.0	71	1.29	0.05	1.45	39.4
6	8.6	16.5	5.2	11.0	1.6	40.1	86	1.80	0.06	0.88	38.5
7	8.5	16.0	4.2	9.5	1.9	38.6	82	2.09	0.07	0.71	36.2

PROFILE S: PARTICLE-SIZE ANALYSIS (%)

		TOTAL <2-MM FRACTION								SAND-FREE			
		Without Carbonates Removed				*Carbonates Removed*				*Without Car-bonates Removed*		*Carbonates Removed*	
Sample	*Depth (cm)*	*<2µm*	*2-16µm*	*16-62µm*	*>62µm*	*<2µm*	*2-16µm*	*16-62µm*	*>62µm*				
S1	0-20	20.9	31.0	21.3	26.8	22.6	23.9	14.4	39.1	<2µm	2-62µm	<2µm	2-62µm
2	20-40	24.9	26.3	13.7	35.0	25.6	33.1	18.6	22.7	29	71	37	63
3	40-55	23.9	26.3	16.3	33.5	25.1	28.7	16.2	30.0	38	62	33	67
4	55-70	22.2	23.4	15.0	39.5	24.2	31.7	18.4	25.7	36	64	36	64
5	70-85	19.2	29.7	15.8	35.3	21.8	30.9	17.8	29.5	37	63	33	67
6	85-90	30.4	27.4	16.3	25.9	26.7	23.3	14.8	35.1	30	70	31	69
7	90-100	27.2	20.6	11.3	40.9	34.4	20.7	11.3	33.6	41	59	41	59
										46	54	52	48

PROFILE S: CHEMISTRY

Sample	pH (1:1)	Extractable Bases (me/100g)					Base Sat.				
		Ca	Mg	Na	K	CEC	NH$_4$OAC	Fe$_2$O$_3$	MnO$_2$ (%)	Organic C	CaCO$_3$
S1	7.2	15.7	5.9	8.8	1.3	45.7	69	1.44	0.04	1.32	44.3
2	6.7	24.4	6.8	5.9	1.4	50.1	77	1.34	0.05	1.26	39.7
3	7.1	20.2	5.3	12.0	1.4	47.3	82	1.45	0.04	1.04	39.5
4	7.1	17.1	6.0	10.7	1.4	42.5	83	1.79	0.05	1.45	39.5
5	7.2	23.6	4.9	11.9	1.4	50.7	83	1.30	0.05	1.41	37.1
6	7.4	21.2	5.0	8.6	1.4	41.3	88	1.81	0.06	1.44	36.0
7	7.5	18.8	4.3	8.7	1.5	41.1	81	1.79	0.07	0.47	36.8

PROFILE T: PARTICLE-SIZE ANALYSIS (%)

		TOTAL <2-MM FRACTION								SAND-FREE			
		Without Carbonates Removed				*Carbonates Removed*				*Without Carbonates Removed*		*Carbonates Removed*	
Sample	Depth (cm)	<2µm	2-16µm	16-62µm	>62µm	<2µm	2-16µm	16-62µm	>62µm	<2µm	2-62µm	<2µm	2-62µm
T1	70-92	25.2	32.7	19.5	22.6	26.6	31.3	17.8	24.3	33	67	35	65
2	92-125	25.4	27.9	18.5	28.3	26.8	24.4	11.5	37.3	35	65	43	57
3	125-160	29.1	34.9	20.8	15.2	30.6	27.9	21.3	20.2	34	66	38	62
4	165-175	30.2	25.6	12.6	31.5	33.1	20.5	11.2	35.2	44	56	51	49
5	175-200	35.5	24.7	11.7	28.2	38.4	26.4	17.1	18.0	49	51	47	53

PROFILE T: CHEMISTRY

		Extractable Bases									
Sample	*pH (1:1)*	*Ca*	*Mg*	*Na*	*K*	*CEC*	*Base Sat. NH_4OAC*	*Fe_2O_3*	*MnO_2*	*Organic C*	*$CaCO_3$*
				(me/100g)					*(%)*		
T1	7.8	17.8	4.8	9.2	1.5	41.0	81	1.65	0.05	0.83	39.3
2	8.0	19.0	6.1	7.5	1.3	42.0	81	1.49	0.05	0.67	37.9
3	8.4	16.5	5.4	9.6	1.4	41.2	80	1.59	0.06	0.56	37.2
4	8.4	13.7	3.8	11.0	1.7	36.0	84	2.04	0.07	0.50	37.4
5	8.3	15.3	3.4	8.9	2.0	33.9	87	2.20	0.10	0.31	35.7

PROFILE L: PARTICLE-SIZE ANALYSIS (%)

		TOTAL <2-MM FRACTION								SAND-FREE			
		Without Carbonates Removed				*Carbonates Removed*				*Without Carbonates Removed*		*Carbonates Removed*	
Sample	*Depth (cm)*	*<2µm*	*2-16µm*	*16-62µm*	*>62µm*	*<2µm*	*2-16µm*	*16-62µm*	*>62µm*	<2µm	2-62µm	<2µm	2-62µm
L1	0-20	32.9	25.9	14.8	26.3	39.2	16.9	13.5	30.4	45	55	56	44
2	20-35	29.2	38.9	13.8	18.0	43.9	18.3	11.6	26.1	36	64	59	41
3	35-65	24.2	41.3	16.0	18.4	37.9	18.0	14.8	29.3	30	70	54	46
4	65-85	31.1	30.8	17.5	20.7	35.4	24.5	13.3	26.8	39	71	48	52
5	85-100	20.6	34.2	21.6	23.6	21.0	25.0	12.9	41.2	27	73	36	64
6	100-120	17.5	32.6	20.0	29.8	21.5	27.8	15.7	35.1	25	75	33	67
7	120-140	18.2	33.2	18.9	29.7	19.6	30.5	20.7	29.1	26	74	28	72
8	140-170	26.3	23.4	12.6	37.6	34.1	22.0	10.8	33.1	42	58	51	49
9	175-200	35.0	26.3	11.0	29.1	45.3	16.5	9.3	28.9	48	52	64	36

PROFILE L: CHEMISTRY

Sample	pH (1:1)	Extractable Bases					Base Sat.				
		Ca	Mg	Na	K	CEC	NH_4OAC	Fe_2O_3	MnO_2	Organic C	$CaCO_3$
		(me/100g)					(%)				
L1	7.5	21.2	4.7	10.7	1.2	49.4	76	1.84	0.02	2.78	41.1
2	7.4	22.8	3.3	11.4	1.0	52.6	74	1.77	0.01	1.51	64.9
3	7.5	21.2	3.6	15.0	1.3	53.4	77	1.84	0.01	0.64	71.8
4	7.4	17.3	4.1	10.9	1.1	43.2	77	2.22	0.04	0.72	44.4
5	7.4	21.3	4.1	8.4	0.8	46.1	75	1.66	0.03	1.22	43.1
6	7.4	23.3	3.1	12.2	0.8	48.2	82	2.02	0.04	1.24	43.4
7	7.4	20.7	5.2	13.5	0.9	53.2	76	1.53	0.03	1.60	45.8
8	7.6	16.4	3.8	9.9	1.2	38.3	82	2.66	0.02	0.60	52.9
9	7.6	14.8	3.8	12.7	1.7	43.7	75	2.55	0.03	0.55	53.2

SAMPLES A, B, C, D: PARTICLE SIZE-ANALYSIS (%)

	TOTAL <2-MM FRACTION								SAND-FREE			
	Without Carbonates Removed				*Carbonates Removed*				*Without Carbonates Removed*		*Carbonates Removed*	
Sample	<2µm	2-16µm	16-62µm	>62µm	<2µm	2-16µm	16-62µm	>62µm	<2µm	2-62µm	<2µm	2-62µm
A	38.9	28.0	16.1	17.0	36.8	29.6	18.9	14.7	47	53	43	57
B	29.9	30.8	15.4	23.8	27.3	28.6	14.2	29.8	39	61	39	61
C	28.5	28.0	15.3	28.2	29.2	35.3	18.7	16.9	40	60	35	65
D	25.6	26.0	15.6	32.8	33.0	20.1	10.7	36.2	38	62	52	48

SAMPLES A, B, C, D: CHEMISTRY

		Extractable Bases									
Sample	*pH (1:1)*	*Ca*	*Mg*	*Na*	*K*	*CEC*	*Base Sat. NH_4OAC*	*Fe_2O_3*	*MnO_2*	*Organic C*	*$CaCO_3$*
		(me/100g)					(%)				
A	7.6	14.4	3.2	9.7	1.7	38.8	75	1.82	0.06	0.43	32.7
B	7.4	13.2	3.3	10.3	1.3	40.0	70	2.23	0.05	0.66	39.8
C	7.3	16.2	3.7	10.2	1.3	37.0	85	2.19	0.07	0.57	38.2
D	7.4	4.8	6.0	19.3	1.4	31.3	100	1.03	0.02	0.34	66.5

CLAY MINERALS

	K	*I*	*P*	*C*	*M*	*X*
Profile Q						
Q1	24	34	6	27	—	9
2	21	29	4	31	—	15
3	25	23	5	15	3	30
4	39	37	5	19	—	—
5	37	33	6	15	—	8
6	20	34	6	40	—	—
7	30	41	13	15	—	—
8	35	25	7	13	—	20
9	44	31	8	17	—	—
10	51	32	3	12	—	2
Profile R						
R1	20	22	3	13	5	36
2	14	18	6	14	—	49
3	22	28	12	21	—	18
4	19	22	6	10	—	43
5	33	38	15	12	—	2
6	34	37	12	6	—	11
7	28	24	8	20	—	20

K = Kaolinite *M* = Smectite
I = Illite *P* = Palygorskite
C = Chlorite *X* = Other expanding

Note: Numbers represent a comparison of peak areas.

CLAY MINERALS

	K	*I*	*P*	*C*	*M*	*X*
Profile L						
L1	32	26	10	10	—	23
2	27	20	6	8	25	14
3	14	10	—	3	57	15
4	24	24	10	12	13	18
5	38	29	7	5	10	11
6	25	34	15	3	—	24
7	32	27	10	—	—	32
8	30	28	11	23	—	8
9	50	28	10	8	—	4
Profile S						
S1	20	26	8	23	—	23
2	17	27	5	19	—	33
3	29	35	3	17	—	15
4	31	28	11	20	—	11
5	29	28	4	14	—	25
6	25	21	10	11	—	33
7	44	28	7	12	—	9

K = Kaolinite
I = Illite
C = Chlorite
M = Smectite
P = Palygorskite
X = Other expanding

Note: Numbers represent a comparison of peak areas.

CLAY MINERALS

	K	*I*	*P*	*C*	*M*	*X*
Profile T						
T1	21	23	10	7	—	39
2	29	33	18	19	—	1
3	30	32	7	11	—	20
4	41	32	12	4	—	10
5	36	25	9	29	—	<1
Samples A, B, C, D						
A	31	31	6	9	—	24
B	35	31	17	11	—	6
C	36	25	16	8	—	14
D	46	25	15	14	—	—

K	= Kaolinite	*M*	= Smectite
I	= Illite	*P*	= Palygorskite
C	= Chlorite	*X*	= Other expanding

Note: Numbers represent a comparison of peak areas.

NOTES

1. Included among Final Neolithic finds from L5NE are some coarse, crudely fired sherds. The clay from one of these sherds was analyzed using the same x-ray diffraction methods as were used in the previous analyses. Qualitative results were obtained as follows. The principal clay minerals present are kaolinite, illite, and smectite. Mixed-layer expandable material is also an important component of the suite. Chlorite is present in trace amounts. Figure 23 shows the smoothed trace of glycolated x-ray diffraction pattern for the F.N. sherd aligned with a similar trace for sample L3 from L5NE. Similarity between the two is apparent. The somewhat more rounded illite (I) peak and the less sharp and defined smectite (M) peak of the former may be due to its having been fired or heated. Since kaolinite (K) is still present, prolonged heating at temperatures of 400°C or greater is ruled out. Brief heating (ca. 15 minutes) to the 400-500°C range, however, would not have destroyed the kaolinite. For comparison, similar tracings for the complete sample profiles Q (Q5N, N scarp) and L (L5NE, E scarp) are provided in Figures 9 and 18, respectively.

A notable difference between the results obtained from the F.N. sherd analysis and the L3 sample is the relative abundance of calcite (calcium carbonate) in the latter. The ratio of calcite to quartz (based on peak height of the glycolated samples) of the F.N. sherd is about 0.3. The calcite to quartz ratio of sample L3 is about 3.

2. The following comments are based upon notes provided by K. D. Vitelli which furnish details of individual contexts containing worn sherds.

3. Archaeological sediment classes, as classified in Chapter 3, are given in parentheses, where the strata fall within these classes.

4. Strata X-XIII are all located in L5NW, for which no master section drawing exists. A secondary section of L5NW appears in Jacobsen and Farrand 1987 (Plate 58), with the strata not numbered. The relevant unit numbers are given in Appendix B.

5. Unfortunately, it has not been possible to construct a similar stratigraphic sequence for grid square Q4.

6. There is a difference of 1.3 m between sea level given by the Greek Army Geographical Service (0 m) and estimated sea level obtained by five weeks of approximate tide gauging in May and June 1974 (*ESL* = estimated sea level, given on Figure 34 as a tidal range of 40 cm). This is confirmed by the general position of sea level on Paralia. We cannot explain this disparity.

The sea floor as extrapolated from van Andel (1980:Figure 5) did not coincide with that taken from the 1:200 site map by F. Cooper. This might result from the disparity between the sea levels used. For the extrapolation, we have therefore chosen to use sediment depth as measured below the sea floor because these will both refer to the same sea level. [For more on this problem, see Jacobsen and Farrand 1987:17. —EDITOR]

7. In what follows, B.P. dates are in uncalibrated radiocarbon years and B.C. dates are in calendar years.

8. Walls A, B, and C were initially called Walls 1, 2, and 3, respectively. See, for example, Jacobsen 1979:271-272.

9. For terminology and abbreviations used in Appendix B, see "A Note on Terminology" (*supra*).

10. Strata X through XII all have weak stratigraphic control. Descriptions and stratigraphy are based purely on the excavation notebooks, but the interpretations are our own.

11. "Cultural Material" is omitted for this trench. All data are based upon field descriptions of 1974.

12. Strata III-X are associated with talus accumulation or localized aggradation of finer sediments. The latter frequently lens or interdigitate with the stony deposits. The stony talus deposits will have been

subjected to continuous re-sorting. These stratigraphic units were difficult to differentiate in the field; therefore, in addition to suffering mixing in antiquity, they may have been mixed during excavation. Due to this uncertainty, discussion of context quality and cultural materials has been omitted from the description of strata IV-X.

13. Soil descriptions from stratum XI onwards are partly based upon descriptions in excavation notebooks.

14. Strata XXI through XXIV were drawn in 1973 but were not present during final redrafting of the section drawings. All descriptions are from excavation notebooks and original drawings.

15. Based upon field descriptions from 1974 by T.J. Wilkinson.

16. This section is transverse to the slope.

17. This section is transverse to the slope.

18. All contexts contain cultural material.

19. This section is transverse to the slope.

REFERENCES

Anthanasiadis, A.

1975 Zur postglazialen Vegetationsentwicklung von Litochoro Katerinis und Pertouli Trikalon (Griechenland). *Flora* 164:99-132.

Baillie, M.G.L., and M.A.R. Munro

1988 Irish Tree Rings, Santorini and Volcanic Dust Veils. *Nature* 332(6162):344-346.

Bear, Firman E. (editor)

1964 *Chemistry of the Soil*. 2nd ed. Reinhold, New York.

Biggs, Robert B.

1978 Coastal Bays. In *Coastal Sedimentary Environments*, edited by R.A. Davis, Jr., pp. 69-99. Springer-Verlag, New York.

Black, C.A. (editor)

1965 *Methods of Soil Analysis*. American Society of Agronomy, Madison.

Borchardt, G.A.

1977 Montmorillonite and Other Smectite Minerals. In *Minerals in Soil Environments*, edited by J.B. Dixon and S.B. Weed, pp. 293-330. Soil Science Society of America, Madison.

Bottema, S.

1974 *Late Quaternary Vegetation History of Northwestern Greece*. Ph.D. dissertation, University of Groningen, Groningen.

1979 Pollen Analytical Investigations in Thessaly (Greece). *Palaeohistoria* 21:19-40.

1980 Palynological Investigations on Crete. *Review of Palaeobotany and Palynology* 31:193-217.

1982 Palynological Investigations in Greece with Special Reference to Pollen as an Indicator of Human Activity. *Palaeohistoria* 24:257-289.

1988 A Reconstruction of the Halos Environment on the Basis of Palynological Information. Appendix I in *New Halos, A Hellenistic Town in Thessalia, Greece,* by H.R. Reinders, pp. 216-226. Thesis, University of Groningen, Groningen.

Bottema, S., and Y. Barkoudah

1979 Modern Pollen Precipitation in Syria and Lebanon and its Relation to Vegetation. *Pollen et Spores* 21:427-480.

Bottema, S., and H. Woldring

1984(1986) Late Quaternary Vegetation and Climate of Southwestern Turkey. Part II. *Palaeohistoria* 26:123-149.

Bryson, R.A., H.H. Lamb, and D.L. Donley

1974 Drought and the Decline of Mycenae. *Antiquity* 48:46-50.

Caillère, S., and S. Hénin

1961 Palygorskite. In *The X-Ray Identification and Crystal Structures of Clay Minerals*, 2nd ed., edited by G. Brown, pp. 343-353. Mineralogical Society, London.

Carpenter, R.

1966 *Discontinuity in Greek Civilization*. Cambridge University Press, Cambridge.

Childe, G.

1958 *The Prehistory of European Society*. Pelican Books, Harmondsworth, Middlesex.

Cooper, F.A.

1987 The Engineering Survey. In *Franchthi Cave and Paralia: Maps, Plans and Sections*, by T.W. Jacobsen and W.R. Farrand, pp. 10-14. Excavations at Franchthi Cave, Greece, fasc. 1. Indiana University Press, Bloomington and Indianapolis.

Creer, K.M., P.W. Readman, and S. Papamarinopoulos
1981 Geomagnetic Secular Variations in Greece through the Last 6000 Years Obtained from Lake Sediment Studies. *Geophysical Journal of the Royal Astronomical Society* 66:193-219.
Cullen, Tracey, and Della Cook
Forthcoming *Mortuary Practices at Franchthi Cave* (title provisional). Excavations at Franchthi Cave, Greece. Indiana University Press, Bloomington and Indianapolis.
Darwin, C.
1945 *Darwin on Humus and the Earthworm.* Reprinted. Faber and Faber, London. Originally published 1881, *The Formation of Vegetable Mould Through the Actions of Worms with Observations on their Habits*, John Murray, London.
Davison, Charles
1888 Note on the Movement of Scree-Material. *Quarterly Journal of the Geological Society of London* 44:232-238, 825-826.
Drost, B.
1979 *Late Quaternary Stratigraphy of the Southern Argolid* (Peloponnese, Greece). Unpublished Master's thesis, Department of Geology, University of Pennsylvania, Philadelphia.
Duhon, Susan T.
1982 *Soils and Surficial Deposits of an Archaeological Site: The Paralia at Franchthi Cave, Greece.* Unpublished Master's thesis, Department of Geology, Indiana University, Bloomington.
Evenari, Michael, Leslie Shanan, and Naphtali Tadmor
1971 *The Negev: The Challenge of a Desert.* Harvard University Press, Cambridge.
Faegri, K., and J. Iversen
1973 *Textbook of Pollen Analysis.* 3rd rev. ed. Hafner, N.Y.
Fairbridge, R.W.
1987 Quasi-Equilibrium in Holocene Climate Change: Astronomic Framework and Terrestrial Inertia. *Programme XII, International Congress, International Union for Quaternary Research*, p. 164.
Farrand, William R.
1982 Palaeoenvironments from 25,000 to 5,000 BP in Southern Greece as Seen from Sediments in Franchthi Cave (Argolidos). In *Palaeoclimates, Palaeoenvironments and Human Communities in the Eastern Mediterranean in Later Prehistory*, edited by J. Bintliff and William van Zeist, pp. 273-274. British Archaeological Reports, International Series, Vol. 133, Oxford.
Forthcoming *General Geology, Sedimentology, and Lithostratigraphy of Franchthi Cave.* Excavations at Franchthi Cave, Greece. Indiana University Press, Bloomington and Indianapolis.
Fladmark, Kurt R.
1982 Microdebitage Analysis: Initial Considerations. *Journal of Archaeological Science* 9(2):205-220.
Flemming, Nicholas C.
1983a Survival of Submerged Lithic and Bronze Age Artifact Sites: A Review of Case Histories. In *Quaternary Coastlines and Marine Archaeology*, edited by P.M. Masters and N.C. Flemming, pp. 135-173. Academic Press, New York.
1983b Preliminary Geomorphological Survey of an Early Neolithic Submerged Site in the Sporadhes, Northern Aegean. In *Quaternary Coastlines and Marine Archaeology*, edited by P.M. Masters and N.C. Flemming, pp. 233-268. Academic Press, New York.
1985 Preliminary Geomorphological Survey of the Neolithic Site of Agios Petros. In *Agios Petros: A Neolithic Site in the Northern Sporades*, by Nikos Efstratiou. British Archaeological Reports, International Series, Vol. 241, Oxford.
Food and Agricultural Organization (FAO)
1966 *Economic Survey of the Western Peloponnesus, Greece*, Vol. 4 (II): *Land and Water.* United Nations Special Fund, Rome.

Frye, John C., H.D. Glass, A. Byron Leonard, and Dennis D. Coleman

1974 *Caliche and Clay Mineral Zonation of Ogallala Formation, Central-Eastern New Mexico*. New Mexico Bureau of Mines and Mineral Resources, Circular 144, Socorro, NM.

Gagliano, S., C.E. Peason, R.A. Weinstein, D.E. Wiseman, and C.M. McClendon

1982 *Sedimentary Studies of Prehistoric Archaeological Sites: Criteria for the Identification of Submerged Archaeological Sites of the Northern Gulf of Mexico Continental Shelf*. National Park Service, Preservation Planning Series. Coastal Environments, Inc. Baton Rouge, La.

Galili, Ehud, and Mina Weinstein-Evron

1985 Prehistory and Palaeoenvironments of Submerged Sites along the Carmel Coast of Israel. *Paleorient* 11:37-52.

Gifford, John A.

1978 *Paleogeography of Archaeological Sites of the Larnaca Lowlands, Southeastern Cyprus*. Ph.D. dissertation, University of Minnesota. University Microfilms, Ann Arbor.

1983 Core Sampling of a Holocene Marine Sedimentary Sequence and Underlying Neolithic Cultural Material off Franchthi Cave, Greece. In *Quaternary Coastlines and Marine Archaeology*, edited by P.M. Masters and N.C. Flemming, pp. 269-281. Academic Press, New York.

Gifford, John A., George Rapp, Jr., and Carol M. Moss

1982 The Sedimentary Matrix. In *Troy: The Archaeological Geology*, edited by George Rapp, Jr., and John A. Gifford, pp. 61-103. Troy Supplementary Monograph 4. Princeton University Press, Princeton.

Glass, H.D., John C. Frye, and A. Byron Leonard

1973 *Clay Minerals in East-Central New Mexico*. New Mexico Bureau of Mines and Mineral Resources, Circular 139, Socorro, NM.

Green, F.J.

1979 Phosphatic Mineralization of Seeds from Archaeological Sites. *Journal of Archaeological Science* 6:279-284.

Halstead, P.

1982 Review of *Thera and the Aegean World I & II*, edited by C. Doumas and *Papers in Cycladic Prehistory*, 2nd ed., edited by J.L. Davis and J.F. Cherry. *Antiquity* 56:142-143.

Hansen, Julie M.

1978 The Earliest Seed Remains from Greece: Palaeolithic through Neolithic at Franchthi Cave. *Bericht der Deutsche Botanische Gesellschaft* 91:39-46.

1980 *The Palaeoethnobotany of Franchthi Cave, Greece*. Ph.D. dissertation, University of Minnesota. University Microfilms, Ann Arbor.

Forthcoming a Franchthi Cave and the Beginnings of Agriculture in Greece and the Aegean. In *The Prehistory of Agriculture: New Experimental and Ethnographic Approaches*, edited by P. Anderson-Gerfand. CNRS, Paris.

Forthcoming b *The Palaeoethnobotany of Franchthi Cave, Greece*. Excavations at Franchthi Cave, Greece. Indiana University Press, Bloomington and Indianapolis.

Harding, A., G. Cadogan, and R. Howell

1969 Pavlopetri, an Underwater Bronze Age Town in Laconia. *Annual of the British School of Archaeology at Athens* 64:113-142.

Harris, Edward C.

1979 *Principles of Archaeological Stratigraphy*. Studies in Archaeological Science. Academic Press, London.

Hassouba, H., and H.F. Shaw

1980 The Occurrence of Palygorskite in Quaternary Sediments of the Coastal Plain of North-West Egypt. *Clay Minerals* 15:77-83.

Hooghiemstra, H., C.O.C. Agwu, and H.-J. Beug

1986 Pollen and Spore Distribution in Recent Marine Sediments: A Record of NW African Seasonal Wind Patterns and Vegetation Belts. *"Meteor" Forschungs-Ergebnisse* 40:87-135.

Hopf, M.

1964 Nutzpflanzen vom Lernaischen Golf. *Jahrbuch der Romische Germanische Zentralmuseums Mainz* 11:1-19.

Howarth, P.J., and J.G. Bones

1972 Relationships Between Process and Geometric Form on High Arctic Debris Slopes, South-West Devon Island, Canada. In *Polar Geomorphology*, compiled by R.J. Price and D.E. Sugden, pp. 139-152. Institute of British Geographers, Special Publication No. 4, London.

Jackson, M.L.

1979 *Soil Chemical Analysis: Advanced Course*, 2nd ed. M.L. Jackson, Madison.

Jackson, M.L., and G.D. Sherman

1953 Chemical Weathering of Minerals in Soil. *Advances in Agronomy* 5:219-318.

Jacobsen, T.W.

1969 Excavations at Porto Cheli and Vicinity, Preliminary Report, II: the Franchthi Cave, 1967-68. *Hesperia* 38:343-381.

1973a Excavations in the Franchthi Cave, 1969-1971, Part I. *Hesperia* 42:45-88.

1973b Excavations in the Franchthi Cave, 1969-1971, Part II. *Hesperia* 42:253-283.

1974 New Radiocarbon Dates from Franchthi Cave: A Preliminary Note Regarding Collection of Samples by Means of Flotation. *Journal of Field Archaeology* 1:303-304.

1976 17,000 Years of Greek Prehistory. *Scientific American* 234(6):76-87.

1979 Excavations at Franchthi Cave, 1973-1974. *Arkhaiologikon Deltion (Khronika)* 29:268-282.

Jacobsen, T.W., and Tracey Cullen

1981 A Consideration of Mortuary Practices in Neolithic Greece: Burials from Franchthi Cave. In *Mortality and Immortality: The Anthropology of Death*, edited by S.C. Humphreys and H. King, pp. 79-101. Academic Press, London.

Jacobsen, T.W., and W.R. Farrand

1987 *Franchthi Cave and Paralia: Maps, Plans, and Sections*. Excavations at Franchthi Cave, Greece, fasc. 1. Indiana University Press, Bloomington and Indianapolis.

Keller, J., W.B.F. Ryan, D. Ninkovich, and R. Altherr

1978 Explosive Volcanic Activity in the Mediterranean over the Past 200,000 yr as Recorded in Deep-Sea Sediments. *Geological Society of America Bulletin* 89:591-604.

Kraft, John C.

1985 Marine Environments: Paleogeographic Reconstructions in the Littoral Region. In *Archaeological Sediments in Context*, edited by J.K. Stein and W.R. Farrand, pp. 111-125. Institute for Quaternary Studies, University of Maine, Orono.

Kroll, H.

1982 Kulturpflanzen von Tiryns. *Archäologischer Anzeiger* 3:467-485.

Leatham, J., and S. Hood

1959 Submarine Explorations in Crete, 1955. *Annual of the British School of Archaeology at Athens* 53-54:263-280.

McLean, S.A., B.L. Allen, and J.R. Craig

1972 The Occurrence of Sepiolite and Attapulgite on the Southern High Plains. *Clays and Clay Minerals* 20:143-149.

Meusel, H., E. Jäger, and E. Weinert

1965 *Vergleichende Chorologie des zentraleuropäischen Flora*. Fischer Verlag, Jena.

Millot, G., H. Paquet, and A. Ruellan

1969 Néoformation de l'attapulgite dans les sols à carapaces calcaires de la Basse Moulouya (Maroc oriental). *Comptes Rendues de l'Académie Scientifique de Paris* 269, Série D:2771-2774.

Paquet, H., A. Ruellan, Y. Tardy, and G. Millot

1969 Géochemie d'un bassin versant au Maroc oriental. Evolution des argiles dans les sols des montagnes et des plaines de la Basse Moulouya. *Comptes Rendues de l'Académie Scientifique de Paris* 269, Série D:1839-1842.

Payne, Sebastian

1975 Faunal Change at Franchthi Cave from 20,000 to 3,000 B.C. In *Archaeozoological Studies*, edited by A.T. Clason, pp. 120-131. Elsevier, New York.

Polunin, O.

1980 *Flowers of Greece and the Balkans*. Oxford University Press, Oxford.

Pope, Kevin O., Curtis N. Runnels, and Ku Teh-Lung

1984 Dating Middle Palaeolithic Red Beds in Southern Greece. *Nature* 312:264-266.

Pope, Kevin O., and Tjeerd H. van Andel

1984 Late Quaternary Alluviation and Soil Formation in the Southern Argolid: Its History, Causes, and Archaeological Implications. *Journal of Archaeological Science* 11(4):281-306.

Pyle, D.M.

1989 Ice-Core Acidity Peaks, Retarded Tree Growth and Putative Eruptions. *Archaeometry* 31:88-91.

Rackham, O.

1983 Observations on the Historical Ecology of Boeotia. *Annual of the British School of Archaeology at Athens* 78:291-351.

Rapp, Anders

1960 *Talus Slopes and Mountain Walls at Tempelfjorden, Spitsbergen: A Geomorphological Study of the Denudation of Slopes in an Arctic Locality*. Norsk Polarinstitutt, Skrifter Nr. 119, Oslo.

Reinders, H.R.

1988 *New Halos, A Hellenistic Town in Thessalia, Greece*. Thesis, University of Groningen, Groningen.

Reinders, H.R., and S. Bottema

1983 Investigations at Halos and Zerelia. Preliminary Report 1982. *Bulletin Antieke Beschaving* 58:91-100.

Renfrew, Jane

1973 *Palaeoethnobotany*. Columbia University Press, New York.

Rikli, M.

1943-1948 *Das Pflanzenkleid der Mittelmeerländer*. Verlag Hans Huber, Bern.

Schumm, S.A.

1967 Rates of Surficial Rock Creep on Hillslopes in Western Colorado. *Science* 155:560-561.

Selby, M.J.

1982 *Hillslope Materials and Processes*. Oxford University Press, New York.

Shackleton, Judith C.

1988a Reconstructing Past Shorelines as an Approach to Determining Factors Affecting Shellfish Collecting in the Prehistoric Past. In *The Archaeology of Prehistoric Coastlines*, edited by G. Bailey and J. Parkington, pp. 11-21. Cambridge University Press, New York.

1988b *Marine Molluscan Remains from Franchthi Cave*. Excavations at Franchthi Cave, Greece, fasc. 4. Indiana University Press, Bloomington and Indianapolis.

Shackleton, Judith C., and T.H. van Andel

1980 Prehistoric Shell Assemblages from Franchthi Cave and Evolution of the Adjacent Coastal Zone. *Nature* 288:357-359.

1986 Prehistoric Shore Environments, Shellfish Availability, and Shellfish Gathering at Franchthi Cave, Greece. *Geoarchaeology* 1(2):127-143.

Shackleton, Nicholas J.

1969 Preliminary Observations on the Marine Shells. Appendix I in Excavations at Porto Cheli and Vicinity, Preliminary Report, II: The Franchthi Cave, 1967-68, by T.W. Jacobsen. *Hesperia* 38:379-380.

Shaw, Joseph W.

1972 Greek and Roman Harbourworks. In *A History of Seafaring Based on Underwater Archaeology*, edited by G.F. Bass, pp. 87-112. Thames and Hudson, London.

Sheehan, Mark Charles

1979 *The Postglacial Vegetational History of the Argolid Peninsula, Greece*. Ph.D. dissertation, Indiana University. University Microfilms, Ann Arbor.

Soil Conservation Service

1972 *Soil Survey Laboratory Methods and Procedures for Collecting Soil Samples*. USDA Soil Survey Investigations Report No. 1, Washington, D.C.

Stibbe, C.M.

1964 *Kreta en Mykene. Aspecten van de Minoisch-Mykeense cultuur*. Zeist, Antwerp.

Sullivan, D.G.

1988 The Discovery of Santorini Minoan Tephra in Western Turkey. *Nature* 333:552-554.

Sweeting, Marjorie M.

1973 *Karst Landforms*. Macmillan, London.

Thornton, Scott E., Orrin H. Pilkey, Larry J. Doyle, and Patrick Whaling

1980 Holocene Evolution of a Coastal Lagoon, Lake of Tunis, Tunisia. *Sedimentology* 27:79-91.

Turner, J., and J.R.A. Greig

1975 Some Holocene Pollen Diagrams from Greece. *Review of Palaeobotany and Palynology* 20:171-204.

UNESCO/FAO

1968 *Carte de la végétation de la région méditerranéenne* 1:500.000. Feuille occidentale, Paris.

United States Department of Agriculture (USDA)

1951 *Soil Survey Manual*. United States Department of Agriculture Handbook, No. 18, Washington, D.C.

1962 Supplement replacing pp. 173-188 of *Soil Survey Manual* (1951).

van Andel, Tj. H., T.W. Jacobsen, J.B. Jolly, and N. Lianos

1980 Late Quaternary History of the Coastal Zone near Franchthi Cave, Southern Argolid, Greece. *Journal of Field Archaeology* 7:389-402.

van Andel, Tjeerd H.

1987 The Adjacent Sea. In *Landscape and People of the Franchthi Region*, by Tjeerd H. van Andel and Susan B. Sutton, pp. 31-54. Excavations at Franchthi Cave, Greece, fasc. 2. Indiana University Press, Bloomington and Indianapolis.

van Andel, Tjeerd H., and Nikolas Lianos

1983 Prehistoric and Historic Shorelines of the Southern Argolid Peninsula: A Subbottom Profiler Study. *International Journal of Nautical Archaeology and Underwater Exploration* 12:303-324.

1984 High Resolution Seismic Reflection Profiles for the Reconstruction of Postglacial Transgressive Shorelines: An Example from Greece, *Quaternary Research* 22:31-45.

van Andel, Tjeerd H., and Judith C. Shackleton

1982 Late Paleolithic and Mesolithic Coastlines of Greece and the Aegean. *Journal of Field Archaeology* 9:445-454.

van Andel, Tjeerd H., and Susan B. Sutton

1987 *Landscape and People of the Franchthi Region.* Excavations at Franchthi Cave, Greece, fasc. 2. Indiana University Press, Bloomington and Indianapolis.

van Andel, Tjeerd H., and Charles J. Vitaliano

1987 Water and Other Resources. In *Landscape and People of the Franchthi Region*, by Tjeerd H. van Andel and Susan B. Sutton, pp. 17-20. Excavations at Franchthi Cave, Greece, fasc. 2. Indiana University Press, Bloomington and Indianapolis.

Vanden Heuval, R.C.

1966 The Occurrence of Sepiolite and Attapulgite in the Calcareous Zone of a Soil near Las Cruces, New Mexico. *Clays and Clay Minerals* 13:193-207.

van Zeist, W., and S. Bottema

1977 Palynological Investigations in Western Iran. *Palaeohistoria* 19:19-95.

van Zeist, W., H. Woldring, and D. Stapert

1975 Late Quaternary Vegetation History of Southwestern Turkey. *Paleohistoria* 17:53-143.

Vernet, J.L., S. Thiebault, and C. Heinz

1987 Nouvelles données sur la végétation préhistorique postglaciaire méditerranéenne d'après l'analyse anthracologique. In *Premières Communautés Paysannes en Méditerranée Occidentale*, pp. 87-93. CNRS, Paris.

Vitaliano, Charles J.

1987 Geological History. In *Landscape and People of the Franchthi Region*, by T.H. van Andel and S.B. Sutton, pp. 12-17. Excavations at Franchthi Cave, Greece, fasc. 2. Indiana University Press, Bloomington and Indianapolis.

Vitelli, Karen D.

Forthcoming a *Franchthi Neolithic Pottery.* Vol. 1, *Classification and Ceramic Phases 1 and 2.* Excavations at Franchthi Cave, Greece. Indiana University Press, Bloomington and Indianapolis.

Forthcoming b *Franchthi Neolithic Pottery.* Vol. 2, *Ceramic Phases 3-5.* Excavations at Franchthi Cave, Greece. Indiana University Press, Bloomington and Indianapolis.

Voliotis, D.

1973 Beziehungen zwischen Klima, Boden und Vegetation und Vegetations-Zonen in Griechenland. *Scientific Annals of the Faculty of Physics and Mathematics, University of Thessaloniki* 13:221-228.

Wijmstra, T.A.

1969 Palynology of the First 30 Metres of a 120 Metre Deep Section in Northern Greece. *Acta Botanica Neerlandica* 18:511-528.

Wilkinson, T.J., and Karen D. Vitelli

1979 Selected Unit Sequences and Associated Pottery. Unpublished report in Franchthi archives at Indiana University.

Wright, H.E., Jr.

1968 Climatic Change in Mycenean Greece. *Antiquity* 42:123-127.

1972 Vegetation History. In *The Minnesota Messenia Expedition: Reconstructing a Bronze Age Environment*, edited by W.A. MacDonald and G. Rapp, Jr., pp. 188-199. University of Minnesota Press, Minneapolis.

Zelazney, L.W., and F.G. Calhoun

1977 Palygorskite (Attapulgite), Sepiolite, Talc, Pyrophyllite, and Zeolites. In *Minerals in Soil Environments*, edited by J.B. Dixon and S.B. Weed, pp. 435-470. Soil Science Society of America, Madison.

Plates

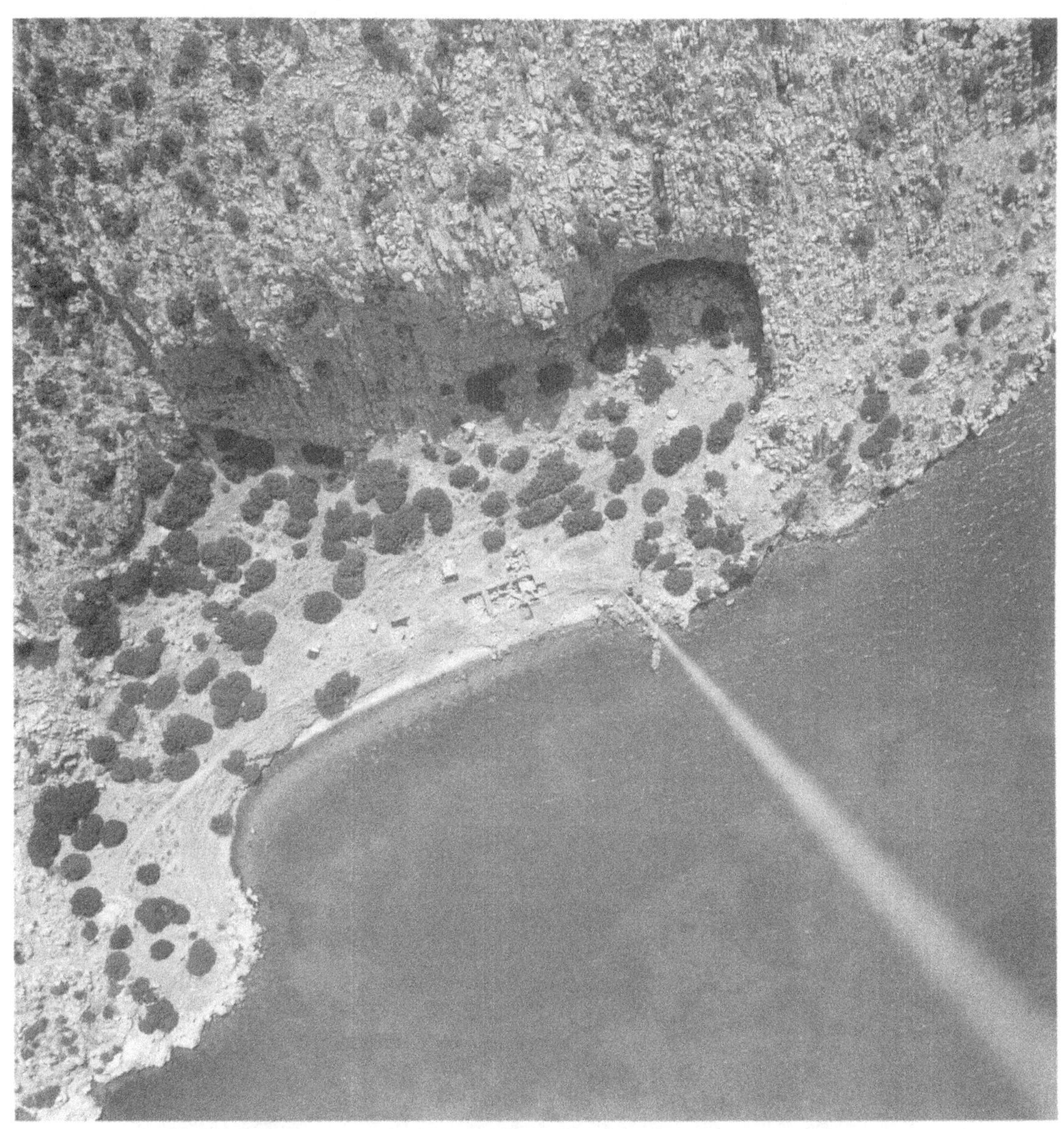

Plate 1. Balloon photograph of Franchthi Paralia (1976).

Plate 2a. View of Paralia from the sea (northwest) looking towards backwall and cave mouth (1976).

Plate 2b. View of backwall, cave mouth (in shadow), and Paralia from the north (1976).

Plate 3. View of outer Kiladha Bay, looking northwest from outside the entrance to Franchthi Cave. The Paralia excavation trenches are visible along the narrow shoreline in the (right) foreground, and an inflatable boat is anchored over the 1981 coring location FC 2. The island of Koronis is in the background (left).

Plate 4. Components of the Eykelkamp pulse-type hand-operated corer. From left to right: 4-cm-diameter piston corer; bailer; auger (below) and T-shaped handle (above); six 1-m-long steel extension rods; four plastic core-casing tubes (with casing handle above); and three core-transport tubes.

Plate 5. Coring operations at FC 2, 1981. The diver is holding the bailer above the top of the casing string (already sunk several meters into the bottom), prior to lowering it down the casing string and removing more sediment by bailing.

Plate 6. Coring operations, 1981. Recovery of a 2-m-long outer casing (with handle still attached) at FC 1 site, ca. 100 m west of Paralia. Franchthi Cave entrance is visible to the right of the standing figure. Water depth is 4.5 m.

Plate 7. Core FC 1 (1981), 540-560 cm sample. Photomicrograph of mud plaster fragments. Scale bar (copper wire fragment) is 1 mm long.

Plate 8. Closeup of Neolithic sherds recovered from the bulk basal sediment sample of core OK85/5. The three largest sherds are of Andesite Unburnished (Pink) Ware, characteristic of the Middle Neolithic. Scale in cm.

www.ingramcontent.com/pod-product-compliance
Lightning Source LLC
LaVergne TN
LVHW082004060826
844660LV00031B/1273

* 9 7 8 0 2 5 3 3 1 9 7 8 4 *